The Official
Andy Griffith Show
Scrapbook

by Lee Pfeiffer

A Citadel Press Book
Published by Carol Publishing Group

To Barbara and Charlie Sciangula, for making my real life so rewarding, and to Andy Griffith for doing the same for my "reel life."

Carol Publishing Group Edition - 1994

A Citadel Press Book
Published by Carol Publishing Group
Citadel Press is a registered trademark of Carol Communications, Inc.

Editorial Offices:
600 Madison Avenue
New York, NY 10022

Sales & Distribution Offices:
120 Enterprise Avenue
Secaucus, NJ 07094

In Canada: Canadian Manda Group
P.O. Box 920, Station U
Toronto, Ontario, M8Z 5P9, Canada

Queries regarding rights and permissions should be addressed to: Carol Publishing Group
600 Madison Avenue, New York, NY 10022

Published in cooperation with Viacom International Inc. and Mayberry Enterprises.

Book design: Morris Taub

Manufactured in the United States of America
ISBN 0-8065-1449-3

10 9 8 7 6 5 4 3

Carol Publishing Group books are available at special discounts for bulk purchases, sales promotions, fund raising, or educational purposes. Special editions can also be created to specifications. For details contact: Special Sales Department, Carol Publishing Group, 120 Enterprise Ave., Secaucus, NJ 07094

Library of Congress Cataloging -in- Publication Data

Pfeiffer, Lee.
The official Andy Griffith show scrapbook / by Lee Pfeiffer.
    p. cm.
"A Citadel Press book."
1. Andy Griffith show (Television program) I. Title.
PN1992.77.A573P44 1993

Contents

Interviews

Mayberry Hall of Fame

ACKNOWLEDGMENTS

There are many people the author wishes to thank for their help in making this homage to Mayberry a reality. I am extremely indebted to the enormously talented individuals who helped make this possible: Don Knotts, who gave up valuable time while touring in *Last of the Red Hot Lovers*; Ron Howard, who interrupted directing *The Paper* to discuss the show in detail; Jim Nabors, a man whose reputation as one of the nicest guys in show business is well deserved; the multitalented George Lindsey; Howard Morris, who's still crazy after all these years; the lovely ladies of Mayberry: Aneta Corsaut, Betty Lynn, and Jean Carson; Hal Smith, who personifies "wonderful"; Jack Dodson, Denver Pyle, Rance Howard, Everett Greenbaum, Jack Prince, Rance and Clint Howard, Parley Baer, and Howard McNear's son, Kit.

Thanks also to my wife Janet and daughter Nicole who endured hearing the show's title song 249 times. From Viacom: Howard Berk and his secretary, Sandie Cooper, who were an absolute joy to work with; Laura Siegal; and Robin Mansfield. From Citadel Press: Steve Schragis, Bruce Bender, Gary Fitzgerald, Al Marill, Mike Lewis, Allan J. Wilson, Don Davidson, Steve Brower, Lisa Cushine, and designer Morris Taub. Many thanks also to my friend Dr. Frank A. Klump (can you imagine if he had married Helen Crump? She would have been Helen Crump-Klump!); Dennis Hasty; Golden Richards; David Browning; Matthew Mead of TBS; Neal Brower, Jack Fellenzer; Bill Williams, Phyllis Rollins; Lyle Fales; Keith Bragg, Mike Boldt; Ron Plesniarski; Laura Flashberg; Bob Scheib; United American Video; Pacific Trading Cards; Warner Brothers; Universal Pictures; ABC-TV; CBS-TV, NBC-TV; *TV Guide*; Sue Rauf; Dick and Jeff Stout; Jerry Ohlinger's Movie Material Store in New York; Howard Frank of Personality Photos; Phil Shepp, Jr. Movie Collectibles, Box 253, Codorus, Pennsylvania 17311. A most special thanks to "The Andy Griffith Rerun Watchers Club," 42 Music Square West, Suite 146, Nashville, Tennessee 37203 for their use of valuable archival material and to Greg Akers and Mendy Abrahamson of Hometown TV, 347 Stanley Ave, Cincinnati, Ohio, 45226, which produces "The Mayberry Collection," a remarkable catalog of licensed products no Griffith fan can be without.

Finally, my warmest thanks to "The Big Guy" himself, Andy Griffith, who entrusted me with this homage to a show he justifiably has a great deal of pride in. Andy participated in this project from the very beginning, and helped sow the seeds for its success. It's with good reason that his colleagues and coworkers over the years have held him in such esteem. In addition to being a legend, he happens to be a nice guy. I hope this scrapbook brings back some warm memories for him and the other members of the cast and crew, as well as the millions of "Honorary Mayberrians" who have insured that the show remains a daily part of American culture.

In 1993 *The Andy Griffith Show* celebrates the thirty-third anniversary of its premiere. During those ensuing years, the show has aired literally every day on television stations throughout the United States, and has cultivated a substantial following in foreign markets despite the series' unabashed love affair with rural Americana. It's doubtful there exists anywhere a hamlet so removed from modern social problems as leisurely paced Mayberry. In retrospect, it's also doubtful such a place existed even back in innocent 1960 when Sheriff Andy Taylor first walked into our living room with his picturesque Mayberry denizens. Certainly, it would be virtually impossible for such a show to be launched successfully today, unless it was structured as a total mockery of rustic existence. Why, then, has *The Andy Griffith Show* remained such a main part of American culture? The obvious answer: we have a nostalgic and quixotic desire to return to a simpler, less demanding era.

In reflecting on *The Andy Griffith Show*, we prefer to remember the series airing during a period of time in which life seemed less complicated, even though society was indeed turbulent in those days, and would become increasingly so as the series matured. By the time the last episode aired in 1968, consider just a few of the events that shook the world: the building of the Berlin Wall; the assassinations of JFK, Bobby Kennedy, and Martin Luther King, Jr.; the escalation of the Vietnam War, and the subsequent protest movement which shattered the nation; the emergence of the hippie culture; the Chicago riots, and the (not yet culminated) race to the moon. Nevertheless, each Monday night, America had an anchor of stability in the form of mythical Mayberry, North Carolina. Here, the fiery passions that disrupted everyday life were absent. No drugs would enter "our" town, the killings of world leaders would not intrude on the characters' weekly shenanigans, and Gomer Pyle would join the Marines, but did we ever really think he'd be seen hunting "Charlie" in the rice paddies of Vietnam? No, Mayberry

Andy, Barney, and Opie in an early 1960s publicity photo.

was—and is—a place of escapism, and if we can't identify with the lifestyle, we can at least revel in its pleasures. In the classic "Man in a Hurry" episode, the stranded big-city businessman shouts in frustration at his eccentric Mayberry benefactors, "You people are living in another world!" Indeed, but, oh, what a glorious world it is.

Most shows have their supporters and detractors, but the series remains among that small, elite number of sitcoms that appear to be universally loved. Yes, there are those urban sophisticates who denounce the show as being hopelessly corny and outdated—the pseudo-intellectuals who pretend to watch some stodgy documentary about techniques to block your hat, while secretly yearning to watch Floyd the Barber. It's doubtful these misguided souls will ever overtly express their admiration for the folks of Mayberry, but then their endorsement is irrelevant. *The Andy Griffith Show* never catered overtly to urbane types, but rather to the man who will wear his Barney Fife T-shirt in public with pride.

In recent years, enthusiasm for *The Andy Griffith Show* has escalated to such heights that even those involved with the series can scarcely rationalize the reasons why. Ratings for the reruns are higher than ever, fan conventions abound, and Mayberry-related licensed merchandise (virtually unheard of in the 1960s) is selling faster than Rafe Hollister's moonshine. Certainly the dismal state of most modern sitcoms contributes to our appreciation of vintage series like this one. The other factors for the series' popularity are obvious but should be stated regardless. *The Andy Griffith Show* was created, produced, and enacted by an ensemble of professionals the likes of which the medium rarely sees. Executive producer Sheldon Leonard, producers Aaron Ruben and Bob Ross, and of course, Andy Griffith himself devoted their time and talents to ensuring that each episode met their own rigid litmus test for good taste and gentle humor. They were aided by a cast and crew of gifted individuals who contributed in their unique ways to the success of the series. Perhaps it was an old-fashioned viewpoint, but these people regarded themselves as weekly guests in the households of America. Like most good guests, they strove to make sure they were never rude or offensive. Such values may be scoffed at today, but have we really prospered as a society using inverse philosophies? In *The Andy Griffith Show* there was mutual respect not only for the viewing audience, but between the characters as well. Certainly, they had to have their exasperations with each other, but underneath, we knew these people loved and cared for each other. How many other sitcoms in recent years reflect even these very basic values?

This leads to the question: Why a book about *The Andy Griffith Show*? The answer may sound corny, but it is sincere. After spending my entire working career as an executive, I was becoming distanced from my family and friends and preoccupied with details that seem quite irrelevant today. I left my job and, with my family, took a leisurely drive through the southeastern United States. My wife and daughter and I had no particular destination. Instead, we pointed the car south and drove, vowing to stop at any points of interest. Now, I will admit to being the ultimate urban dweller. My brushes with small-town life were few and far between, and compared to me, Woody Allen looks like Grizzly Adams. Yet, I was consistently charmed by the towns I visited on our "vacation to nowhere." It was odd to have strangers say hello to you when they weren't trying to sell you Hare Krishna literature. It was pure heaven to have a waitress with a beehive hairdo prepare an old-fashioned malt in a greasy-spoon diner. And, in our own way, we "roughed" it—at least by our standards, by staying in local motels whose names faded the minute we drove away.

Throughout our journey I kept telling my wife, Janet, "Mayberry does exist." I felt like Ronald Colman in *Lost Horizon*, having found my personal Shangri-la. Lest I lose it as Colman did in the movie by trying to overstay my welcome, I returned home, comfortable with being a stone's throw from Manhattan, but determined to pay homage to the small-town culture that we had found so appealing. Simultaneously, I began to watch reruns of *The Andy Griffith Show* on a nightly basis. I was amazed at how each episode withstood the test of time, and decided to use the series as a catalyst for paying tribute to rural America. There have been other books about the show, but I wanted to take a different slant and make this a true "scrapbook" of Griffith lore, exploring not only key individual episodes, but also the cultural impact the series has had on its fans. This is by no means a definitive history of the show (for that I recommend Richard Kelly's book *The Andy Griffith Show*). Rather, it is a collection of facts and subjective opinions that, hopefully, will induce readers to appreciate the brilliance of those who created the series. Most of all, it is designed to allow the reader to have fun browsing through its pages. As long as the series remains popular, it will always be appropriate for it to be reexamined at different periods by different writers. Nevertheless, this might just be the only volume in which so many individuals speak at length about their experiences on the show. I am most grateful for the level of enthusiasm all of these talented people have shown. To ensure I had a total feel for the show, I watched all 249 episodes. Interviews with some very busy talents had to be researched and scheduled. In addition to asking for their comments about the show, I have also tried to place it in perspective relating to the various actors' careers before and since. Despite our love of these people's work on the series let us not forget they are all professional performers with many other achievements to discuss. Many of the show's actors were trained in the theater, and quite a few were skilled in performing the classics. As George Lindsey pointed out, they may have played their roles "too well," leaving the mistaken belief that their characters were merely extensions of their real-life personas. If there is a down side to their success on *The Andy Griffith Show*, it is that some of these actors have not had ample opportunities to extend their talents to different roles. Writing and assembling *The Official Andy Griffith Show Scrapbook* was a true delight. The opportunity to speak to so many people whose work I've admired for so long left me appreciative and humbled. Many of these people have indicated they want to keep in touch and maintain a friendship. While this may be unusual by the standards of most celebrities, it is par for the course with alumni of *The Andy Griffith Show*. The sincere love and appreciation these individuals have for each other comes to be understandable. The only disagreements to be found are when they try to credit virtually anyone but themselves for the success of *The Andy Griffith Show*. This includes Andy himself, who habitually deflects most of the praise to his fellow players and his crew. The relationship among these folks is basically a carbon copy of their roles on the show. Their mutual love is only outdone by their love for their fans—those legions who have kept the show thriving for so long.

The overriding quality of *The Andy Griffith Show* is its appreciation of joy found in the small, everyday things in life that we all seem to overlook or take for granted. In "The Sermon for Today" episode, the residents of Mayberry are admonished by their pastor to slow down. The advice is ludicrous when applied to the townspeople, of course. If they slowed down any more, they would be in a mausoleum. But the message is really being directed at the viewing audi-

It's not all work and no play for Mayberry's finest, as evidenced by these publicity shots from "A Wife for Andy" episode.

ence, though as Andy Griffith points out, trying to emulate the town in real life is largely an exercise in "wishful thinking." Sheriff Andy Taylor and his fellow Mayberrians would solve all their problems in a half hour—the script writers would guarantee that. There are no such guarantees in reality. Yet, we can learn a lesson from *The Andy Griffith Show* and it is as timeless as the show's comedic aspects. That is, mutual respect and an appreciation for life's qualities should never be considered outdated values. The huge audience for the series today indicates this principle is not as foreign to most people as some would have us believe.

The Andy Griffith Show did not cause a cultural revolution, nor did it start any fashion trends (our streets were never filled with millions of people sporting Goober Pyle beanies). The show's plots never explored the fantastic or the shocking aspects of life. Yet, in its own way, it has aged far more gracefully than many other shows whose reliance on timely topics have rendered them to the "My Mother the Car Graveyard for Forgotten Sitcoms." Despite the frustrations of our daily grinds, we can relax for a short time with friends like Andy, Barney, Goober, Gomer, Aunt Bee, Opie, Floyd, Otis, Howard, Emmett, even Ernest T. Bass, and for that brief period, remind our-

selves not to take life too seriously.

I am grateful for the years of entertainment that *The Andy Griffith Show* has brought to my family and so many others. The series is a link between generations. When I was seven years old, I'd squeeze onto the couch next to Mom and Dad and chuckle at the show's gentle humor. Today, my daughter, Nicole, does the same, and I realize, as do the array of fans who experience the same ritual, that this is a tradition which will endure—a small but charming method of allowing families to relax together with the sheer purpose of laughing. As Howard Morris told me, a day without laughter is indeed a wasted, tragic day. Fortunately, there is a place we can escape to where laughter reigns supreme; a place where friends and family bond for life; a place where time has stood still, and perhaps the last place where the good guys most assuredly will win. The place is called Mayberry.

LEE PFEIFFER
Piscataway, New Jersey

INTERVIEW WITH ANDY GRIFFITH

"Andy Taylor"

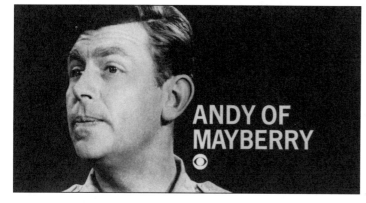

In some syndication markets, *The Andy Griffith Show* was retitled *Andy of Mayberry*.

Growing up in the town of Mount Airy, North Carolina, in the thirties, Andy Griffith found that the path to success in movies and television did not seem like an inevitability. His family lived modestly, but his father's longtime job at a chair-making factory spared the Griffiths the poverty that afflicted so many others during the Depression. Young Andy Samuel initially wanted to be a musician, and Ed Mickey, a local minister at a Moravian church, took the boy under his wing and helped him develop talents in that area. Such was the influence of the reverend that Andy considered a career in the ministry. Instead, he attended the University of North Carolina.

Upon graduation, Andy taught high school for a while, but simultaneously developed an act consisting of comedy and song which he would play to local civic groups, and he broke into show business with a preacher act on the Rotary circuit. His first big break came with release of an "instructional" record called "What It Was Was Football," which became a comedy classic. Going from stand-up comedy in the late forties and early fifties, he was cast in a TV production of Ira Levin's service comedy *No Time for Sergeants*. He later starred in the hit Broadway staging of it, and a couple of years later, the movie. His motion picture debut was as the folksy but dark-sided country singer Lonesome Rhodes in Elia Kazan's *A Face in the Crowd* (1957).

Andy returned to Broadway in 1959 as the star of *Destry Rides Again*, a musical based on the old Jimmy Stewart–Marlene Dietrich film classic. It was received with lukewarm reviews, but proved to be a hit with audiences. During this run, he shot the pilot for *The Andy Griffith Show*, which aired as a segment of *The Danny Thomas Show* in February 1960. The episode was well received, and led to Andy's own series. *The Andy Griffith Show* would run eight years and become one of the most beloved television series of all time, thanks in no small part to Andy's obsession with ensuring quality control, coupled with his hiring of some of the most creative talent around. When Andy finally left the series in 1968, the show was number one in the ratings and had spun off the very successful *Mayberry R.F.D.* Eager to embark on a feature-film career, Andy made *Angel in My Pocket*, a mildly successful comedy which capitalized on his Mayberry image. (Earlier he had followed up *No Time for Sergeants* with *Onionhead*, another service comedy, and a lighthearted western, *The Second Time Around* in 1961.) However, his attempts to

deviate from that image did not meet with success. A short-lived dramatic series titled *The Headmaster* (1970) was a ratings disappointment, as was the hastily conceived follow-up sitcom, *The New Andy Griffith Show* (1971). In 1979, a show called *Salvage One* cast the former Mayberry sheriff as a space junkman who constructed rockets to the moon out of refuse. This unique concept failed to "fly" with audiences.

Yet during the 1970s, Andy had proven he could handle a variety of different on-screen personas. He evoked sympathy as the meek building super who heroically battles terrorists in *The Strangers in 7A* (1972), and scored as the savage motorcycle gang leader in *Pray for the Wildcats* (1974). In 1977, he received wide praise for his performance as the thinly veiled LBJ figure in *Washington: Behind Closed Doors* and an Emmy nomination (incredibly, his only one to date) for his superb portrayal of the father obsessed with bringing his daughter's killer to justice in *Murder in Texas* (1981). He went on to play the despicable political boss in *Murder in Coweta County* (1983), and gained praise for his hilariously understated performance in feature films *Hearts of the West* (1975) and *Rustlers' Rhapsody* (1985). It was his role as the sly country lawyer in the TV miniseries *Fatal Vision*, aired in 1984, that led to the development of his hit series *Matlock*, which has been on since 1986. The character of Ben Matlock fit Andy like a glove, allowing him to use his wry sense of humor to outfox his worthy opponents. In 1993, the show moved from NBC to ABC, and production shifted to Andy's home state of North Carolina. Never one to indulge in the Hollywood lifestyle, he now claims he is living his dream of working on a quality series while enjoying the state he loves so much in the company of his wife, Cindi.

Interviewing Andy Griffith is not without its difficulties. First, he is such a master storyteller, the interviewer tends to lose track of prepared questions and just sit back and revel in his wonderful anecdotes. Ask Andy what time it is and he'll tell you how to build a watch. He may go the long way around the barn, but what a journey it is! Second, he is so genuinely funny, it is difficult to transcribe the interview tapes because uncontrollable laughter stops the work in its tracks. Fortunately, there were enough gaps between the guffaws to enable me to present the following interview.

Andy's career was followed by his high school paper in Mount Airy, N.C.

Q: Can you recall your early years in show business and how this eventually led to your initial appearance as Andy Taylor on Danny Thomas's show? **AG: It's kind of complicated to comprehend. Understand, I had never been offered to do a television series before, and I had never pursued it. I had kind of a fast rise in that I didn't go into show business until I was twenty-six, and I went into it in a very small way—entertaining civic clubs around North Carolina. During that period, my former wife, Barbara—who was also my partner—accepted a second show for a group we had performed for previously—and we only had one show! We had a piano player who could also sing a little bit—Larry Stith was his name—and he and Barbara worked out some songs— duets and things. On the way to the performance, I pulled out some old material that hadn't scored before and thought I'd try it again. On the way over to the job, I made up a monologue about a country fella's first experience seeing a football game and not knowing what was going on. And it scored—heavy! So, I continued to do it.** Q: That was your "What It Was Was Football" sketch? **AG: Right. I did that act once in Chapel Hill, and a man who had a little record label told me he'd like to record it, and we'd split the profits. Capitol Records then bought it and signed me to the label. It eventually sold a million copies or more. It's just been rereleased on a CD, along with some of my other stuff—some funnier than others. There's also some songs. All these things were recorded from 1954 up into the 1960s, at odd times when I would be appearing somewhere, occasionally on TV.** Q: Not all of these records were hits, however. I seem to recall a rather ill-fated version of "House of the Rising Sun." **AG: (laughs) Yeah, but that isn't on this new CD! I must confess to you that I thought I was—but I'm not—a well-equipped blues singer. I don't have it in my soul! I should stay away from that area! After I made that record, I thought, "Lord God, what did I do???!" But some of the things on** it I liked and wish they were on the CD—like "Just a Closer Walk With Thee." Anyway, I had only been in show business for four or five years before I was on Broadway in a big hit—*No Time for Sergeants*. Then I met Elia Kazan, and after several meetings with him, he decided to go with me as Lonesome Rhodes in *A Face in the Crowd*. While all the actors got great notices, the picture did not. Q: Today, it is regarded as a classic and one of Kazan's best achievements. **AG: It is now, but it got only mixed notices at the time, and as a result did not do big business. Any way you look at it, that doesn't help anybody—I don't care how good a movie is. Then I did another picture—*Onionhead*—which was a real piece of junk, and that did nothing [at the box office]. I couldn't get a job for about a year. I just stumbled around doing guest shots on variety shows, which I thanked God they had. I did 'em all, including the *Ed Sullivan Show*.** Q: It's rumored you were not very pleased with your appearance that night. Why? **AG: It was the first [TV] job I ever had. I was terrified. When Ed Sullivan first heard of my record, he wanted to tie me up for eighteen guest shots. William Morris [Agency] would only give him four. After my first appearance, he called and wanted out of the next three! I never got a single laugh. I wasn't ready. Now, if Letterman goes into that [Ed Sullivan] theater, they'd better make some major changes, because that's the worst comedy house I've ever played in my life! In fact, it's the worst comedy house that ever was! Now they have the big screen for people in the balcony, but in the old days if you played where you should play—for people in the front row—the people in the balcony couldn't see you. So they would yell at you! The comic would have to stand maybe twenty feet back from the front row, which makes it tough! I just died that night, I absolutely died! I can still go in that theater now and get an upset stomach!** Q: How did you regain enough confidence to go back on TV? **AG: That was due to Steve**

Floyd to Andy: "Did you know the dingo dog was indigenous to Australia?" (*pause*) "Well, it is!"

Andy was a hit with his broadway debut in *No Time for Sergeants*. This page is from the original *Playbill*.

Myron McCormick, Andy Griffith and Roddy McDowall in "No Time for Sergeants"

WHO'S WHO IN THE CAST

MYRON McCORMICK (Sgt. King)

Mr. McCormick has worn the uniform of both the U.S. Army and Navy on Broadway with notable comic distinction. As a Seabee he served on Broadway for the entire run of the prize musical, "South Pacific," as big-dealing Luther Billis. Of durable stuff, his feat of not having missed a performance hereabouts for more than 1,300 times as the "South Pacific" ventral dancer may be an all-time attendance record in a major role. He first donned Army Khaki in "Yellow Jack," subsequently played military gents in "Storm Operation," "Paths of Glory" and "Soldier's Wife." Last season he portrayed a philosophic bartender at City Center in Saroyan's "The Time of Your Life" and a crop trader in Tennessee Williams' "27 Wagons Full of Cotton." He also found time to play in Hollywood recently in "Not As a Stranger" and "Three for the Show," and trouped the summer circuit opposite Maureen Stapleton in "Come Back, Little Sheba."

Born in Albany, Indiana, he had his first brush with theatricals at New Mexico Military Institute. At Princeton he was active in undergraduate plays, but he didn't let his interest deter him from winning a Phi Beta Kappa key, which he promptly mislaid. Along with other collegians he was a charter member of the University Players on Cape Cod. He came to town with his classmates James Stewart and Joshua Logan to make his bow in "Goodbye Again," and has been around ever since in such fare as "Small Miracle," "Thunder Rock," "Wingless Victory," "The Damask Cheek," "State of the Union" and "Joy to the World."

ANDY GRIFFITH (Will Stockdale)

Mr. Griffith, who is here making his first New York stage appearance as a Georgia draftee, actually hails from North Carolina. Having graduated from the University at Chapel Hill where he was initiated into the theatre by the Carolina Playmakers, he was teaching

(Continued on page 34)

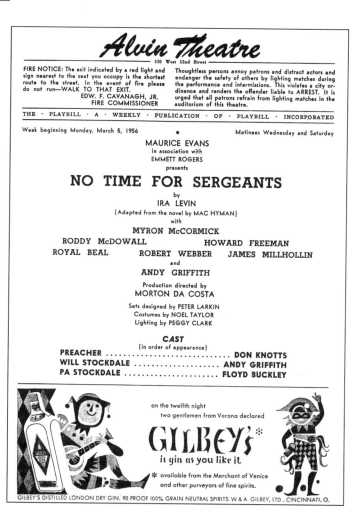

Onionhead capitalized on the success of *No Time for Sergeants* with Andy's misadventures in the Coast Guard.

Andy's first feature film following the series was *Angel in My Pocket*, an underrated comedy with Mayberryian overtones.

Despite the abundance of humor in Mayberry, Andy often faced danger as the "Sheriff Without a Gun."

Elia Kazan's *A Face in the Crowd* with Patricia Neal provided Andy with his skyrocket to stardom. Here, boxing champ Rocky Marciano visits the set.

Allen. Steve had *The Tonight Show*, and the Henry Hudson Theatre [where the show was filmed] was a wonderful comedy house. The audience was right on top of you. Instead of putting me out by myself, they brought out two stools, where Steve and I would sit. I would do these monologues to Steve, and Steve would get tickled and laugh out loud. The more he'd laugh, the more the audience would laugh. So Steve booked me a lot. Anyway, I went back to Broadway in a show called *Destry Rides Again*, which was half-a-hit. The dancing was good, the music was fair, but the book was nothing because the audience already knew the story. I decided during that period that it was time for me to try TV again. I'd struck out everywhere else. In a little while, Sheldon [Leonard] came and told me his story for the pilot [of *The Andy Griffith Show*]. It seemed contrived. Q: Did Sheldon initially conceive of a series or merely a recurring guest role on *The Danny Thomas Show*? **AG: No, this was to be a spin-off of the Danny Thomas appearance. I played this country sheriff who was also justice of the peace and editor of the paper. This was what made me think it was pushing it a bit. I asked Sheldon to come back to New York a second time to tell me the story. I still was very unsure of the idea, but I took an immediate liking to Sheldon and had an immediate trust in him. So, I agreed to do it. I had a week off from *Destry* in January 1960. That's when I shot the spin-off. They shot with three motion picture cameras, which was a technique that Desi Arnaz had created. The first day was a script day—you read and worked on the script all day. Talk about somebody who was terrified—that was me!** Q: What in particular unnerved you? **AG: The first day, Danny Thomas, Artie Stander, who wrote the script, and Sheldon Leonard screamed at each**

other all day long! I sat there in total silence. At the end of the day, I asked Sheldon if I could speak with him. Now, Sheldon is a very wise man with a lot of intuitive knowledge. I told him, "If this is what television is about, I don't think I can do it!" He said, "Andy, the star of the show controls the attitude on the set. Danny likes to yell, so we all yell. If you don't want to yell, nobody will yell." And, do you know, that's exactly the way it turned out. Q: One assumes the atmosphere on *The Andy Griffith Show* was low key? **AG: Whenever it was loud, it was laughter! We never fought, and none of us said, "I said that a half hour ago!" We didn't care who came up with the idea, or who had the joke— as long as somebody did. We didn't have ego problems. I'm not saying Danny Thomas did, I don't know about that. Sheldon didn't have an ego problem with us, either. Sheldon would come down and read the script. He'd say what he'd have to say about it and get up and leave.** Q: *The Andy Griffith Show* script conferences were supposedly highly collaborative affairs involving everyone including little Ron Howard. **AG: Oh yes, everybody was invited. A lot of people came up with ideas. Usually, everybody would say what they'd have to say and leave. Don Knotts usually stayed a long time after and he's a very good sketch writer.** Q: That's a talent many people may not be aware Don possesses. In fact, you also contributed a great deal to the scripts, yet you never received a writing credit. **AG: At that time, my name was all over the screen anyway. I never felt I needed a writing credit. See, the people on that show—Aaron [Ruben] and Sheldon—they allowed me the time to learn television writing. Obviously, you can't learn to write comedy if you don't already have a funnybone to start with. But, I remember the very first show we shot. It was called "The**

Andy as *Sheriff Taylor*, the world's best-loved lawman.

Housekeeper," and after I first read the script, I said "Something about this bothers me, but I don't know what." I couldn't put my finger on it, but I kept saying it as the show went on. Finally, I was able to say what bothered me. Then I was able to say, "Maybe we can fix it this way." Then, finally I just took a pencil and a piece of paper and started to write. It was their patience with me that allowed me to do that, and I'm very grateful to them, and will always be. Q: That first episode introduced Frances Bavier as Aunt Bee. Frances had originally appeared on the pilot episode, but in a different role. **AG: Yes, and her appearance in the pilot was inspired by an old joke. She played a woman who had rented a tuxedo for her husband's funeral, but they buried him in it! So, she'd been paying rent on that tuxedo all those years.** Q: Was it ever considered to have *The Andy Griffith Show* filmed before a live audience? **AG: I think Sheldon had a lot to do with that decision. We needed a town and we needed to go outside and to go to a body of water—all things like that. One camera is the only way you can do that. They can't afford to do one-camera shows now.** Q: Is it true that you originally wanted to use your own name on the show? **AG: I don't remember. I may have asked why I couldn't, but I wasn't insistent. In fact, Taylor is a family name—my grandmother was a Taylor.** Q: Although Mayberry is a fictitious town, were there elements based upon your upbringing in Mount Airy, North Carolina? **AG: I'm glad you asked that question, because it's something I'd really like to clarify. Many people have built a myth that Mayberry was based on Mount Airy, which it was not. I cannot deny that the person I am was born and raised in Mount Airy, and I was therefore influenced in many ways by that town. I will tell you that it was not *all* positive. I was actually called "white trash" at**

one point. This was said by a young girl I was stuck on, and she probably wasn't thinking. And we did come from the wrong side of the tracks. But I was stuck on her and kept hanging around her, even though I was only in the fourth grade! She kinda wished I'd leave her alone. But, when she said, "Get away from me, white trash," I did. Q: I guess that illustrates the painful power of prejudice. **AG: Yes, that remark has stuck with me my entire life. But, I knew I wasn't second class. Some people in Mount Airy gave me a great boost when I was in high school. See, I'm not athletic in any way. And I was not intellectual—I wasn't a good student. My mother's family was always musically inclined, while my father's family had a great sense of humor. This was a good blend for me. I started looking in the Spiegel Catalog at musical instruments, as big bands were the rage at the time. I'd go to every movie that had a big band in it. One day I saw Jack Teagarden take a trombone apart in a movie called *Bourbon Blues* and put a glass over the end of the slide and play a tune, and I thought, "Well, this is it!" I got a job with the N.Y.A. [National Youth Administration], which was an offspring of the W.P.A. I got six dollars a month which I used to buy that horn.** Q: So you envisioned becoming a professional musician? **AG: A wanted to, but I didn't know how to play it, even after two months! Then I heard about this Moravian preacher. Now, I hadn't heard of a Moravian church in my life. But all Moravian churches have a band, so I caught hold of that man and went to see him. He started teaching me to play that horn and I don't think it was two months before I played "Moonlight Sonata" in church. Then, after about a year or two, he talked me into studying voice and I wound up singing solos all over Mount Airy. The people in that town were very encouraging**

Andy and Don Knotts teamed with Tennessee Ernie Ford for a 1967 variety special.

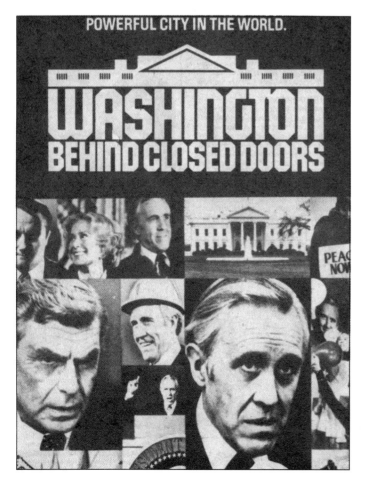

Andy's performance as the thinly veiled L.B.J. character in *Washington: Behind Closed Doors* reminded viewers of his skills as a dramatic actor.

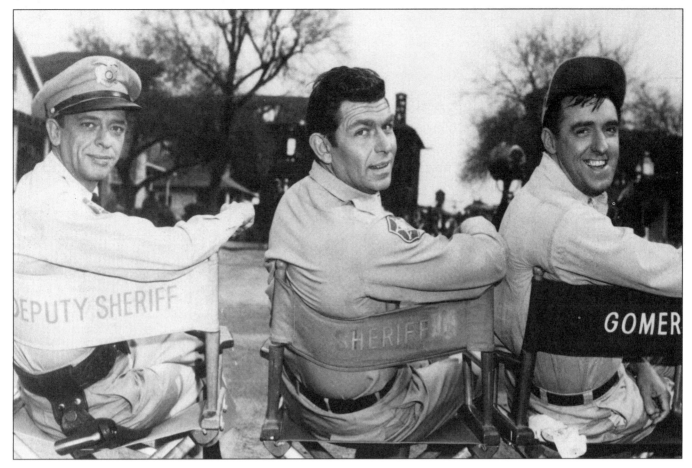

The Andy Griffith Show premiered in 1960 and became an instant hit. Here Andy poses on the set with Don Knotts and Jim Nabors.

Friends since their Broadway days in *No Time for Sergeants*, Andy and Don found *The Andy Griffith Show* to be a labor of love.

Salvage I, the 1979 comedy sci-fi series, cast Andy as an eccentric junkman who constructs a rocket to the moon.

The role of wily, countrified Atlanta lawyer Ben Matlock fit Andy like a glove, and the hit series proved Griffith remains one of the most popular actors on TV.

to me. There was a barber at a Baptist church who would slip me five dollars every time I sang. So, there were many good things about Mt. Airy. But, you have to know that Mayberry was formed when we would all sit down and talk about the script. It was formed right around that table from the imaginations of Don Knotts, me, Aaron Ruben, Sheldon Leonard, and whoever was writing or directing. Other main contributors were Harvey Bullock, who happened to come from North Carolina, and Jim Fritzell and Everett Greenbaum—all brilliant comedy writers. Q: Maybe the reason Mayberry became so beloved is because, as you've said in the past, all of the townspeople's problems could be resolved in a half hour. **AG: That's right—all the problems *would* be resolved in a half hour. Mayberry was a perfect Utopia, even though that's a redundant description.** Q: How do you feel about actual towns that try to emulate the fictitious qualities of Mayberry? **AG: There's some towns that have discussed renaming themselves Mayberry and I raised hell about that. All these towns have their own history, their own problems, and their own pride. Naming them Mayberry is not going to help, although I hear there is some tiny community that has recently done so.** Q: You consistently praise the writers of *The Andy Griffith Show*. Although there were many, there seemed to be a seamless transition over the years. How was that achieved? **AG: That was always something that amazed**

me. Harvey Bullock was usually on the money, as were Jim and Ev, although some of the other fellas would miss. They'd think about Andy and Barney's relationship as very simple and transparent. It was actually very complicated, and it was not easy to write. So Aaron Ruben did massive rewrites, as did I, on much of the material. Aaron and I would work together almost every weekend—sometimes we would work seven days in a row, often for twelve hours. Q: It's safe to say that virtually every episode of the series maintained the high standards you insisted upon. Arguably, the only other program that achieved that quality was the original *Honeymooners*. **AG: *The Honeymooners*, like *Fawlty Towers*, is a whole special thing where one central character would set himself up at the beginning of the show for this horrible downfall. Every time Jackie Gleason went into that bedroom, you knew he was going to hurt himself!** Q: For quite some time Gleason and yourself were sort of the Kings of CBS. Did you know him well? **AG: Well, *he* was, anyway. I only met him once—when he had his show in New York in the same place the Sullivan show was at. His summer replacement one year was Tommy and Jimmy Dorsey's *Stage Show*, which I did once. I had to go up to see Gleason [who was producing it] in order to get on it. That was pretty early in my career, although I think I may have already been on Broadway.**

Don Knotts was born on a farm in the hills of West Virginia, but his father's health problems resulted in his moving the family to Morgantown when Don was an infant. Here, the family made a meager living by running a boardinghouse for students at the nearby University of West Virginia. Don felt the urge to enter show business while still in his teens. He developed a ventriloquist act which failed to elicit much excitement. He toyed with the idea of becoming a teacher, but when World War Two broke out, the underweight [109 pounds!] patriot joined the army and was assigned to Special Services where his talents were used to provide entertainment for other GIs. Following his stint in the service, he completed his education at the University of West Virginia, chucked his ventriloquist act, and went to New York to seek fame and fortune.

The gamble paid off and Don landed the role of a psychologically disturbed character on the soap opera *Search for Tomorrow*. Another break came with a supporting role as the camp psychiatrist on Broadway in *No Time for Sergeants*. He was also with Andy in the 1958 film version. It was on the stage where Don met Andy Griffith for the first time, and developed a close friendship that lasts till this day. Don later proved to be a popular regular on *The Steve Allen Show*, where he capitalized on the "nervous milquetoast character that would become his trademark. When Don heard about the forthcoming *Andy Griffith Show*, he suggested that his old friend needed a sidekick and so began the career of Deputy Bernard P. Fife—one of the best-loved characters in television history. Knotts would win five Emmys (three in consecutive years) for his inspired portrayal of the hapless lawman.

In 1965, at the peak of his popularity as Barney, Don made the decision to leave the show he loved so dearly to pursue a career in feature films. (He had already starred in the hit feature *The Incredible Mr. Limpet* while on hiatus from *The Andy Griffith Show*.) From 1966 to 1971 he made a series of modestly budgeted films for Universal: *The Ghost and Mr. Chicken, The Reluctant Astronaut, The Shakiest Gun in the West* (a remake of Bob Hope's *The Paleface*), *The Love God?*, and *How to Frame a Figg*. Most of these were enormous successes at the box office outside of the big cities. He later went against instinct and starred in a TV variety series that proved to be his first career misstep.

Don resumed concentrating on feature films and appeared in a number of Walt Disney hits, as well as *The Prize Fighter* (1979) and *The Private Eyes* (1980), both with Tim Conway. In 1979 he joined the cast of the hit sitcom *Three's Company* and contributed appreciably to the long run of that series. Don reassumed the role of Barney Fife in *Return to Mayberry* in 1986. He has concentrated on his stage career in recent years, and has toured in a variety of well-received productions. A warm, modest man with a self-deprecating sense of humor, Don Knotts is a gentleman in every sense of the word. He is deeply appreciative of the fans who have remained so loyal to him, and there is a growing sentiment that he is one of the great comedic actors of his time. Indeed, it is not without good reason that he has been compared with Chaplin. The word "genius" might be used a bit too frequently these days, but in the opinion of the author, it is appropriate when applied to Don Knotts. I interviewed Don while he was in the midst of his 1993 tour of Neil Simon's *Last of the Red Hot Lovers* with former *The Andy Griffith Show* alumna Barbara Eden ("The Manicurist" episode).

Don as Mayberry's resident Casanova, Barney Fife, showing the effects of a passionate evening with Thelma Lou.

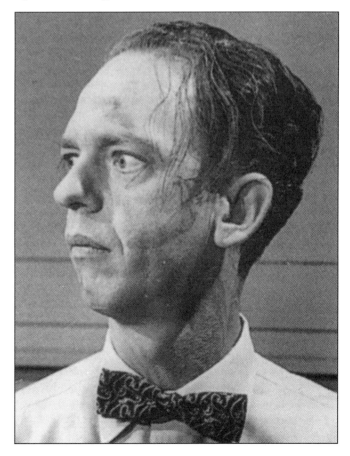

Q: Growing up in Morgantown, West Virginia, did the prospect of achieving success in show business seem like an impossibility? **DK: Well, my folks were farmers, but around the time I was born [mid-1920s] they sold their farm and moved into town, so I didn't actually grow up in a completely rural area. I wouldn't say that it was an impossible dream to go into show business, as I started thinking about becoming an actor when I was about five years old. In the back of my mind, I think I always believed I could achieve something, but I didn't know exactly what. A lot of the humor I learned came from my own family. I had an older brother who was extremely funny. I can remember back in grade school when I was getting up and doing little comedy things for the class.** Q: Even then you were the class clown? **DK: That's right! Then I remember when I was about thirteen, I started doing ventriloquism, and I would entertain at parties.** Q: You later developed a comedy act when you went into the service, did you not? **DK: Yes, I paired with two guys. The first was named Red Ford, and then Mickey Shaughnessy [later a successful character actor in films—Ed.]. Later, I used a comedy act to audition for *Arthur Godfrey's Talent Scouts*. I then got my first real good break in New York with the role of Windy Wales on the *Bobby Benson* western radio program which was on the Mutual network. I got that break fairly early, and I stayed with the show for five years.** Q: What many people don't realize is that you had a recurring role on *Search for Tomorrow*. **DK: Yes, I played a neurotic character who would only really talk to his sister. Lee Grant played the sister part of the time, and then she left the show for some reason. Nita Talbot took over. I stayed with that show off and on for three years.** Q: Is it true that origins of the nervous character which would

become your trademark stemmed from an actual incident? **DK: I attended a banquet once and saw a man speaking who was very nervous. I made note of the fact that when he'd get up to speak, he was visibly shaking—especially his hands! Later, I wrote a monologue based upon this incident. However, when I auditioned the act at the Blue Angel, they didn't like it at all, so I put it away for a long time. By that time, however, I was already doing *No Time for Sergeants* on Broadway.** Q: When did you revive the nervous character? **DK: It was on the daytime version of *The Garry Moore Show*, then I took it to *The Tonight Show* when Steve Allen was there.** Q: Returning to *No Time for Sergeants*, this was the first time you met Andy Griffith. Did you have an immediate rapport with him? **DK: I don't know if it was apparent from day one that we had this chemistry together, but we did get acquainted and became friends pretty fast. I loved appearing on Broadway—I enjoyed it very much. Andy, of course, left after the first season and I stayed on pretty much through the second season.** Q: Did you remain in touch with Andy frequently after you parted paths? **DK: I didn't have too much contact with him during that time. He did make an appearance on *The Steve Allen Show* when I was there. But, we had really lost track of each other because I had moved out to the Coast for Steve Allen and Andy was doing the Broadway musical *Destry Rides Again*.** Q: How did it come about that you landed the role of Barney? **DK: I kind of suggested myself! (*laughs*) I didn't know that Andy had done the pilot, and I happened to see it on the Danny Thomas program. I thought, "Well, he might need a deputy!" So I called Andy up, and he thought that sounded like a good idea.** Q: Is it true that in the beginning of the series, Barney was only supposed to appear periodi-

CAMPAIGN UP IN KNOTTS

't Be Chicken About It!

1R. CHICKEN, Don Knotts is cast in a role made-to-measure for his
:omic—and an exploitation star. This provides made-to-measure
showman.

hrough his long time, three Emmy award winning role on the "Andy
"), and earlier, his appearance with Andy Griffith in both the movie
versions of "No Time For Sergeants." So, start with your local TV
promotion—a plug in the lobby and on your screen, for on-the-air
advertising to the local shows in which Knotts appears.

POTS
DIFFERENT!
NARRATES
S IN THESE
VER-SELLERS!

Free! Hilariously Narrated
By DON KNOTTS!
RADIO SPOTS

Above: Marketing ideas from the pressbook for *The Ghost and Mr. Chicken*, the hit that launched Don's string of films for Universal in the late sixties.

cally? **DK: I think that's true, although I don't know for certain if they had made up their minds about what to do with Barney. If I remember, I only had a contract for ten out of thirteen episodes. Back then, they'd do thirty-nine shows, but I was only guaranteed appearances in ten out of every thirteen. They changed that pretty quickly after we got into the shows, however. We didn't know the audience reaction right away, because we had done quite a number of episodes before the first one aired—I believe it was around ten shows.** Q: In the first episode Barney refers to Andy as "Cousin Andy," yet that relationship was dropped henceforth. Any idea why? **DK: I don't think they felt it was necessary to make us relatives. I don't know why they even did that in the first show.** Q: As the role of Barney became more integral to the comedic content of the show, Andy began to play more or less the straight man. A lot of stars might have had an ego problem with voluntarily giving up the laughs, but apparently not Andy. **DK: Andy was very encouraging to me. I always have to hand it to Andy for that. A lot of stars wouldn't do that. But, he told me that when it looked as though I was going to be the funny guy he quickly switched to playing it straight. He also changed his dialect quite a bit.** Q: Andy has frequently stated that the quality of the scripts was due to collaborative efforts of everyone on the show. What do you recall about those "think tank" sessions? **DK: I never worked anywhere where the work on the scripts was so thorough. By the time we would see a script, it would already have been polished. Then we would read it with the cast, and it was like an open session. Anyone who wanted to could voice an opinion about anything in the script.** Q: Andy Griffith recalls that you made a lot of significant writing contributions to the show. **DK: Thanks to Andy, I was able to. I can't**

praise him too much. He's such a good guy and a great boss. He ran the show so well that everyone was so happy being there. As far as the writing goes, we always read the script a week in advance and then we'd do the next show before we'd do the script we were currently studying. Usually, Andy and I, along with [director] Bob Sweeney and [producer-writer] Aaron Ruben, would sit and do what we felt were necessary polishes and rewrites. Sometimes, Andy would say, "Why don't you see if you can write up a funny little thing to put in there." So, I ended up doing a lot of writing.** Q: Did you bring any inspirations from real life into your contributions to the show? **DK: Absolutely. Andy and I had similar backgrounds, and we would discuss the way some of those people we knew acted and we would laugh about it and put it into the script.** Q: As we all know, the *Griffith* set was an unusually close one in terms of relationships. Is it true that the one person who did not generally indulge in after-work activities was Frances Bavier? **DK: You know, surprisingly, I don't recollect too much about Frances. For some reason or another, I didn't see her too much. She didn't sit out on the set a great deal unless she was actually working. She was always very affable and nice, and a wonderful actress, but she would sort of disappear when she wasn't needed. Frances was always a bit mysterious to me! I was more acquainted with the other cast members. Jim Nabors, for example, was always fun to be around a really good guy. And Ron Howard, who was always a very gifted child. Although, I never saw him directing in my imagination, as you know he is a major force in this industry today.** Q: You enjoyed a remarkable chemistry with Howard McNear. Andy admits Howard would consistently crack him up whenever he enacted the character of Floyd. Did Howard

As *The Incredible Mr. Limpet* Don was literally between a rock and a hard place when he joined some illustrious companions on Mt. Rushmore.

Enjoying a laugh on the set with Andy and Jim Nabors.

have a similar effect on you? **DK: (***laughs***)** Oh, yeah—he did! I remember in one episode I had to deputize him and someone else. Well, we just had to do that scene over and over and over again. I couldn't even look at him, because he would cause me to break up! Q: There were initially problems finding a suitable love interest for Andy in the early episodes prior to Aneta Corsaut's joining the cast. Were there similar problems for you? **DK: No, Betty Lynn worked out just fine. She was really easy to work with. Betty had been a very experienced actress when she came to us, and she had done lots of movies. Again, we were blessed with a really wonderful cast and every single one of them was so good, which was why the show was so successful.** Q: Let's mention the legendary, but unseen seductress of Mayberry, Juanita from the diner. Was it ever considered to have her? **DK: Talk about someone who was very easy to work with! (***laughs***) But I don't think it was ever suggested that we bring her to life. Interestingly, when I did my first movie for Universal after the show—*The Ghost and Mr. Chicken*—we incorporated an unseen character in the movie who yelled "Atta Boy, Luther" to me. Well, Andy came out to help us with a rewrite on that movie. We had gotten into some trouble, and I asked him to help us out, so he did. He suggested that we make more of that guy. So, we worked him in throughout the movie. Strangely enough, it was Universal that wanted to finally show that guy at the end, but I refused! I felt really good about that movie.** Q: Getting back to *The Andy Griffith Show*, you won five Emmys for your performance as Barney Fife. Do you recall your reaction when you were nominated the first time? **DK: I couldn't believe it. I hadn't even thought about being nominated—it hadn't even occurred to me! In fact, I remember I was painting a fence at my home,**

when I was called in to the phone. When I was told the news I went, "What the . . . ? ? ? ? ?" I was totally flabbergasted. The show certainly should have won other awards, and I have no idea why it didn't. Who can figure out those things?** Q: You said earlier in your career that you preferred feature films to TV. Was this the motivating factor in your leaving the *Griffith Show* in 1966? **DK: Well, actually I left the show at the time because Andy had said he was only going to go for five years. I talked to him in the middle of the fifth year, and he said he still intended to stop. So I had started to look around and I interviewed with a bunch of people, as I was hot, of course, at that time. Universal offered me a picture contract, and that was something that I'd always wanted. But then Andy turned around and changed his mind. (***laughs***) But I was already so far along with Universal, that I just went ahead with them.** Q: Were you satisfied with the films you made at Universal? **DK: Yes, the first three films I made out there I was very pleased with—*The Ghost and Mr. chicken, The Reluctant Astronaut,* and *The Shakiest Gun in the West*. the last two I wan not.** Q: Those would have been *How to Frame a Figg* and *The Love God?* **DK: Right.** Q: Many of your fans consider *The Love God?* a cult movie that ranks with your funniest efforts. **DK: Maybe, but many people thought it was to risqué for my image at that time. Most of the theaters that showed my films would not even book it because they thought it would not be acceptable to audiences.** Q: Speaking of bucking the traditional Don Knotts image, is it true you were the idol of a commune of hippies around the time of *The Love God?* **DK: That's true, I ran into a guy in Hawaii—on Waikiki. He was a hippie and he invited me to his "pad." When I got there, I found all these guys hanging out passing around marijuana. (***laughs***)**

Don returned for the premier episode of *Mayberry R.F.D.* to be best man at Andy and Helen's wedding

However, I only spent the day with them—I never moved in! Q: What was your view of *The Don Knotts Show,* which premiered in 1971? **DK: It just didn't work. I was not cut out for that. That's not something I do well—come out and be a host. I simply wasn't comfortable in that role, and it showed. I prefer to be seen as an actor.** Q: In the seventies you made a number of hit films for Disney. What were your thoughts about returning to the small screen for *Three's Company?* **DK: Well, I was very tickled to do it, really. Of course I was walking into a hit. The show was already very popular. It was quite pleasant.** Q: For many years, you and Andy refused offers to do a reunion film. What motivated you to change your mind for the *Return to Mayberry* movie? **DK: Actually, Andy put that whole thing together. I didn't even know he was planning it, frankly. One day he called me and said, "Listen, I've got this reunion going. Let's do it." So I said "Okay." So, it was really all his doing.** Q: Andy told us he was inspired by a get-together with you and Ron Howard at an Emmy Awards broadcast and the subsequent conversation the group enjoyed at a dinner after the show. **DK: Oh, really? I didn't know that's what did it. He never mentioned that to me. Working on that movie was very nice. We went up to that little town near Santa Barbara—Los Olivos, and it was fun. We were up there for about four weeks. I had stayed in touch with some of the cast more than with others, so I enjoyed being with them all again.** Q: Were you pleased with how the reunion turned out as a finished film? **DK: Yes, I really was. The only thing that bothered me was that I thought that the scene where Andy and I first meet at the office wasn't quite funny enough. Otherwise, I thought it was a very good show.** Q: Of course, you team up fairly regularly with Andy on *Matlock.* How did that come about? **DK: Oh, Andy just asked me to come in and do it. It was just that simple. But, it's always a great deal of fun. I don't know if I'll be able to do anymore, however, as he's now filming in Wilmington, North Carolina.** Q: Andy Griffith told us you're the best friend he has in the world. Is it safe to assume the feeling is mutual? **DK: Oh, absolutely! I just love Andy. You know, that was one of the things that was so enjoyable about the show. We had so much fun on the set, and we always kidded around constantly. Again, Andy is such a good guy to work for and makes it so pleasant on the set that you don't want to go home! I can't say enough good stuff about him. I just saw him when I played on tour in Charlotte and Winston-Salem. He's certainly my best friend.** Q: Many people may not be aware that you have been doing a great deal of work on the stage throughout your career—including some drama as well. **DK: Well, the drama you're referring to is *A Good Look at Boney Kern* which was written for me some years ago. It's both a comedy and a drama. There are a lot of laughs in it. It was by a wonderful writer named Jonathan Daly. I play a man who falls in love with his landlady's daughter or granddaughter—I forget which, as I haven't done the show in a long time. Anyway, she is blind. It's a very sweet story, but there are a lot of laughs in it too. Right now, I'm also very pleased with the reaction to *Last of the Red Hot Lovers,* in which I'm costarring with Barbara Eden. You might remember she made an appearance on *The Andy Griffith Show* playing a manicurist!** [episode 48, telecast in January 1962— Ed.] Q: Do you have a favorite episode from your years as Barney Fife? **DK: I'd have to say I have two. One of them was about Aunt Bee's pickles** [episode 43: "The Pickle Story"—Ed.]. **I always really liked that one. Another of my favorites was "Barney and the Choir"** [episode 52—Eds.]. Q: How would you summarize what *The Andy Griffith Show* meant to you? **DK: Well, it was a real springboard for my career—no question about it. It was also the highlight of my career. I haven't done anything since that I enjoyed as much. It was a thorough enjoyment. I didn't think I'd ever do a show where I couldn't wait to get to work!**

Knotts, Don   **LExington 2-1100**
TELEPHONE EXCHANGE

COMEDY - CHARACTER - JUVENILE

RADIO: Currently featured as: Windy Wales on Bobby Benson's B-Bar-B Ranch, The Lanny Ross Show, Experience Speaks, This is Nora Drake.

TELEVISION: Kenny Delmar's Schoolhouse, Arthur Godfrey, Magic in the Air, Bobby Benson.

STAGE: Featured comic and actor with the Army Review "Stars & Gripes," two years. Featured comic in Vaudeville and Nite Clubs four years. Summer Stock - Two Seasons.

Height	5'8''
Weight	125
Hair	Brown
Eyes	Blue
Age	25

2/51

This card was used by Don for publicity purposes early in his career.

"REMARKABLE"

Knotts as Knotts.   Knotts as Zhorka.

Dear Sirs:

I thought you might be interested in seeing the remarkable resemblance between Don Knotts of The Steve Allen Show and the Soviet interrogator in Part III of THE CHAINS OF FEAR [by Nikolai Narokov, May 24–July 12].

Don . . . is a very talented comedian who can portray many different types of characters. He could also have posed for the illustration.

ERNIE OTTO
New York, N.Y.

● *He did, for artist Stevan Dohanos, who picked Knotts as a model after seeing him on television—as Steve Allen's Press Agent Ernie Otto knows very well.* —ED.

"Mayberry, U.S.S.R": Yup, that was the future Barney Fife depicted as a Communist torturer in a 1958 *Saturday Evening Post* article. (Well, at least it wasn't Floyd the Barber!)

Don and Andy in the classic "Haunted House" episode.

A perfect match—Don with one of his five Emmys.

Learning the fine art of yo-yoing from Ron Howard between takes on the show.

Don's periodic appearances as the eccentric Les "Ace" Calhoun on Andy's *Matlock* series always were a delight.

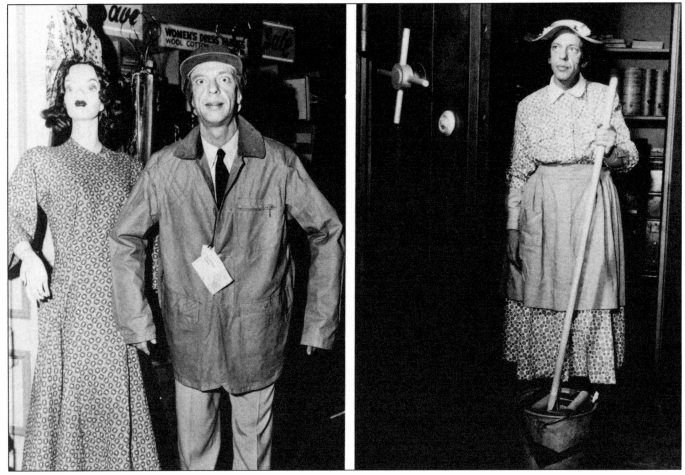

Mayberry's "Man of a Thousand Faces," Barney Fife, always aware that "It's a jungle out there," adopts some ingenious disguises to thwart the bad guys.

How to Frame a Figg continued Don's winning ways at the box office.

Don's 1993 tour of *Last of the Red Hot Lovers* with Barbara Eden (Mayberry's sexy onetime manicurist!) proved to be a sellout everywhere.

INTERVIEW WITH RON HOWARD

"Opie Taylor"

By the age of ten, Ron Howard had amassed an impressive résumé of acting credits and quickly became one of the most sought-after child stars of the 1960s. He leaped to stardom in the role of Opie Taylor on *The Andy Griffith Show*. Ron loved every minute of the series, as it allowed him to spend time with his real family (his mom or dad were consistently on the set to offer him advice and support) as well as a cast and crew he regarded as a second family. Ron stayed with the series from its premiere episode in 1960 to its final broadcast in 1968. Throughout this time, audiences saw young Ronny Howard grow from a tyke to a teen. Ron escaped typecasting that proved fatal to so many other young stars. In 1962 he appeared with Robert Preston and Shirley Jones in *The Music Man*. He starred with legends like Henry Fonda and John Wayne, as well as in George Lucas's landmark *American Graffiti* in 1973. From 1974 to 1984 he was America's favorite teenager in TV's *Happy Days,* while also taking lead parts in the low-budget box-office hits like *Eat My Dust!* and *Grand Theft Auto.* The latter allowed him to make his directorial debut, and he proved to be an emerging talent as a filmmaker. His body of work to date as director includes such diverse hits as *Night Shift, Splash, Cocoon, Gung Ho, Willow, Parenthood, Far and Away,* and more recently *Backdraft.* He remains on the short list of major power players in Hollywood, a status not reflected in his affable nature and ability to joke about himself. All who know him agree that "ego" is a word not in Ron Howard's vocabulary. I interviewed him as he prepared to film *The Paper* in Manhattan.

Looks like Andy doesn't have time to "deal" with Opie in this publicity shot from the set of *The Andy Griffith Show*.

Q: Andy Griffith maintains that a significant reason for your success in show business was the relationship you shared with your father [actor Rance Howard] **RH: Andy's always been very outspoken in his admiration of my dad. It was my dad who said, "Yeah, wouldn't it be great if on the show the boy respected his father and wasn't allowed to wise off to him." That concept seemed to take hold. Now, I don't want to overstate this, but Andy has kind of credited the basis of the Andy-Opie relationship as having been inspired by the relationship between my father and me.'** Q: Andy told me that he felt all along that, despite your success, your mom and dad would have allowed you to quit show business any time you wanted. **RH: That's interesting that he picked up on that. My parents would go out of their way periodically to say, "If you're not enjoying this, you shouldn't be doing it." At the same time, there was an understanding that if I was going to act, I had responsibilities to live up to.** Q: You gave some very moving performances even before you learned to read. Is it true your dad would rehearse plays with you at that early age? **RH: Well, he's actually quite a gifted teacher, although he never had any interest in pursuing that as a career since he likes to act, and that's what he's done all his life. He's also directed a lot of stage productions. I had been watching him rehearse a summer stock production of *Mr. Roberts* and apparently started picking up some of the dialogue. He loved that show, as he had toured with Henry Fonda in it. We used to do a scene together between Roberts and Ensign Pulver. When I auditioned for my first movie role in *The Journey*, we did that scene from *Mr. Roberts*.** Q: How were you cast as Opie in *The Andy Griffith Show*? Did you do a screen test? **RH: No, I didn't. I had been in a pilot—actually a *General Electric Theatre* episode**

hosted by Ronald Reagan—and I didn't get screen credit. Ronald Reagan went out of his way in the end to say, "We owe a special thanks to little Ronny Howard who played Barnaby." The show was a pilot with Bert Lahr called *Barnaby and Mr. O'Malley* that was based on a comic strip. It was a big part for me. By that time, I had already been doing *Playhouse 90* and *The Red Skelton Show* live on CBS and I'd been able to make some kind of impression because I hadn't horribly screwed up any of the live productions! (*laughs*) Q: Weren't there *any* screw-ups you can confess to? **RH: Well, yes! On *Playhouse 90*, I was doing an episode that was supposed to be a seasonal thing. They had fake snow, but the scene changed to summer and I was supposed to come bounding out and jump into a convertible. In the back of the car was fake snow, and I apparently jumped into it and started throwing the fake snow in the air on live TV. Since they said it looked like I was throwing stuffing from the seats, my career survived! (*laughs*) Going back to *The Andy Griffith Show*, my father was a great director and intermediary, without stepping on anybody's toes. He used to interpret a lot and walk me through things. The great thing that he had, that a lot of child actors don't have the advantage of, was the ability to relate to me as an actor, because he was one himself. Anyway, getting back to how I got the job as Opie, I had done a lot of shows like *Dobie Gillis, Dennis the Menace*, and *The Twilight Zone*—a lot of classic shows, and that helped get me some attention. Sheldon Leonard had seen *Barnaby and Mr. O'Malley* and called to say he wanted to meet with me for *The Andy Griffith Show*. He was told I was committed to the *Barnaby* series, but Sheldon said, "I don't think that series is going to sell." At the time that seemed absurd, as the**

Behind the scenes on *The Andy Griffith Show* with dad Rance and little brother Clint, Ron shows early interest in a possible directing career.

network had very high hopes for the show. As it turned out, he was right. I do remember going into a meeting for *The Andy Griffith Show*, but I don't remember auditioning, per se. Q: Let's talk about one of your favorite episodes, "The Ball Game" [episode 193—Ed.] which your dad cowrote. This was apparently based on a real incident. RH: That was the first time I had ever been involved with anything that had evolved from a personal life experience. We had this birthday party ball game with my dad as an umpire. He's not a knowledgeable baseball man, but he's been around Little League enough that he can umpire. My dad's a very fair, moral midwestern man and he takes everything he does very seriously. I hit what I thought was going to be the game winning home run in the last inning—a grand slam, no less. I belted it over the left fielder's head, rounded second, rounded third, and had a close play at the plate. I thought I was safe, but he called me out. I was really furious and hurt and I thought he ruined my birthday. But he said, "I gotta call it as I see it." So, the next day he came to the set shaking his head and he said to Andy, "I can't believe what I just went through!" So, they turned it into an episode that was a lot of fun to do. Q: Let's talk about another classic episode—"Opie, the Birdman" [episode 96—Ed.], one of the most touching of the series. How were you able to convey such emotion in the scene in which Opie accidentally kills the mother bird? RH: By that time, I was eight or nine and could read as well as feel very comfortable. In retrospect, I think I had begun to develop some technique. I loved doing that episode as I hadn't been specifically through anything like that. Through the years, whenever I had an emotional scene to play, my dad would take me off to the side and we would talk about this dog I had that had been

run over. It wasn't a bludgeoning kind of thing, but more of a discussion. We would talk about the scene in a pure Actors Studio type of way, and discuss what the character was feeling. I would then relate it to that memory. So, usually when I was crying, it wasn't fake tears—they were real and they evolved out of these memories. I seem to remember in that particular episode that I kind of put myself through that exercise instead of being talked through it. I remember being kind of proud of that episode. It was very well written. Q: How did you enjoy the atmosphere on the set, which apparently was a lot of fun, but also quite demanding? RH: I can't think of more than two or three times when I thought there was tension on the set—at least where I noticed it. I remember a kind of balanced approach. I wouldn't call it controlled chaos, but it was very loose, although there were clearly defined work patterns. There really was never a question about behavior and showing up and knowing your lines. That was always taken for granted. I wouldn't say that Andy in any way insisted upon a set like that or dressing anyone down, but he was clearly the leader and he really did lead by example. Later, when I was doing *Happy Days*, it was a one-camera show [not shot before a live audience—Ed.] for a season and a half just as The Andy Griffith Show was. In some ways I was like Andy, being the straight man. I was nineteen years old, and when we would wrap up for the day, I remember being absolutely whipped and I wasn't creatively involved with that show the way Andy was with his. I recall thinking that at the end of his day, Andy would then go off and work on scripts! He had boundless energy, commitment, and dedication. I give him a tremendous amount of credit for the show maintaining the level of quality that it did. I also give him a lot of

Between takes, Ron demonstrates his bike-riding skills to an impressed Don Knotts.

credit because, as a kid, he gave me this wonderful experience every week. I was allowed to go to the cast read-through and then hang around while everyone pitched their ideas. And I'll never forget the first time they took a suggestion of mine! I felt great. Q: The show never stooped to slapstick and always maintained a certain dignity. RH: I remember Andy saying on many different occasions, "This show is not *The Beverly Hillbillies*. I want people to laugh at this show, but I don't want people to laugh *at* these characters. I grew up with these types of people. I want people to laugh *with* them." Of course, we had a great cast, too. Don, Frances, Howard McNear. It was an extraordinary experience for me. I think that as a director today, I'm always aware of the systematic approach to storytelling, characterization, and entertainment that we had on *The Andy Griffith Show*. Later, I learned a lot from *Happy Days* about a broader, faster pace of comedy. So now, I have a pretty good ear for that kind of urban comedy rhythm. But my own sensibilities about creating a work environment and the problem-solving aspects of making a movie and telling a story and finding characters' motivations all go back to experiences from [the show]. I did not do any intellectual analysis at the time, but I did gain instincts from osmosis. Q: Was it your intention from your early days in show business to become a director? RH: By the time I was eight, if people asked me what I wanted to do when I grew up, my pat answer was "actor/writer/producer/director/cameraman." (*laughs*) Oh, and "baseball player!" Q: Not a bad prediction, although I guess it's a little late to make the last one come true. RH: Yeah, it's a little late for that one. I just couldn't hit those curve balls! But I think I was influenced by watching my dad direct, and also Bob Sweeney,

who had been an actor as well as a fantastic director. I always thought the directing job would be a fascinating one. Q: You were fortunate in that you never suffered from typecasting. RH: What is interesting is that I will be walking in Manhattan and one block people want to talk about *The Andy Griffith Show*. The next block they want to talk about Backdraft. The next block they want to talk about *Parenthood* or *Happy Days* or once in a while they'll pull out *The Music Man* or *American Graffiti*. Q: In order to get a chance to direct you had to commit to act in a low-budget film. RH: That's right. I had to act in *Eat My Dust!* in order to get to direct *Grand Theft Auto*, which I cowrote with my dad. They were very successful, and helped open up that whole genre which lasted about five years. Q: Let's talk about some of the legends you've either costarred with or directed. As a young director, you worked with Bette Davis in *Skyward* on TV. Were you intimidated by her reputation? RH: I was terrified, and intimidated! But my dad gave me a great piece of advice on that one. He said, "Actors want to be directed, so don't be afraid." I found that to be the best advice anyone could have given me. She was very concerned about my age. For a while, she kept calling me "Mr. Howard." I said, "Miss Davis, please call me Ron." She said, "No, I'll call you Mr. Howard until I decide if I like you or not." Things like that. She was a real character. It was 108 degrees where we were filming out on this tarmac in Dallas. I had to wear a sport coat and a nice shirt, because in my mind I had to dress up for my first day with Bette Davis. Everyone was making fun of me for trying to look older. I had grown a mustache also. So, as I walked toward her she pretended to be startled and she said, "I thought you were a child walking toward me!" She got a big laugh from the

Ron is surprised with a birthday cake on the set of *Return to Mayberry*, courtesy of Andy Griffith, George Lindsey, and Jim Nabors.

The relationship between Andy and Opie was based on something rarely depicted in TV sitcoms: mutual respect.

crew. **But I persevered, and kept directing. She would listen and ended up liking what I told her. At the end of the day I said, "You can go home now, Miss Davis." She said "Okay, Ron," and literally patted me on the ass. It was a great moment for me. She later told me to stick with it, as she thought I could be a terrific director. Years later, when I was directing Don Ameche and Hume Cronyn and the others in** *Cocoon*, **it was great having that experience with Bette Davis under my belt.** Q: You costarred with Henry Fonda in the TV series *The Smith Family*. What was your working relationship like with him? **RH: He was a very private man, but I had a huge advantage because he had a warm spot for my father from doing** *Mr. Roberts* **with him. At that time, my mom had been pregnant with an older brother who died at birth. Hank always thought he had been around when my mom was pregnant with me. We never told him otherwise. He took me under his wing and was a bit more open with me than he was with others. He really encouraged me to go into directing. He always told me that film was a director's medium and if he had to do his career over again he would have either remained exclusively on the stage or become a film director.** Q: You were the last actor to share the screen with John Wayne, having costarred in *The Shootist*. Wayne referred to you as one of the finest actors he had ever worked with. How did you regard him? **RH: You know, I've only seen that film once when it came out. I remember being proud because I received a Golden Globe nomination for it. The movie has its own kind of following. So many people made reference to it in the last year for some reason. I'm going to have to see it again, because I don't remember it that well. At the time I thought the plot was a little slow, but I liked the performances very much. John Wayne was great to**

work with. Q: Contrary to popular opinion, Wayne did not regard *The Shootist* as his last film and had purchased a script called *Beau John*, which he intended to make with you. It was a comedy centering on an Irish family in the 1920s, I believe. **RH: I never knew what that property was about until you just told me that. I saw him looking quite frail at a Henry Fonda tribute about six months before he passed away. He said to me, "Hey, kid! I found a book. It's you and me or nobody!" That was the last exchange I ever had with John Wayne. What impressed me most about him was he was much more methodical and conscientious about his acting than I expected him to be. I think one of the reasons we got along so well was because we both liked to rehearse. I was impressed about the way he would seek out opportunities to use that John Wayne rhythm—you know, that pause in his sentences. Wayne was kind of intimidating on that picture, but not to me. He was at war with the director [Don Siegel] and I felt the heat between them.** Q: Let's discuss *American Graffiti*. Did you have any idea the film would become a massive hit? **RH: No, but I did love the script. I remember my dad saying he didn't care for it too much, but I thought it was honest and captured a lot of the things I was feeling. It turned out to be much more entertaining—explosively so—than I thought it would be. I thought it was a modest "theater-near-you" thing we would all be proud of, but I had no idea it would turn out to be so big.** Q: Do you miss acting, or ever have the urge to appear in one of your own films? **RH: I don't miss it too much. Once in a while I do, though. I don't miss it as a career, but I do sort of miss it as an experience. I know I'll feel that way on this new film [*The Paper*] because it's got a great cast: Michael Keaton, Robert Duvall, Glenn Close, Marisa Tomei, Randy Quaid,**

Ron starred with Candy Clark and Charles Martin Smith (among many others) in George Lucas's *American Graffiti* in 1973.

Jason Alexander, Spalding Gray, Jason Robards. I know I'm going to have pangs, watching them act. They'll be cooking away on the scenes, and I'll be worrying about the weather! Q: Andy informs us that you were a prime mover and shaker in getting *Return to Mayberry* off the ground. Yet you were reportedly quite nervous about resuming the role of Opie. **RH: It wasn't so much resuming the role, because by that time my career as a director had been established. I didn't have any trepidations about revisiting the role. My trepidations were more personal, and had to do with revisiting these people. You know, I don't see Andy all that much. I bump into him at a function once in a while and that's about it. I realized that I was really carrying around a fourteen-year-old's perception of all these people. I wondered whether all that would be lost, as my memories of the show were so precious to me. I soon realized that even then they had already been treating me as an adult, so I had already seen their strengths and foibles. I realized that my memory of them was not through rose-colored glasses. I think I came away with greater respect for** Andy and his overview and sense of vision as a storyteller. I really enjoyed a couple of conversations that we had, and I think he probably would have made an extraordinary director as well. Although I don't think the tone of *The Andy Griffith Show* holds up as well over two hours as it does in a half-hour segment, the end result of *Return to Mayberry* was nostalgic and charming. I was proud to be a part of it. I only saw it once, but for me the most important element was the experience of being around all those people again. *The Andy Griffith Show* was an important part of my life and I'm very proud of it.

Ron's *Happy Days* series continued his winning ways on the tube. Here he poses with (from left) Donny Most, Henry ("The Fonz") Winkler, and Anson Williams.

Ron the director on the set of his Oscar-winning *Cocoon*.

On hiatus from *The Andy Griffith Show*, Ron costarred with Glenn Ford in *The Courtship of Eddie's Father* in 1963.

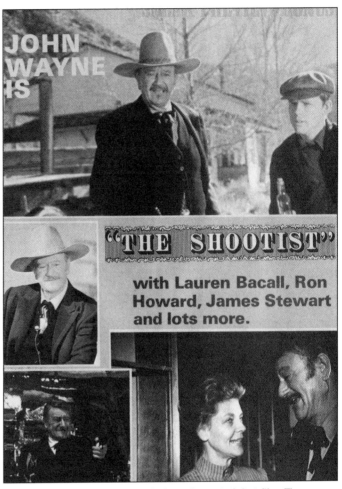

Ron starred with John Wayne in the legendary actor's last film, *The Shootist*. The Duke regarded Ron as one of the finest actors he had ever worked with.

"Goober Pyle"

Prior to becoming Goober Pyle on *The Andy Griffith Show*, George Lindsey had already established himself, appearing in everything from broad comedies to dramatic TV shows. Like many of the cast of *The Andy Griffith Show*, initially he was not envisioned to be a recurring character, but his successful interpretation of his role led to a long association with the series. In fact, George stayed on through the *Mayberry R.F.D.* years, providing a vital link to the *The Andy Griffith Show*. In recent years, George has remained a popular entertainer on stage as well as on TV, through such shows as *Hee Haw* and *Nashville Now.* Being typecast as Goober has at times frustrated him, as many people forget he is an accomplished actor capable of playing a wide variety of roles. He is also grateful, however, for the success Goober Pyle has brought him. He adopts that persona at numerous fan conventions and other venues, where he delights in seeing the joy it brings to his legions of fans. In 1992, George Lindsey received an honorary doctorate from his alma mater, the University of Northern Alabama, in recognition of his many fund-raising drives for the school. George's proudest accomplishment, though, is his extensive work on behalf of the retarded, specifically for the Special Olympics. He has raised enormous sums to benefit this organization since 1972, when he initiated a celebrity golf tournament that would remain an annual charity event for the next seventeen years.

Q: Is it true you originally intended to be a teacher? **GL: Well, I only taught for a year in order to get enough money to go to acting school. My other goal was to play first-string college football. My main motive, however, was to be successful in show business. I went to New York for the American Theatre Wing and attended the professional course for the actor for two years. For eight hours a day, we practiced voice, diction, the Russian theatre, the French theatre, and makeup. Two interesting things happened during that period of my life. The first is that I completely lost my accent. The second is that I auditioned to be Andy Griffith's understudy in *No Time for Sergeants*. They told me I wasn't big enough physically, and I wasn't "country" enough!** Q: You later landed a spot on *The Tonight Show With Jack Paar.* **GL: Yeah, that should have been wonderful. Unfortunately, that was the night he asked for contributions for tractors for Castro!** *(laughs)* **That sort of overshadowed my appearance a little! As I look back on it, I suppose it took a lot of intestinal fortitude, guts, blind ambition, and ego to go to New York and say, "I'm going to be famous!" However, it never even dawned on me at the time that you couldn't do that. In any event, I had done a Broadway show called *All American* for Joshua Logan. Carol Haney, who had been the star of *Pajama Game*, had seen me in that and asked me to do a show called *Wonderful Town*.** Q: How did you end up in California? **GL: I was signed for a pilot called *My Fifteen Blocks* for Sheldon Leonard. It didn't sell. Neither did a pilot I did called *Butterball Brown* about a minor league baseball team. Mickey Shaughnessy was in it, so was Jim Nabors. I ended up doing about forty TV shows prior to *The Andy Griffith Show*, including *The Rifleman, The Real McCoys* and *Voyage to the Bottom of***

***the Sea.* I played a lot of different roles—killers, dopers, and so on. I played in an episode of *Alfred Hitchcock Presents* called "The Jar," which was a real classic. I also did the movie *Ensign Pulver* [1964] for Josh Logan. By the way, the other sailors in that picture were Jack Nicholson, Jimmy Farentino, Peter Marshall, Jimmy Coco, and Larry Hagman. Josh would have us audition for lines every day. One day there was a big scene and I beat out Nicholson!** *(laughs)* **Of course, Nicholson was on the *Griffith Show* twice after that.** Q: You originally auditioned for the role of Gomer on *The Andy Griffith Show*. **GL: I actually got the role. They put a hold on me, but at the time it was for a onetime appearance. Then Andy saw Jim Nabors at The Horn nightclub and recommended him for the part. So they had a dilemma— whether to go with a professional actor who had a lot of credits, or go with the untrained guy who was a diamond in the rough. Well, as we all know, Jim got the part. But after that, they offered me the part of a soldier who was returning to marry Charlene Darling. I turned them down because my intuition told me that if I took the part, I'd never be a regular on the show.** Q: We can't overlook discussing Goober's popular imitation of Cary Grant. Was that improvised? **GL: That will go with me to my grave! Cary Grant wasn't ad-libbed, but the Edward G. Robinson imitation was. So was the bit where I "sew" my fingers together. My mother had shown me how to do that. That was in my first episode, "The Fun Girls". You know, Andy didn't really like what I did too much in that show. Later he told me to stop trying to act and be myself. It took me about a year to get Goober down right and stop being a caricature of Gomer. I eventually did over one hundred shows. After Don Knotts left, I seemed to take his place,**

Things get hairy in Mayberry when Goober fancies himself a rural Einstein in "Goober Makes History."

Not even Andy and Howard can persuade Goober to allow them into the "Regal Order of the Golden Door to Good Fellowship" without saying the password: "Geronimo!"

George was outstanding in the seriocomic episode "A Man's Best Friend," wherein Goober was convinced his dog could talk.

Goober doesn't mind Andy interrupting his reading (chances are it's not War and Peace anyway!).

George featured in a 1970 promo flyer for *The Andy Griffith Show* in syndication.

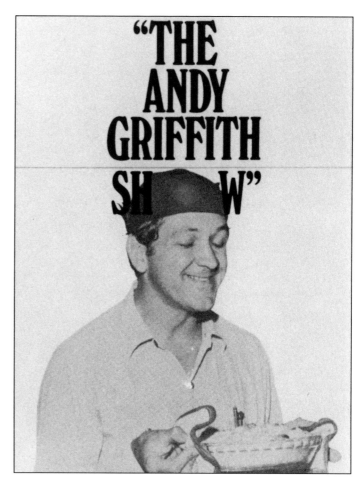

maybe because the Jack Burns experiment didn't work. Q: What are your recollections of the atmosphere on the set? **GL: Griffith, of course, was responsible for everything. I remember everyone used to wait home on Monday nights, because if he liked the show, he would call you. If he didn't call, that meant he didn't like the show. He was the toughest taskmaster I had ever worked for. He demanded a hundred and twenty percent, but he didn't demand any more of anyone else than he did for himself. We had a chance to go to Rome, Paris, and London to do six shows, but he wouldn't go because the scripts weren't right. That's how much care he put into the show. We would go for hours trying to change one word. Andy lives by that old motto, "If you're going to plow the field, you'd better be in charge of the mule." Now as for Don Knotts, I didn't know him socially, but he was absolutely brilliant to work with. So was Howard McNear. Like many of the actors on the show, he always gave you more than needed when you shared a scene with him. The scripts we had were so good . . . There wasn't much ad-libbing. We'd sit at the table for eons making suggestions. It was about two or three years before they let me participate, but they always let me sit in. Besides, I always wanted to go because I'd get a free Cobb salad!** Q: Did anyone play practical jokes on the set? **GL: Oh, we had high-jinks all the time! They'd love to play practical jokes on me because I was initially so intense with my role, they didn't think I had much of a sense of humor. One time Andy and [makeup artist] Lee Greenway sneaked into my dressing room while I was asleep, and covered the whole place with duck guts. When I woke up it looked like I was inside someone's intestine! Other times they'd drop bags of water on me, and once they tried to distract me during a scene by** having a girl in a bikini stand right out of camera range. I always had to have my pencils and tire gauge in a certain order. I couldn't function unless they were. Well, they would always move them around to mess me up. Q: You actually only appeared in one episode with Jim Nabors—your first show, "Fun Girls," in 1964. **GL: Yeah, but we've worked together many times since. We did a Minnie Pearl tribute, *Sally Jessy Raphael,* and a show in Branson at the Roy Clark Theater called *Gomer and Goober.* Hopefully, we'll do more stage work together in the future.** Q: Why did you decide to stay on with *Mayberry R. F. D.?* **GL: I wasn't originally supposed to be on that show, and that's why they did the pilot without me. Then they said they didn't want to do the show without me.** Q: How did you feel when the show was canceled, even though it was in the top ten: **GL: One day Griffith called up and told me it was over. It didn't dawn on me right away that my career had been terminated. I always just thought I'd move right into another show, but of course it didn't turn out that way. You know, I would have liked being nominated for an Emmy for my work as Goober. But, for some reason, the only people who received any awards were Don and Frances Bavier. I think the reason is that we did it too well and people just didn't think we were acting. A lot of people in the industry even thought we were actually like the characters we played. But look at our backgrounds . . . mine was in theater, Jack Dodson's was in theater, Griffith's was on Broadway, Don had been entertaining since he was about fourteen, and let's not forget Aneta Corsaut had done *The Blob* with Steve McQueen! But I can say that everybody who worked on that show really appreciated each other's talent.** Q: What was it like to work with everyone again on *Return to Mayberry?* **GL: I don't know**

George displays the ol' school spirit in the 1993 reunion special.

if it was just me, but I never really understood the script very well. *(laughs)* For instance, I can't understand why Goober and Gomer—the two nosiest people in the world— weren't out in that boat on the lake looking for the sea monster. The movie was a huge success—it drew a forty-nine percent [market] share. But that movie, just like the reunion show we did for CBS [in 1993], made me think that all we'd have to do is slip on our old clothes and it would have seemed like we had never left *The Andy Griffith Show*. Except now, everybody was groveling at Ron Howard's feet hoping he'll get us a role in one of his pictures! *(laughs)* I make sure I refer to him now as "Mr. Howard"! Q: We can't omit talking about your work on *Hee Haw*. How long were you with that show? **GL: Twenty-two years. It's the closest thing to vaudeville I'll ever be on. It was wonderful. I even got to do my own wardrobe. We only worked twice a year, in June and October. There were wonderful guest stars like Henny Youngman and Ethel Merman. You know, between *The Andy Griffith Show* and *Hee Haw*, I've been on the number-one Nielsen-rated show and the number-one syndicated show. I've been on TV every single week since 1964, which might be some kind of a record.** Q: How would you describe that character of Goober? **GL: I've said this many times, but Andy gave me the best insight into his character. He said, "Goober's the kind of guy who'd go into a restaurant and say, "Hey, this place has got great salt!" That one line gave me my interpretation of what Goober was all about. He always had a** lot of irons in the fire—working at the fillin' station, being a church elder . . . Goober was always more complex to me than Gomer was. I always pictured him going home at night and trying to figure out life. When you look at those scenes between Opie and Goober, Goober would just turn himself around and become a little boy. My favorite show of all time had Goober with the talking dog. [episode 171: "A Man's Best Friend"—Ed.] The moral of the show was how cruel kids can be to adults. They were very, very cruel to Goober. Now, Goober didn't want to hurt the kids' feelings. When they apologize to him, he takes the onus off of them by immediately kidding around, despite the fact he's very hurt.** Q: Can you sum up your feelings about *The Andy Griffith Show*? **GL: I always felt that Goober played a big part in the show's success. I'm proud of that. And Griffith always gave me and the rest of the cast our due. He made sure each of got a number of shows where we could demonstrate our strength. The way he ran the whole thing was just so terrific—I give him all the credit for the way the show worked out. I guess if I could sum up my feelings in one sentence it would be, "I wish it hadn't ended." It was a wonderful experience. It got me to where I wanted to be in the business. I was proud to be part of the whole thing. People are watching it thirty years later. I don't think they'll be doing that with most of the shows on today. As for my own personal epitaph, I think I'd like my headstone to read either "I'M HAPPY I MADE YOU LAUGH," or "I TOLD YOU I WAS SICK!"**

INTERVIEW WITH JIM NABORS

"Gomer Pyle"

Jim Nabors, born in the small town of Sylacauga, Alabama, never considered himself a "natural" for the show-business world. He moved to California, where he created a well-received act consisting of storytelling, jokes, and singing. Although he tried his hand at acting, several pilots he did failed to sell. Lightning struck the night Andy Griffith saw his performance at The Horn nightclub. Andy envisioned Jim for the role of Gomer Pyle, and the rest was TV history. Although Jim was on *The Andy Griffith Show* for only one season, his contribution to the show was so successful that in 1964 he was able to spin off into his own highly rated *Gomer Pyle, U.S.M.C.*, which ran for six seasons. Jim has always countered his hayseed image of Gomer with his remarkable baritone singing voice, and has had enduring success with his dozens of record albums and concert appearances. In the 1970s, he also had a popular variety show which costarred his *Gomer Pyle* foil, the late Frank Sutton. He occasionally ventures into feature films, and has costarred with Burt Reynolds in *The Best Little Whorehouse in Texas* (1982), *Stroker Ace* (1983) and *Cannonball Run II* (1984). Jim's passion for Hawaii is well known, and, between tours, he spends his time at his residence in Honolulu or his macadamia nut plantation on Maui.

Mayberry's most eligible bachelors—*not!*

Q: Having been born in a small, rural Alabama town, did the prospect of entering show business seem remote to you? **JN: I wanted very much to be in the business, but realistically, I didn't really think I had a shot at it. I didn't feel I was that gifted or talented. I knew I wasn't a leading man.** Q: Then what prompted you to move to California? **JN: I had had asthma since childhood, and it had always been suggested to me that if I moved out of the South, I could possibly get rid of it. That's really what prompted me to move more than anything else. Otherwise, I would have been too frightened to just say, "I'm going out to California and get into show biz!" My first job was at NBC, working at their warehouse stacking film and making deliveries. Then I learned how to edit and became a film editor. I never was very good at it!** Q: Simultaneous to this, you were performing your nightclub act. **JN: In my early night club act, I wasn't a singer or a stand-up comic. I was just sort of a character. It was the silliest act you ever heard of. I'd sing like this [his regular voice], and talk like this [his Gomer Pyle voice]. But, Andy Griffith saw me at The Horn, and had a great line about my work. He said, "I don't know what you do, but you do it very well?" That night was really the kick-off to my career, although a year before that I had been on *The Steve Allen Show,* which was the first thing I had ever done professionally. This was a very short lived show on ABC that originated from California. It was not only my first TV appearance, but Tim Conway and The Smothers Brothers also started on that show.** Q: On that all-important night when Andy say your act, did you know he was in the audience? **JN: Oh, sure. He was brought to The Horn by some friends from my hometown that I knew. I had met Andy prior to this, but he had not seen me work or knew what I did. I had always been a fan of Andy's since he did "What It Was Was Football." I thought he was great.** Q: You also had done a pilot called *Butterball Brown.* **JN: You must have been talking to George Lindsey!** *(laughs)* Q: In fact, I was. **JN: I knew it, because nobody else remembers that show! It wasn't very good. George and I are the only people who even know about it!** *(laughs)* **I was doing anything that came along at that time. I had already made my first appearance on *The Andy Griffith Show.* It was my first acting job and I was a "special guest star" on the number-two show in the nation. It was quite a break. Then, they decided to use me as one of the town characters. After I had done about two or three shows, Frances Bavier asked me if anyone had recognized me. I said, "Yeah, the girls in the drugstore. I was never so thrilled in my life." I then mentioned that I had been offered four television series, and everyone started to laugh. Then they realized I was serious. They had offered me *Butterball Brown,* and I had read for the *No Time for Sergeants* TV series, which I could have gotten if I wanted it. Andy asked me to do his show for another year and get some experience. He promised me that after that, they'd do a pilot with me and I'd be a partner. I didn't even understand what he meant. I was just looking for work.** Q: So, Gomer wasn't originally envisioned as a recurring character? **JN: No, not at all. After I had done the first show that's when they decided to keep me.** Q: Ironically, George Lindsey was also being considered for the role of Gomer at the same time you tested for it. **JN: Right! As a matter of fact, George had a lot of experience that I never had. He'd done some Broadway, a couple of *Alfred Hitchcock* shows, and all sorts of other things. He read for the part, and they had taken a hold of him [a procedure that preced-**

Above: Jim's runaway success as Gomer landed him on magazine covers throughout the nation.

Left: Jim's periodic concert tours on mainland U.S.A. continue to sell out.

"Gomer the Houseguest" proves to be too much to handle for even the normally hospitable Taylors.

THE MARINES HAVE LANDED

By FRANK JUDGE

THE MARINES have lost a dashing, suave, sophisticated officer and gained a well-meaning, bumbling recruit.

Around the Pentagon, they may not consider it an even swap.

But the idea spells success for Jim Nabors, surprise comedy hit of "The Andy Griffith Show," and Robert Vaughn, a fine actor whose talents stood out like a signal flare on "The Lieutenant," a mediocre effort which NBC is dropping.

Nabors, the Gomer Pyle of Griffiths' CBS series, is landing in the Marines as the star of his own show, "Gomer Pyle, USMC."

Vaughn, a dashing Marine in "The Lieutenant," will be a dashing international intelligence agent in a new NBC spy thriller series, "Solo."

As "The Andy Griffith Show" finishes its season, Nabors, who is Gomer Pyle, service station attendant in the series, joins the Marines. He disappears from that show, only to turn up next fall as the star of his own series.

Nabors, whose corn-pone talk and sense of humor matches Griffiths', is a plain living fellow who was editing film at NBC a couple of years ago. He tried his comedy in California nightclubs, impressed Griffith and was cast as Gomer Pyle.

Future superstars Jim Nabors and Robert Vaughn, circa 1964. (The *Solo* series referred to was the original title of *The Man From U.N.C.L.E.*)

ed offering an actor a formal contract]. Then I read for the part, and somehow I got it. I didn't know any of this, until George told me. He asked me, "Are you the one who got that part?" When I told him I was, he said "You son-of-a- . . . *(laughs)* In fact, George used to visit me on the set of *The Andy Griffith Show*, and that's how that Gomer and Goober relationship came about. Q: Did you draw on any real-life influences for your interpretation of Gomer Pyle? **JN: Sure I did. That's what acting's all about—drawing on things you know and people you know. I was influenced by a mixture of a lot of people I had known since childhood.** Q: *The Andy Griffith Show* was known to be one of the most demanding shows on the air when it came to quality control. Did you find the pace intimidating, as a young, inexperienced actor? **JN: No, as a matter of fact, looking back on it I thought that was the way all shows were. You see, Andy was very precise as to what he thought these characters should be like. To me, this was wonderful. You knew where you stood. It gave me direction. I'll be honest with you, I have never had that kind of direction even in the several series I'd done since that time. I think Andy is one of the best people I've ever known in terms of those qualities. I can't thank him enough for directing me the way he did. Also, you had an incredible talent in Aaron Ruben. He was also very much responsible for setting up *The Andy Griffith Show*. His talent is as big as anyone else's in Hollywood in terms of writing and creating. He was marvelous.** Q: One assumes that, in addition to the hard work, there were plenty of good times on the set. **JN: Oh, sure. Andy always created that kind of atmosphere. As long as you were professional, and you did your work, you were fine. It was basic professionalism that he expected of you. There was always fun and laughter on the set. Everyone really got along great.** Q: What are your recollections of working with Don Knotts? **JN: Don Knotts was probably the funniest and best comedic actor that I've ever worked with. He's just incredible. One time I asked him how he managed to be so funny and he said [imitates Knotts]: "It helps when you look like I do!" Another great talent was Ron Howard, who was blessed with two wonderful parents. They weren't your typical show-business father and mother team. They were very family oriented and his father was almost always with him. Even though there was a father-son relationship between Ron and Rance Howard, they were also good friends. Ron was always a great kid, and I never saw him get out of line. It was really a good time on that show, although I probably am more aware of it now than I was then. I was too busy trying to touch all the bases.** Q: do you have an episode that is a particular favorite? **JN: I don't watch the reruns because when you see yourself so young there, and then so old in the mirror, it's depressing! *(laughs)* It's okay if you've stayed on the air over the years like Andy has. Then, it's a natural progression and everyone sort of grows old with you. But, if you've been off the air a long time, and suddenly you go back on, people say, "Oh, my God! Look at him *(laughs)* As for a favorite episode, as an actor, not a viewer, I'd have to say "Citizen's Arrest" [episode 106—Ed.]. I had been very insecure up to that point with my situation. I didn't know if they were going to keep me or let me go. But, after they wrote that episode, I thought they really did like me and I had a chance with the show. . Also, there was the fun of working with Don Knotts. I didn't know about the discipline of not laughing. But, when I had to look at him carrying on, I kept cracking up. He was brilliant.** Q:

Jim and Andy on the set of *Return to Mayberry*.

In "The Songfesters" episode [115—Ed.], you were able to display your singing talents. I remember at the time, many of us were convinced your singing voice had been dubbed because it was so unlike the Gomer we all knew. **JN: (*laughs*) That's why they were a little hesitant about letting me sing more on the show. They felt people wouldn't believe it was really me. They just let me do it a few times.** Q: However, those episodes did go a long way in launching your professional singing career. **JN: They sure did! It helped me land guest spots on other people's variety shows, and that was really great for me and my career.** Q: Were you nervous about leaving the series to start the *Gomer Pyle, U.S.M.C.* show, where you basically carried the weight of the show's success on your own shoulders? **JN: I didn't realize that responsibility at the time. I was just so thrilled to have my own show. It just meant to me that I would have to work harder and longer. I didn't really feel the pressure of carrying the show at first, but I did after a while because I was in almost every scene.** Q: Were you involved with the creative elements of the *Gomer Pyle* series: **JN: Not really. The character's traits came from me, but Aaron Ruben really was responsible for the show. I wasn't involved creatively with my show the way Andy was with his. I didn't feel I was good at that. We'd all make some suggestions about our characters occasionally, but Aaron had it so firmly in mind as to where everything would go, that he was the chief carpenter of the whole show.** Q: You had a wonderful rapport with your costar, Frank Sutton, whose Sergeant Carter was the perfect foil for Gomer. **JN: Frank and I were both working actors. Looking back on those years, I can say I appreciated everything about Frank. He was a good guy and we worked very well together. We approached our roles in totally different ways. He was a**

studied actor with a masters from Columbia in theater arts. Of course, I had never acted and my degree was in business. I came out of nightclubs, and that's a whole different ball game. Frank later appeared on my variety series, and became a part of everything I did after *Gomer Pyle*. I was very saddened by his untimely demise. Q: You resumed playing Gomer again in *Return to Mayberry* in 1986. How did it feel going back into that character? **JN: I just shifted into gear naturally. I didn't do that much in the show, but it was wonderful to get together with everyone again. It's like Ron Howard said, "If you're going to have a reunion, it's better to have a working reunion." That way, you can always catch up with each other between shots. It's more fun than sitting around a barbecue somewhere. I had pretty much only stayed in touch with Andy on a regular basis over the years, although I would see George Lindsey occasionally. I also kept in touch with Frances Bavier, who would write to me now and then. I was very fond of her. She was very good to me on a personal level. On weekends, she used to take me "antiquing" with her. She taught me a lot. You know, we always used to joke that nobody could figure out where Aunt Bee was from. Most of us had these deep southern accents, and all of a sudden Aunt Bee would come in and call "Awnnndeee! . . . " in that sophisticated voice. (*laughs*) She was truly everybody's aunt.** Q: Having played Gomer for many years, were you concerned about typecasting? **JN: No, because I knew I just wanted to sing and do variety. I always had that in the back of my mind. Music was always the number-one thing with me. I never thought I was a very good actor.** Q: Even though people are still enjoying your work from so many years ago? **JN: Well, I hope they are. But, I'm very limited as an actor because I've really only**

Publicity shot to cross-promote two hit CBS series: *The Andy Griffith Show* and *Gomer Pyle, U.S.M.C.*

played the one character. I never really tried anything else, with one exception. I played a killer on *The Rookies*. It got great reviews, but it wasn't my cup of tea. I'd much rather be singing! Q: Do you enjoy touring? **JN: I don't like it as much as I used to. The travel is very, very hard these days. It used to be much easier. Of course, you're away from home and it's not the same. I like to do so much work a year, and then stay home for the rest of the year.** Q: "Home," of course, is Hawaii. **JN: Yes, I'm sitting on my porch in Honolulu right this second watching them surf. I also have a place in Maui, and a ranch in Montana where I spend about four months a year.** Q: Are your surprised about the enduring enthusiasm for *The Andy Griffith Show*? **JN: I'm amazed at it, really. It's a timeless show. It reminds us of "Never-Never Land." It was like that for all of us on the show, too. Each of us saw Mayberry in different ways. It's flattering that the work we did so**

many years ago is still viable, but I try not to look at it in an egotistical way. In fact, I was recently in Atlantic City having breakfast in the coffee shop of the Trump Plaza. There was an elderly Jewish couple sitting next to me. The woman kept turning around and staring at me. She kept doing this until she turned around and asked [imitates accent]: "Are you the von on the TV?" I said, "Yes, ma'am." Well, she resumed eating her breakfast a while, then turned around again and asked, "Are you the only von still living?" (*laughs*) Talk about feeling old! I said "No, ma'am." She waited a few more minutes, then turned around and said, "What ever happened to the funny von??" (*laughs*) Maybe she was talking about Don, I don't know. The guys who were sitting with me fell down laughing. All during my appearance at the casino, they'd ask me, "What ever happened to the funny von?" That helps make sure you don't develop any ego problems!

"Helen Crump"

With Aneta, Andy Griffith finally found the right chemistry
to allow Sheriff Taylor a sustained romantic relationship.

Aneta Corsaut joined *The Andy Griffith Show* in its third season with episode 86 "Andy Discovers America," telecast in March of 1963. The show simply needed an actress to portray a schoolteacher—Helen Crump—but Aneta had such chemistry with Andy Griffith that she was asked to reprise the role. The characters of Andy and Helen gradually became an item, and Aneta would stay with the series until the premiere episode of *Mayberry R.F.D.*, wherein Andy Taylor and Helen Crump finally tied the knot. Prior to it, Aneta Corsaut had done a number of TV shows and motion pictures, the most notable being the 1958 cult classic *The Blob*. Since *The Andy Griffith Show* she has costarred in the successful comedy series *House Calls* and had a recurring role on *Days of Our Lives*. She occasionally appears with Andy Griffith on *Matlock*.

Talk about May–December romances: Ron and Aneta in the "Opie Loves Helen" episode.

At least it wasn't peanut butter! Aneta's big-screen debut found her menaced by an extraterrestrial ball of jelly in the 1958 cult classic *The Blob* and had her last name misspelled as well!

Q: What inspired you to enter the acting profession? **AC: Because I couldn't fulfill my dream of becoming the first woman pitcher in the major leagues! My other goal was to be the lady who wore a tutu and rode between two horses in the circus! As it turned out, I attended Northwest University, and then went straight to New York where I appeared on quite a few shows, including** *Sergeant Bilko*. **I believe my first paid appearance was on** *The Imogene Coca Show*. **Actually, my background has been in drama, and yet I'm known for comedy series!** Q What are your recollection of making the infamous film *The Blob*? **AC: (***laughs* **It was done by a group of very religious people who thought if they made a science-fiction film, they could raise enough money to do religious movies. Everyone connected to it was so religious.the producers, the director. I remember Steve McQueen drove the producers crazy! He was more of a maverick in those days real hell on wheels. Every day the filmmakers would go into prayer meetings—they would pray to everything, including the makeup brushes! They would always finish by saying, "And save us from Steve McQueen!" They worked us about eighteen hours a day on that picture. I ended up with pneumonia from the scene where we were locked into a freezer. They gave me two hours off so I could get a shot from a doctor! When we were filming, I always kept moving around so may back was to the camera as much as possible. When it opened, I left the country and hoped it would blow over. Of course, it became a big hit, quite by accident. I haven't personally seen it in about fifteen years.** Q How did you become involved with *The Andy Griffith Show*? **AC: My mother had moved out to California after my father had died. I joined her in 1960, when I moved from New York. I loved New York, and didn't want to leave, but I thought I should be with my mother. I got an agent, and started doing some shows,**

including *Mrs G. Goes to College* [with Gertrude Berg] **which lasted only one year. One of the people who wrote it was Jim Fritzell, and he introduced me to Bob Sweeney. They had already gone through three very good actresses on** *The Andy Griffith Show* **who had played Andy's girlfriends. My role was originally supposed to be a one-shot appearance as a schoolteacher. I remember Andy and I got into an argument my first day on the set! I don't know if he remembers the incident, but it was about women's lib. I was for it and he was against it. It obviously wasn't that brutal of an argument, because by the end of the week we had become good friends. I had seen the show previously because Jim Fritzell and Everett Greenbaum had been writing it. I always enjoyed it, but I never thought I would ever become involved with it. It was a very wonderful show to work for. It was really like a family on the set. We would come very early to work, regardless of whether we were in the first shot or not. Then, even if you finished about three o'clock, you still stayed around to watch everybody else work, have coffee, and talk. You'd never know we had just been together for twelve hours!** Q: Did you have any creative input regarding the scripts? **AC: We all did. We would all occasionally suggest plot lines, some of which worked out, and some of which didn't. It was a very democratic procedure, although Andy oversaw everything. He was always a workaholic, but a very talented one. He was able to do writing, rewrites, help direct, and produce! I think the proudest moment of his life is when he got his writer's card.** A: Among the cast and crew, who were you closest to in your personal life? **AC: Andy. We would go to parties and lunches, and always talk politics. He has remained an incredibly good friend. He's a very loyal person.** What was your relationship like with Don Knotts? **OC: I always loved Don, but I never got to know him that well**

Andy and Helen's marriage on *Mayberry R.F.D.* was one of the TV events of the year.

personally, although I don't know exactly why. He was always very shy. With Andy you could joke in a certain way, but if you tried the same thing with Don he might blush! (*laughs*) I consider him to be a true comic genius. That also goes for Howard McNear as Floyd the Barber. He was adored by everybody. You'd fall down laughing just talking with him! [At this point, Ms. Corsaut manages a passable imitation of Howard McNear and laughs at the memory of his characterization of Floyd.] He would always make you feel beautiful and wonderful. Q: Your scenes with young Ron Howard are among the best loved of *The Andy Griffith Show*. AC: Oh, I loved Ron Howard. He was always the sweetest kid who ever lived, and always cooperated with everyone fully. His parents, Rance and Jean, were simply fabulous people. One of them was always with him, and they never left him in the hands of someone else, like a social worker. It was never in his nature to get out of line. Once he acted up a little tiny bit for a second. His dad, Rance, said, "Excuse us," and he took Ron behind the set and had a little conversation with him. When Ronny came out, he just said, "I'm sorry," and that was the extent of the trouble he caused! Q: You also shared some memorable scenes with Betty Lynn. AC: Oh, she's wonderful. We always got along great, but we're completely different. What's ironic is that in real life, she's from a big city and I'm from a small town. On the show, she played more of a rural person, while my character was a bit more cosmopolitan. Q: Were you ever frustrated that it took until the final season for Andy and Helen to get married? AC: No, in fact I was surprised they ever did. I think the reason the characters worked so well together is that they had written Helen to be rather irritating so there would be something for Andy to play off. She was not the sweet little girl who would always say, "Yes, dear." Part of that input was mine, and part of it

was the writers', who wanted to go in a direction different than the girls who had previously been in the shows. It's been said that Andy was stringing along Helen for all those years, but I say maybe it was vice-versa! After all, she never showed any particular interest in getting married. That aggravated some of the people who watched the show, and I'd occasionally get complaints in the mail that I was not very nice to Andy! (*laughs*) Q: Does the extent of the fan movement in the 1990s for *The Andy Griffith Show* surprise you? AC: It's mind-boggling! The first fan convention I went to, I thought very innocently there might be a few people to chat with about the show. I couldn't believe the number of fans who showed up. You know, the fans are so very dear to all of us, because they've kept such an interest in a show that was on so long ago. Q: What have you enjoyed doing most since *The Andy Griffith Show*? AC: Well, *House Calls* was a totally wonderful experience. I've also done a number of dramatic parts on shows, and I still prefer drama to comedy. As funny as *House Calls* and *The Andy Griffith Show* were, I'm still not comfortable with comedy. I'm not a comedian. Maybe that's why a number of comedy pilots I've done over the years have not sold! I really love doing *Matlock* because I get to work with dear Andy. It's always a lot of fun to play a role in which I get to scold him! Playing a judge, I get to sit way up above him and tell him to shut up! (*laughs*) Andy just called and invited me to North Carolina to do another episode. He's got such a beautiful place in Manteo, I'm dying to see it again. Q: Do you have a favorite episode of *The Andy Griffith Show*? AC: I still watch them once in a while if I get a chance. My favorite was the episode in which Helen writes a book [episode 213, "Helen, the Authoress"—Ed.] I also like the same one everyone else does—Ev and Jim's "Man in a Hurry." It was a wonderful part of my life.

INTERVIEW WITH BETTY LYNN

"Thelma Lou"

Betty Lynn had already reached a considerable level of success as an actress in film, stage, radio, and television when she joined *The Andy Griffith Show* as Thelma Lou, the longtime girlfriend of Barney Fife who patiently endured the deputy's fear of marriage—(not to mention Barney's tendency to insist upon going "Dutch" on their dates!). Betty had been a contract player for Twentieth Century-Fox in the late 1940s, and her TV credits both before and after *The Andy Griffith Show* are quite extensive and impressive. This multitalented actress looks back fondly on her days as one of Mayberry's most popular citizens and seems genuinely surprised by the enormous outpouring of love and enthusiasm she receives from fans of the show. Betty's quick wit and down-to-earth charm leave an interviewer with little doubt as to why she is a favorite of the fans.

"Where's the beef?" Certainly not on Barney, as Thelma Lou frantically fattens up her lover boy to pass the police physical exam.

Q: Can you tell us about some of your earlier experiences in show business? **BL: Well, when I was just eighteen I had auditioned for USO camp shows during the war. They said they wanted to send me overseas with a guitarist to do a hospital unit. They said I was a "girl next door" and I could sing and talk to the people in each ward. I was ready to go to Europe, but instead they sent me to China, Burma, and India for eight months. There weren't a lot of people entertaining in that area. It was gratifying, but also sad, emotional, and exhausting. I've never quite gotten over it—seeing the wounded, the dying, the paraplegics, and the young people who were ruined for life. I still cry a lot when I think about it.** Q: Upon your return, what direction did your career take? **BL: I came home to Kansas City, Missouri, for three months, and I went back to New York. The man on the train who took my luggage said, "Well, the little girl is going to try her wings in New York." In fact, I had just completed that tour of the military hospitals on the other side of the world! For the first year, I did hardly anything in New York. I was ready to come home and give up. My mother said, "Let's both make a novena to the Blessed Mother. If it's meant for you to stay there, something will happen in the next nine days. If not, you come home, Betty." Well, I soon signed a contract for a [Broadway] show called *Park Avenue*, which was not a big hit, but it gave me an opportunity. From that, I was approached by five different studios for tests. Fox signed me and I was thrilled. They brought me out to the West Coast, and I picked up my mother in Kansas City, as I was underage.** Q: What are some of the favorite films you did? **BL: Well, *Sitting Pretty* with Clifton Webb and Robert Young was my first film, and it's become a classic. I next did *Apartment for Peggy* with Bill Holden, *June***

***Bride* with Bette Davis, *Mother Is a Freshman* with Loretta Young, *Father Was a Fullback* with Fred MacMurray, *Cheaper by the Dozen* with Clifton Webb, *Payment on Demand* with Bette Davis, *Take Care of My Little Girl* with Jeanne Crain . . . I forget a lot of dates and specifics because some years ago a tornado hit my house and destroyed most of my personal mementos, so I really have nothing to refer to. In 1951, I started doing some television—mostly dramas like *Climax!* and *Wagon Train*. Then I did a series based on *The Egg and I* live for CBS for about eight months in New York. I returned to the West Coast and didn't realize how much the studios hated television, and my work in it hurt me. They considered television to be "beneath" them.** Q: How did all of this experience lead to *The Andy Griffith Show*? **BL: Well, I had managed to resume doing feature films eventually. On TV I did a series called *Where's Raymond?* with Ray Bolger, and then I was a regular on a series for Disney called *Texas John Slaughter*. When they called me in about *The Andy Griffith Show*, I was still under contract for that series. They had had several other women play opposite Don Knotts, but they ended up still looking for someone, and I guess I was it. I really don't know why they chose me. I had seen the show shortly before that. I was home alone, and it made me laugh out loud, which was very unusual. I thought it was a funny, cute show, but I had no idea I would ever be in it. I thought I was just doing a one-shot appearance, but of course, it became a regular thing.** Q: You had a wonderful on-screen rapport with Don Knotts, and the Barney-Thelma Lou relationship became a highlight of the series. **BL: I loved working with Don—and Andy, too. I loved every minute of the show. When they would use me in an episode, I couldn't wait to get**

there. I would sit around when I was through and watch everyone else work. Bob Sweeney was a terrific director, having been an actor himself. I was very privileged to have had the opportunity to work with these people. When we did *Return to Mayberry*, Andy said those were the happiest years of his life, and I think he meant that. Andy made sure that everything went well. He's a perfectionist in his own way, yet he has an easygoing way that is very appealing and fun to be around. I always felt free to throw in suggestions at the script conferences. We could all sit around and read the scripts together and laugh a lot. The writers were terrific, Aaron Ruben was a great producer, and it was very seldom that we encountered any problems with the script. Now and then there would be something that didn't strike me as being true to Thelma Lou's character. I'd open my mouth and say so, and while they may not have always agreed with me, they always listened. Q: Can you tell us about your personal relationships with the cast? **BL:** Most of my work was with Don, Andy, and sometimes with Ron and Frances. Later, when Aneta joined, we worked together frequently. They were all wonderful. I can say that among the other cast members, Jim Nabors was great to work with. Everyone told me what a gorgeous voice he had, but I had never heard him sing. One night, he took me to The Horn nightclub, where he was performing. After dinner, he got up and did his act which started off as a country humor thing. Then all of a sudden he went into *Pagliacci*—I almost fell of my chair! He's a sensational talent and a wonderful guy. I haven't seen him in ages—except for a brief bit during *Return to Mayberry*—but I remain very fond of him. Now Frances Bavier was a person about whom you knew very little when it came to her personal life. She was inclined to drop a few hints about things, then look at you with those dancing blue eyes. She was a real actress and a marvelous one. Every part that woman ever played, I just adored her in. I got along with her very, very well and had a lot of fun on the set. I really liked her a lot, and I wish I had more to do with her away from work. Now, as for Ron Howard, I always considered him and Natalie Wood to be among the best child actors. His parents had been in the business and knew what they were doing. They were always on the set and made sure he had a very good life. He couldn't have been nicer to work with. He was very serious about his work. He always wanted to be a director. I remember saying to him, "when you get to that point, Ronny, don't forget me!" (*laughs*) Because we admired him so much, it's been a great joy to all of us to see his career has gone so well. No one could be happier for him than all of us from *The Andy Griffith Show*. Another wonderful person was Howard McNear, who was the sweetest man you could ever want to meet. We were all crazy about him, and Hal Smith as well. I'd also like to say how adorable George Lindsey was. George is a real talent—he sings, dances, tells jokes, and MC's. Once on a plane, Hal Smith and Howard Morris were seated together, and I was sitting next to George Lindsey. I laughed so hard, I couldn't take it, and I was yelling, "Shut up, George! I can't breathe anymore!" He was giving me his whole routine, and by the time he was through I was hurting! Q: How did you feel when Don left the show? **BL: Well, I** didn't know at first. I was on location and all of a sudden Andy said something about Don leaving and I said, "What???" He said, "Didn't you know? Don's leaving because he has a contract with Universal." I said, "You're kidding! I'm glad you told me!"

Mayberry's sweethearts—Betty Lynn and Aneta Corsaut—reunited for *Return to Mayberry*.

Betty's charming portrayal of Thelma Lou continues to make her a favorite among fans.

(*laughs*) I didn't work on the show after that except for one time when he came back for the reunion, and found that I was married. You'd be surprised at the number of fans who said to me, "How could you have done that?" They thought it was my idea to have Thelma Lou married. But, I wasn't in favor of it. Q: It always seemed a little difficult to believe that the relationship between Barney and Thelma Lou could have deteriorated to such a point that he wouldn't have known she was married. **BL: I originally said, "The only way I can play this is if Thelma Lou had hired this fellow to pretend to be her husband because her feelings had been hurt by Barney's dragging on the relationship in the same way for so long."** Supposedly, this caused Thelma Lou to leave town, and then of course Barney had left town. I insisted the only way I could play that episode was to have my husband turn out to be a fellow I hired. But they said, "Oh, no, you really got married, Betty, you really did." I guess they wanted to end the relationship once and for all, and that was the way to do it. Ironically, that last show was the only color episode I did. Incidentally, the fellow who played my husband thought he was now going to have a steady role. He thought, "Boy, this is great! I'm Thelma Lou's husband!" I thought it was only fair to tell him that chances were that he wouldn't do the show ever again! (*laughs*) Q: In fairness, the Barney–Thelma Lou relationship was resolved very nicely by their wedding in *Return to Mayberry*. **BL: Yes, and it was done in a funny way with Barney pretending he had no interest, and yet knowing how many months and minutes I had been married. I had heard rumors for a couple of years that they were going to do a reunion show, but I didn't know if I would be in it. One Christmas Eve, I got a phone call from Andy, who was in North**

Carolina, and he said, "Betty, it's snowing here and everything. I thought I'd call you and wish you a Merry Christmas, and tell you that we're having a little party and we'd like you to be a part of it." Then he told me about the show. I thought it was sensational and I was glad to be a part. Initially, I didn't know if it was good to bring us back together twenty years later. Would we all work together in the same way? But once I got there and started filming, it was like we never had left each other. It was a great relief, and it felt great to do it. I had a wonderful time. Q: Can you fill us in on your career after *The Andy Griffith Show* **BL: I worked with Fred MacMurray as his secretary on *My Three Sons* for three years. After that I played Brian Keith's secretary on *Family Affair*. In later years, I did a few things but nothing very important. I was later hurt in an accident with a dog. I had an abscessed leg and a bacterial infection. They thought I was going to lose my leg. I was operated on, and then two months later I broke out with shingles. I looked like someone had painted me red, I had lesions all over, and my eyes were swollen shut. That's when all of a sudden, everyone called my agent asking me to do interviews! Before that, I hadn't gotten many calls. I really was very ill for quite a while, but although it was very difficult, I did start doing personal appearances in relation to *The Andy Griffith Show*.** Q: Do you enjoy the fan conventions? **BL: Oh, yes, although when I attended the big one in Nashville, I really didn't do very much. I had wanted to do something different, and come out and do a couple of numbers that would relate to Barney. But I never got the chance, because our time was very limited. Basically, I was just driven out in a squad car and we had a little routine where I was supposedly looking for Barney. It ended with**

Betty and the gang—Hal Smith, Jack Dodson, George Lindsey, and Howard Morris—at the 1990 TBS thirtieth anniversary taping. (photo courtesy of TBS)

George Lindsey and me onstage together, although we hadn't rehearsed anything. But the people were so wonderful! I felt kind of undeserving because they all went wild and I didn't even do anything. I thought I should sing or something, but these wonderful people gave me a standing ovation for doing nothing! They said maybe next time I'll get a chance to perform. Q: You later did some episodes of *Matlock* as Andy's secretary. What are your memories of those shows? BL: Well, there was no part there, unfortunately. Andy did his best, he made up things, took lines from other people, etcetera. But it just didn't work out. But it was a lot of fun working with Andy again. Q: Why do you think *The Andy Griffith Show* remains such a popular favorite among viewers? BL: I think it was based on good values and that it touched people in many ways. It had truth and reality, as well as some crazy things that made you laugh. The relationship between Barney and Andy

was great. So was the relationship between Andy and Opie. Many young fellows used to tell me that their own relationship with their fathers was not what they had hoped it would be, and they would turn on the TV and pretend it was the way Andy and Opie's was. You know, speaking of young men, I often meet fellows in their thirties who come up to me and tell me that when they were ten or twelve years old they were absolutely in love with Thelma Lou..In fact just recently, the cable TV repairman found out I had played Thelma Lou and said, "I was in love with Thelma Lou when I was twelve!" If anyone had known at the time how I was turning on so many ten- and twelve-year-old boys, they probably would have thrown me in jail! (*laughs*) But, these are the kind of sweet people that remember the show. It was truly a wonderful period in my life.

INTERVIEW WITH JACK DODSON

"Howard Sprague"

Jack Dodson was primarily known for his work in the theater prior to his joining the cast of *The Andy Griffith Show* in the series' fifth season, having won acclaim for his role opposite Jason Robards in Eugene O'Neill's *Huey*. It was during the Los Angeles run of the play that Andy Griffith took notice of the young actor and gave him a guest shot in episode 178: "Lost and Found," which aired on January 24, 1966. Although this was a one-shot appearance, Jack was asked shortly thereafter to portray Howard Sprague, the gentle, good-natured town clerk who had to cope with being "square" even by Mayberry standards, as well as the influence of his dominating mother. The character of Howard proved to be so popular that Jack Dodson continued to portray him during the *Mayberry R.F.D.* years. Following this, Jack gave a memorable performances in *The Getaway* and *Pat Garrett and Billy the Kid* (1973) for director Sam Peckinpah. Jack has had many other notable achievements throughout the years on TV, in film, and in the theater. He most recently had a recurring role in ABC's acclaimed *Homefront*.

Q: Is it true you originally never planned to be an actor? **JD: I always wanted to be a filmmaker, but there were very few places you could study film, especially where I was raised in Pittsburgh. I ended up going to Carnegie Tech. I graduated in 1953, went into the army, and did a hitch in Korea. Then I went to New York where I got a job as a night clerk at the Statler Hilton. I later got a part in an Off-Broadway play, and then joined the Circle-in-the-Square theater group. My first play there was *The Quare Fellow* about the I.R.A. We then did a highly acclaimed production of *Our Town* for [director] José Quintero, who was in his prime at the time. I was also in the original company of *The Balcony*, which was twenty years ahead of its time in this country.** Q: Your first big break came when you starred opposite Jason Robards in *Huey*. How did that role come about? **JD: I had been with the Circle-in-the-Square for seven years, but had never been able to crack Broadway. I was about ready to throw in the towel, because although I had worked consistently, I didn't make any money. I had a part-time job with a pipe and tobacco importer, and when they offered me a permanent job, I was going to take it. One day, José Quintero asked me if I wanted to do *Huey*. He said, "This will be on Broadway, and it will be just you and Jason Robards." Robards was the biggest star in the American theater. The play was an extraordinary experience and the beginning of a friendship that has lasted all these years. *Huey* got good reviews, but we didn't do any business, because the play was only a little over an hour long and nothing like that had been done at that time. Even though the tickets were eight dollars, the audience didn't think they were getting their money's worth!** (*laughs*) Q: Yet, the play opened in Los Angeles. **JD: Yes, it was there Andy**

Griffith came to see us and came backstage and raved about what a great evening of theater he thought it was. When the play ended, I stayed in L.A. to see if I could get some work in TV or on stage. I told my agent how Andy had seen the play and loved it, but when he spoke with the casting people, Andy didn't remember my name! My agent thought I was making up stories. Finally, Andy and his wife went to the movies to see *Darling* one night, and he hated it. He started talking about how the best acting he had seen recently was in our play. Then he remembered who I was and called me down to the set. I was embarrassed, and really didn't have anything to say to him! Suddenly, there was a terrible thunderstorm. I had to leave because I had left all the windows open in my car! That was really embarrassing, but they called me back to read for a small role. I didn't realize I was being evaluated for the role of Howard Sprague. Then they asked me if I would be interested in playing Howard. They described the role as a guy who always had a cold and lived with his mother. That was a time in my life when I thought I could play anything, so I said "Yes," even though I had never played a role even remotely like that. Q: Had you been familiar with the show prior to this? **JD: I was strictly a stage actor, and I only had Monday nights off, so I knew very little about TV. I had seen *The Andy Griffith Show* a few times, but my wife was a designer for *The Perry Como Show* which was on opposite *The Andy Griffith Show*, so of course we would watch Como. I was very naive when it came to Hollywood, and I had very little concept of what was being offered to me—a contract for the number-one show on TV.** Q: What are your recollections of the script conferences on *The Andy Griffith Show*? **JD: I participated because I wanted to learn. They didn't want you writing dialogue, but they**

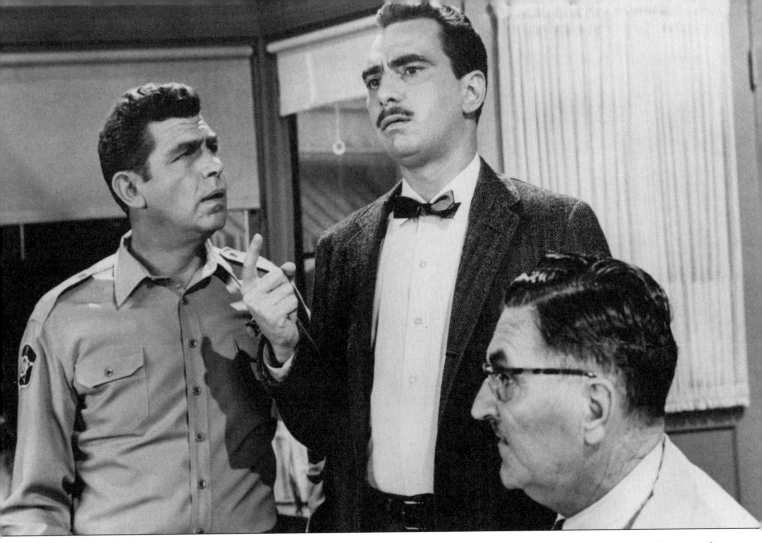

did encourage you to suggest something and let them put it into words. And that's the way it should work. I never realized until it was all over that most shows did not encourage such participation from the actors. It was a rude awakening when I began to work elsewhere to discover most writers don't even want to talk to the actors. On *The Andy Griffith Show*, it was different. You see, Howard Sprague was not a funny character—he was an amusing character. He was going to cease being amusing if he remained under the thumb of his mother. In order for that to work, you'd have to go very, very broad with it. That would get you into an area that wasn't right for that show. So I made a suggestion that we get Howard from under that thumb, and concentrate on his eccentricities—show him as a guy trying to fit in but not quite doing so, and they used that suggestion. Q: In fact, one of the funniest episodes involves Howard hosting an ill-fated party at his new "Bachelor Pad." When somebody finally does decide to show up, Howard utters that great line. " . . . and still they come!" JD: (*laughs*) Yeah, he had root beer and Swiss cheese sandwiches. He even had a beaded curtain on the door, and was saying, "Time flies when you're having fun!" (*laughs*) Who couldn't be pleased with that writing? Our writers were all educated, well read, worldly fellows, you know. Bob Ross, especially. He was very instrumental in the development of Howard's character. Howard was not an easy character to write for and frequently there had to be a good deal of rewriting done to avoid the more clichéd aspects of the character. Q: Are there any episodes that stand out in your memory? JD: I remember very vividly the episode where Howard wants to move to an island to get away from the hurly-burly of Mayberry [episode 234, "Howard's New Life"—Ed.].

Harry Dean Stanton was in that one, playing the guy that owned the bar. We weren't allowed to call it a bar, though. (*laughs*) When Harry walked on the stage the first day, he was very quiet. I remember thinking, "This isn't going to be very funny. He's playing it too low key." Then when we began to work, I saw how wonderful he was. It was a marvelous comedic performance. That episode was a really tough shoot. The sound of the waves caused us to have to loop a lot of our dialogue. They also had to use a lot of lights for balance, and the heat created by those lights was hideous. It was a marvelous show, but the making of it was a nightmare. Q: What are your recollections of *Return to Mayberry*? JD: I had encouraged Andy to do the show. He had been reluctant, but I knew that we were still of an age back then that if it worked, we could go back and make it into a regular series. When Andy finally agreed to do *Return to Mayberry*, unfortunately, the project was initially placed in the hands of people who didn't know what to do with it. Andy had to get rid of the first script, and while he was waiting for a new script, along came *Matlock*. The show was a big hit, and that canceled out any possibility of reviving a show about Mayberry. As for *Return to Mayberry*, I think they should have concentrated more on the election rather than the monster in the lake. Also, there was a pretty standard bad guy, and he didn't really work all that well in Mayberry. If you're going to have a villain in Mayberry, he's got to be as inept as the rest of us. However, that movie did give me an opportunity to write. Andy and I had talked about whether to dye our hair for the show, so that inspired me to write that stuff about Howard dying his hair with Cuban Sunset, and being preoccupied with the possibility of going to a beauty parlor. Q: The movie gave you a rare opportunity

Howard, the most destructive force known to serious fisherman since *Jaws*, actually lands "Old Sam" in Jack Dodson's favorite episode, "Big Fish in a Small Town."

to work with Don Knotts, who had already left *The Andy Griffith Show* when you joined the cast. **JD: Yes, I knew Don but had not actually worked with him before. I wasn't in the shows where he returned to Mayberry. I was in the one where Andy and Helen got married, and Don came back for the wedding. We posed for some publicity pictures together, but we didn't have any scenes together. You know, the *Return to Mayberry* movie was very decent, and of course, the ratings went through the roof. I knew they would, because in my travels, I found that people regarded me as an old acquaintance, and would ask, "Why can't they do it again?" Just one final thought on that picture—I had lost a lot of hair over the years, but when I saw Ron Howard, I realized he had lost even more. I remember thinking, "Man, I never thought I'd live to be *that* old!"** (*laughs*) Q: Were you close with the other actors you worked with regularly on the show? **JD: The whole company was a joy to be around. However, of all the people on the show, I'd say that only Howard McNear was somewhat like his character in real life. Most of us weren't. Andy Griffith is nothing like Andy Taylor, Frances Bavier was nothing like Aunt Bee, and so on. I remember it being extraordinarily difficult to watch when Howard began having trouble right before he left the show. It was all rather sudden. It was toward the end of the day, and Howard was exhausted from having been on the set since that morning. It was the last scene of the day, and he could barely get through it, which had never been the case before. It was very painful to watch. He was a splendid actor, and he and his wife were such lovely people. I also got along very well with Frances, but I never knew anything about her personally. Aneta Corsaut had a party once, and I was quite surprised that Frances came. She had a wonderful time and was very outgoing.**

My wife had never met her, and they had a long conversation. That was my only memory of Frances socializing off the set. Years later, I was working at ABC and a guard told me he used to work with her husband. I never even knew she had been married! It may not have even been true, but she was so private, I can't be sure! But she had a great voice and could read beautifully. She could have made a fortune doing voice-overs. Q: How did you react to the cancellation of *Mayberry, R.F.D.*? **JD: When we were finally canceled, they put out a lot of baloney about canceling all the rural programs to improve the quality of CBS. They really more or less denounced all of us who were in those shows. We were very highly rated when we were canceled, but they put out some press releases that said how ghastly these shows were and how awful it was for CBS to have shown them. The newspapers swallowed this bullshit, but the real reason for canceling them was because the new regime at CBS wanted to clear out the programs from the old regime. Their idea of improving the quality of the shows was to put on a series in which Ted Bessell was living with a monkey. We weren't the only ones who suffered. Look at *The Beverly Hillbillies*. That was excellent farce. The show has been demeaned, but it was brilliantly performed. When *Mayberry* was canceled, many of us were blacklisted. I didn't work much until 1976. Hal Cooper, one of the directors on *Mayberry*, was a big help in getting me back on TV. He introduced me to Norman Lear and I got some guest shots on *Maude* and *All's Fair*.** Q: Right after *Mayberry R.F.D.* was canceled, you appeared in Sam Peckinpah's *The Getaway* with McQueen. What was it like working with the maverick director? **JD: I knew Sam through Jason Robards. When Sam was doing the picture I sent him a telegram that said, "At**

Howard's ability to toss a one-liner is met with typical reaction by Andy.

liberty." He called me in and we talked. The next day, "Bingo!" He gave me the part. We did everything on the first take. Originally, the couple [McQueen and Ali MacGraw] were supposed to be captured, but in the final film they make a clean getaway. That was very controversial at the time. Later, I did *Pat Garrett and Billy the Kid* for Peckinpah. Sam was an interesting guy. He had done a marvelous prologue for that film, but the studio cut it. He began to come apart as far back as *The Wild Bunch*, when the studio cut that, too. He took that really badly. He was a strange fella, but I got along with him very well. He kind of destroyed himself, but the industry helped him to do so. He wouldn't play the game. Q: Can you fill us in on some of your more recent activities, including your recurring role in the TV series *Homefront*? **JD: I did a picture for Propaganda Films called *A Climate for Murder*. It's been on HBO and is out on cassette. It's a good little picture. Last year I did a pilot called *The Sons of Liberty* about small-town guys that belong to a lodge. There were a lot of old character actors, which may be why it didn't sell! As for *Homefront*, I actually enjoyed watching the show, including the episodes I was in. With *The Andy Griffith Show*, I watch the reruns occasionally, but only those I don't appear in. I was only supposed to appear in one episode of *Homefront*, but they liked what I did and I ended up doing eight. It was the best work I've** done in twenty years. I'm also in strong contention for two feature films that will be shot in New York, but I can't be more specific since nothing is definite. I've also done a voice-over in a Keebler commercial with Parley Baer. Other than that, I'd like to do another series so I can make the big bucks for my old age! **(laughs)** Q: Do you have a favorite episode of *The Andy Griffith Show*? **JD: I like them all, but the one I enjoyed most was the one where I caught the fish named Old Sam [episode 200, "Big Fish in a Small Town"—Ed.]. I got to play a serious scene with Ron Howard, and I played that in a way they didn't expect me to play it. It worked well, and that's the one I enjoyed filming the most. However, there were so many that we enjoyed shooting because of all the laughter and shenanigans *off* camera, especially when something would go wrong. We never saved our bloopers, unfortunately.** Q: Are you surprised at the longevity of the fan movement for *The Andy Griffith show*? **JD: Yes, because we never set out to make a classic. We never expected it to have such a long life. The program didn't get the kind of publicity *Cheers* got, for instance. I don't think I did more than a couple of interviews for the show. But *The Andy Griffith Show* changed my life for the better. It's one of the things I'm most proud of in my entire life.**

INTERVIEW WITH HAL SMITH

"Otis Campbell"

Hal Smith was a popular character actor by the late 1950s, owing to his work on a variety of TV series and radio shows, where his versatile speaking ability allowed him to capitalize on his talent for creating memorable voices for the characters he portrayed. In 1961, he joined *The Andy Griffith Show* as Otis Campbell, the most lovable town drunk in history. Instead of portraying Otis as a one-dimensional rummy for slapstick effect, Hal often gave him depth and a sense of emotion that made audiences empathize with the character. During and after the *Griffith* years, Hal found himself in great demand for voice-over work in films, TV, and commercials. Audiences may be surprised to know that the voice of Mayberry's most inebriated citizen gave life to Winnie the Pooh, Barney Rubble, Goofy, and numerous other classic children's characters. In recent years, Hal has maintained a nonstop work schedule, but often finds the time to attend movie memorabilia conventions, where he is inevitably mobbed by fans of *The Andy Griffith Show*.

Q: Is it true that your first acting role was as a "Nasty Little Elf" in a school play? **HS: That's right—it was *The Story of Pandora* in my first year in grammar school in Wilmington, North Carolina, where I lived until I was nine years old. It was a traveling company that came to town and was looking for kids who wanted to play an elf in Pandora's box—if you'll pardon the expression. (*laughs*) It was a little dark in there! We moved to New York State, where my folks owned seventy-five hundred maple sugar trees. My brother and I used to tap those trees for the sap and put it on a sled and take it to the sugar house. We started doing amateur shows and won just about every one we were in. I played a little guitar, and my brother and I would sing duets. We called ourselves "The Smith Brothers"—Cough and Drop. When I got out of the service in 1946, instead of going back to Utica, where I worked in radio, I came to California. I took a gamble, and got a part-time job in radio right off the bat. I also parked cars for months to earn some money.** Q: How did you begin landing acting roles? **HS: Well, being in radio, several casting directors heard about me. I was making a personal appearance in Missouri for the worst picture ever made, called *Down Missouri Way*, which was the first "Francis the Talking Mule" movie. When I got back to California, I got a call from an agent named Betty Wookey who had been told about me. She offered me a role in [a B western] *Stars Over Texas* with Eddie Dean. This led to many TV credits including a role as the neighbor in *I Married Joan* [with Joan Davis and Jim Backus]. We also made a series called *Jefferson Drum* [1958 to '59], which was the first dramatic show produced by Goodson-Todman. Later [1962], I played Barney the photographer in *Saints and sinners* with Nick Adams, and one of the neighbors in *Fair Exchange*. I was also the Pancake Man for International House of Pancakes and Pioneer Pete for Pioneer Chicken.** Q: How did you become involved with *The Andy Griffith Show*? **HS: Someone saw me playing a drunk on *Ozzie and Harriet* and [casting director] Ruth Birch had me come over to read. When I was on, somebody said, "Hey, you're Otis!" I had no idea it would be a running thing. Unfortunately, there was an executive at our sponsor—General Mills, who kept trying to get me off the show because he was an alcoholic, and he saw himself whenever he saw me. But Danny Thomas, Sheldon Leonard, and Andy Griffith insisted that I would stay. They had a lot of guts to fight the sponsor! I ended up doing about fifty episodes.** Q: What are your recollections of the atmosphere on the set? **HS: It was as pleasant as the dickens! It was demanding to a point, but marvelous. We had a dart board where Andy, Don, and I would play. We'd tell stories and laugh and giggle. Andy was a wonderful guy. He'd say to somebody, "Now wait a minute, that line shouldn't be mine. Give it to someone else." He was always so generous. He viewed his role as a philosophical solver of problems. He was great at it, and I think he remains one of the most unheralded actors we have in the business. Many of the best parts of that show were Andy's ideas that were put into the script. I did have to break his balloon one time, though. It was at a party with Ozzie Nelson, who told Andy that I first played a drunk on his show. Andy insisted it was on *The Andy Griffith Show*, but I had to side with Ozzie on that one. (*laughs*) I should also say that Don Knotts was absolutely delightful to work with as well. You know, I appeared as the town drunk in Don's first picture for Universal, *The Ghost and Mr. Chicken*. We still keep in touch frequently**

"Deputy Otis." Andy and Barney assist Mr. Campbell in his ruse to convince his brother-in-law that he is a reputable lawman.

Is Otis off to "Moo York City"? Maybe he should try an "udder" form of transportation!

today. He and I would often think of things to put into the scripts for *The Andy Griffith Show*. I must say, however, that the writing was absolutely great. If it wasn't for the good writers the show wouldn't have been what it was. Q: Were you close with others from the cast on a social basis? HS: Well, although I didn't know him too well on a personal level, I loved working with Howard McNear. He told me a funny story about the day his son was in the back yard with a can of black aerosol spray. The can stopped up on him, so Howard took it into the house to fix it. He ended up putting it on a can opener, which caused it to explode and cover the whole kitchen in black paint. I asked how his wife reacted, and he said in that inimitable way, "Why she hit me with a broom!" (*laughs*) I also should talk about Ron Howard. He was a sharp little kid, but I never thought he'd end up being so big in the business because his dream was to be a baseball player. He talked, slept, and drank baseball. He'd bring bats and balls on the set and we'd play with him. He was a marvelous kid. Q: Did you watch the show regularly with your family? HS: Yes, whenever I was home I would watch it with my son and wife. We enjoyed it very much, but there are many I've never seen so I watch them on reruns. You know, my son, Terry, ended up going into show business. He does prosthetics and makeup. He worked with John Chambers on the makeup for *Planet of the Apes*, and was nominated for an Emmy for *Alice in Wonderland*. He also did the makeup for the science-fiction series *V*. In fact, he's working on a bust of Otis right now that might be marketed commercially in the future. Q: What was it like resuming the role of Otis in *Return to Mayberry*? HS: It was just like we had only been gone from each other a day. It was like no time had lapsed between the last

episode and that movie. The main thing is that they sobered up Otis and made him an ice-cream salesman because drunks aren't prevalent [today] on TV. I said to Andy, "Why can't I say I sell rum ice cream and let it melt so I can drink it in the morning?" He told me, "Oh, we can't do that!" (*laughs*) Q: Since *The Andy Griffith Show* you've been working virtually nonstop. Can you fill us in on some of your more prominent achievements? HS: Well, they wanted me to do a running character as a drunk on *Night Court*, but I was too busy to commit to it at the time. I'm also involved with a radio show and a cartoon show for a group called "Focus on the Family," which Parley Baer is associated with frequently. My character is called John Avery Whittaker, and his coffee shop is called "Whit's End." When little kids have problems, they come to him for help. These are religious shows, but the messages are short and we don't press them too hard. The radio show is on all the Christian stations. I've been doing these for over five years, and I've loved every minute of it. I also do—or have done—the voices of Winnie the Pooh for seventeen years; Flintheart Glombold in *Duck Tales*, Goofy, the horse in *Beauty and the Beast*, and the original Barney in *The Flintstones*. I just did the voice of Santa Claus for Hanna-Barbera's new feature film *Jeremy Creek*. [At this point the interviewer can't resist asking Hal to do a repertoire of his voices for his seven-year-old daughter, Nicole. Hal happily complies, and does a spontaneous and hilarious number of his imitations.] Q: I feel as though I just lived through thirty years of TV history in two minutes! HS: (*laughs*) Those were all fun things to do. I loved every minute of the work I did in those shows. Q: Do you have a favorite episode of *The Andy Griffith Show* HS: I have several, including "Aunt Bee, the

Otis and his fellow moonshiner see visions more frightening than the usual pink elephants in the "Haunted House" episode. Hal Smith would have a supporting role in *The Ghost and Mr. Chicken* which was inspired by this episode.

Warden" and "Dogs, Dogs, Dogs" [episodes 55 and 93—Ed.], both of which were very funny. I also think "Hot Rod Otis" [episode 114] was a great show as well. You know, it's amazing how many people still enjoy *The Andy Griffith Show*. I was back in Charlotte, North Carolina, at the speedway for an appearance. They built a jail in the welcome tent for Otis, and it's a good thing they did, because I was mobbed and ended up signing thirteen hundred autographs. The show is nostalgic even for young people and those people who don't come from little towns. Even today, little kids ask me for autographs. Last week two girls who look like Campbell's Soup twins came up to me in a restaurant and went wild when I gave them autographs. I also attended the Memphis Film Festival with Aneta Corsaut, Betty Lynn, and Howie Morris from *The Andy Griffith Show*, and the reaction was just great. *The Andy Griffith Show* was an important part of my life and I thoroughly enjoyed every minute of it.

INTERVIEW WITH HOWARD MORRIS

"Ernest T. Bass"

Howard Morris was a major name in TV comedy when he assumed the infrequent, but legendary role of Ernest T. Bass in *The Andy Griffith Show*. His first appearance came in episode 94 ("Mountain Wedding") and his grand finale as the kooky mountain hermit was in episode 162 ("Malcolm at the Crossroads"). Howard resurrected the character for a memorable appearance in the 1986 *Return to Mayberry* film. He also contributed greatly to any number of classic TV shows going back to the medium's early days. Morris has worked with the great legends of comedy, many of whom he remains friendly with to this day. In addition to his acting skills, Howard is a noted comedy director and has more credits than are possible to list here. He directed eight episodes of *The Andy Griffith Show*, and has received the Clio award several times for his outstanding direction of TV commercials. The multitalented Morris also has an extensive number of credits in feature films, as both actor and director.

Interviewing Howard Morris is an experience unlike any other. His sarcastic wit mandates that you have a good sense of humor about everything in life—including yourself! He finds humor in literally everything, and remains a zany talent.

Helen Crump's class is turned into a rural blackboard jungle in "The Education of Ernest T. Bass."

Q: Is it true that your first inclination to go into show business came from watching your mother play the organ in movie houses? **HM: Yes, sort of. My first experience with film—silent through it was—was at the Gem Theater on One Hundred and Eighty-first Street in Manhattan. I guess I was seven or eight, and I sat in the dark looking up at this huge screen. It was a movie called *The Last Command* with Emil Jennings.** Q: That couldn't have been remade years later under the same title, with Sterling Hayden? I believe that film dealt with the Alamo? **HM: What the [blank!] could Emil Jennings have to do with the Alamo?** (*laughs*) **No, this was an old silent movie about a Russian film director who came to the U.S. as a refugee from a revolution and ended up as an extra in movies. I remember looking up and saying to myself, "Gee, I could do that!" Although, I guess the jury's still out as to whether I can!** Q: Was it your original intention to become a comedian or an actor? **HM: At that time, I had no comprehension about the difference between the two. I just wanted to be something other than what I was. I got a scholarship to NYU and went to the drama department there. I began to work with a group called the Washington Square Players. The first real performance I ever did was in a play by George Bernard Shaw called *You Never Can Tell*. I remember standing in the wings petrified. I heard my cue, made my entrance, hit my mark, said my first speech, and fainted right on stage. But I learned a lot from that group. For instance, on Saturday nights we would do *Hamlet* and I would play several parts.** Q: How did you go from performing in *Hamlet* to being primarily a comedic actor? **HM: By pure accident. You just fall into things when you're in the theater. I tried a stand-up act, but I was no good at it. I need to work in tandem with other actors. I ended up** doing a lot of "quick" TV programs, as there were very few big shows in those days. There were mostly variety shows like Berle, Gleason, and Sid Caesar. I had done a number of shows such as *Hamlet* with Maurice Evans; *Call Me Mister* with Carl Reiner, Buddy Hackett, and Bob Fosse; and *John Loves Mary*. After that, I was making the rounds looking for work. I was headed down Fifty-second Street toward the bus, about ready to go home. I ran into a guy named Biff Liff, who had been the stage manager of *Call Me Mister*. He said, "If you go across the street and ask for Max Liebman, he's doing a show called *The Admiral Broadway Review* with Sid Caesar." I said "Who?" I didn't know who anybody was. He said, "They're looking for a guy Sid can lift up by the lapels! It's for a TV show." Well, nobody wanted to do TV back then. It was a misbegotten medium. I had a moment to decide whether to continue on my way home, but I was right across the street so I went up there. When I got there, four guys were carrying a woman across the floor while she was singing. It turned out she was Imogene Coca. I met Max Liebman in the ladies' dressing room and he introduced me to Lucille Callan and Mel Tolkin, the writers, Sid Caesar, and a Frenchman who was there studying American theatrical techniques. I read the scene with Sid and he looked over at Max and said, "Him! Get!" For thirty-five dollars I was hired to do that show on a one-shot basis. The next day Max asked, "Can you write?" I said, "I can print!" He said, "All right, you're a writer. Can you dance? If so, it's another five dollars." So I made forty-five dollars. I worked by sign language and sounds with the Frenchman, who didn't speak English, until the next morning I was in the john and the Frenchman said, "Hey, Howie, how ya doin'?" It was Mel Brooks.

The good, the bad, and the ugly? Nah, just the local boys contemplating Ernest T.'s upcoming fight with Malcolm Merriweather.

If love is blind, then Ernest T. must have glaucoma! Howard and Don in the "Mountain Wedding" episode that introduced Mr. Bass.

From that moment, we became very close friends. I stayed with the show until it ended, then I did *Gentlemen Prefer Blondes* on Broadway while simultaneously working on *Your Show of Shows* with Sid and Imogene. Q: How did you become involved with *The Andy Griffith Show*? **HM: Aaron Ruben had been a writer on a program I did with Sid called *Caesar's Hour*. He became the producer of** *The Andy Griffith Show*. **Along came a script with the part of Ernest T. Bass which they wanted me to look at. I wasn't busy, so I did it. However, out of the entire run of** *The Andy Griffith Show*, **I was only on it five times. It had to do with the power of that character [Ernest T. Bass]. When I go south as Ernest T. Bass, kids come up to me and say, "Mr. Bass, when I grow up, I want to be just like you!" It's a tribute to insanity in the nation. One of the reasons Ernest T. Bass was only on five times was because they didn't know what to do with him—he was such a strong character, he overpowered everything around him.** Q? It's been said that certain elements of Ernest T.'s character were improvised by yourself. Is that true? **HM: Well, I used to make up those rhymes he would say. They let me do it because they were wise enough to realize it had some strength. I also was involved in another way, because I directed some of the episodes, although that didn't happen until I had already played Ernest T.** Q: You also made a brief appearance in an episode set out on Myer's Lake, wherein you played a TV repairman [episode 140, "Andy and Helen Have Their Day"— Ed.]. **HM: (*laughs*) Oh, yeah. The word "yeah" became very important in that episode. It hadn't been fully written and they asked me to do it, so [imitates his voice in the episode] I said, "Yeah." And of course, the character kept saying that one word in that same voice.** Q: Had you been a fan of *The Andy Griffith Show* prior to being involved with it? **HM: I had seen it a few times, and had been impressed with the cast, especially Don Knotts. On the set, Andy was a tough taskmaster because he wanted everything right—and there ain't nothin' wrong with that! He always listened to people's suggestions, and that was a quality the show had, but it was so well written to begin with, there wasn't much you had to do. (*sneezes*) Oh, that felt good! (*laughs*) Getting back to the set, I have a tendency to keep going after the director says "Cut!" Andy realized that, and he let me do it. And we found so many good things can happen after the word "Cut!" had been uttered. If an actor has any skill, he can wing stuff that turns out to be vitally useful. When I directed the shows myself, I remember being impressed by the people involved. They were a damned good group of guys, totally professional with good scripts and a great work ethic. What more can you ask for?** Q: Did you find acting more challenging than directing? **HM: There was a difference. As an actor, you are a segment—one instrument in the band. As a director, you're kind of the leader. So, somewhere along the way, I said I'd rather lead the band than play piccolo. That is no longer true, though. I now direct and act with equal zest.** Q: Do you think it was appropriate to film *The Andy Griffith Show* as a one-camera show, as opposed to doing it in front of a live audience? **HM: Sure, it was successful wasn't it? If it ain't broke, don't screw with it. I don't think any value would have been gotten with that show, had an audience been there. Certain textures need certain things. And this is a show of gentle, old-time recollection. That's what we long for today. You know, you could have two guys sit on the porch and just talk about nothing. It was about human beings; about things that could have a revelatory quality to an**

The (almost) civil Ernest T. shows progress under Andy and Helen's tutelage.

audience. They didn't go for jokes. It was all derived out of character and situations, and that's the best kind of comedy. Q: What are your recollections of *Return to Mayberry*? HM: It felt like *The Twilight Zone*. There we were with the same people, the same clothes, the same sets, the same situations. It was wild and really wonderful—like you were dreaming. Bob Sweeney was still living, and as director he had a real feeling of the texture of the show, and was wise enough to let the juices flow. Hmmm, that sounded very poetic! Anyway, by "juice" I mean the talent of the actor to . . . having been given those words and situations . . . provide a little extra "gravy" or "sauce." I was pleased with the movie, and it got one of the biggest ratings ever. Q: Andy says his only regret is not having Ernest T. Bass show up in the last frames to throw some rocks at Barney. HM: Well, if you remember, the last scene showed Don and Andy taking down the flag. They shot a scene of me throwing rocks. For whatever reason, they didn't use it. Q: During the years of *The Andy Griffith Show* you remained one of the most active writers and directors in TV. What was the extent of your involvement with *Get Smart*? HM: Well, Mel Brooks and Buck Henry really came up with something there, especially when you mix in Don Adams's insanity and some wonderful writing. I only directed one episode—the pilot. Q: Why did you not stay on with the show? HM: You can only tell the witch doctor to go [blank] himself once. Thereby hangs a tale I will not elaborate on. I just did the pilot as director and writer, although there were a lot of elements from the show that I invented, such as the cartoon aspect of the show. Carl Reiner had let me direct *The Dick Van Dyke Show* and that helped me establish a reputation, although I had done dozens of other shows like *The Andy Griffith Show* and

Hogan's Heroes. Anyway, Mel had me see someone who had a script for *Get Smart*. He was holding it like it was toilet paper and he said to me, "I don't know if we have a show here or not." I took one look at it and said, "God! This thing is brilliant, and you don't know whether you have a show or not?" It was the best thing I had read in years, and I was thrilled to direct it. This gentleman remained with the show for years. I did not. But I'm very proud of the pilot as it kind of puts everything together in a strange way and sets the style for the series. I also cast Ed Platt as The Chief because the legitimacy of him in contrast to Don and Barbara Feldon was so perfect that it set up a sense of reality. That's what's wrong with comedy today. Comedy only works if it comes off of something real. Q: You also won Clios for your direction of commercials. Can you tell us which specific ads were so honored? HM: You may remember a series of McDonald's commercials which dealt with the employees—guys cleaning up and leaping over tables. And that won a Clio, although I had to fight the ad agency. They said you couldn't have people jumping over counters. So I shot it the way they wanted, but then I scotched the film. I was a nervy little bastard in those days! Back then they allowed you to do things that way. Nowadays, you don't get those opportunities. It's all money and power. I don't do it anymore because of age. That's a syndrome of this business. If you have white hair, they don't even want to see you. It's very scary because it affects you day to day. This is my ego speaking, but in terms of skills and professional techniques, I'm better now than I've ever been in my life. That is a result of years and years of experience. If they don't want to use that experience, then I have to think it's their loss. Jeez, listen to my damned mouth!

Still crazy after all these years. Howard on the TBS thirtieth anniversary special. (photo courtesy of TBS)

(laughs) Q: With TV comedy so poor today, it's a small wonder the reruns of classic shows like *The Andy Griffith Show* remain so popular. **HM: You know, I'll tell you a story. I got a call from Billy Crystal from left field one day. He said, "Howie, we haven't met, but when I was six years old and it was time for me to go to bed, I would lie down on the living-room floor and my father would grab me by the ankles and lug me into the bedroom while I'd yell 'I'm Ernest T. Bass!'" I was so flattered, because I'm such a fan of this guy!** Q: Do you enjoy attending the fan conventions for *The Andy Griffith Show*? **HM: I go south and put on the Ernest T. outfit and they absolutely flood me. After that, I sign autographs and can sit there for four hours doing that. I makes me feel great. You know what else makes me feel great? They're *my* photos they're buying to get autographed! But *The Andy Griffith Show* gave me a sense of reality to deal with. You could take pride from it and learn from it and maybe benefit the world a little bit if only through laughter.** Q: Who makes you laugh? **HM: Oh, the Marx Brothers, Laurel and Hardy, W. C. Fields, Jackie Mason, Jack E. Leonard, and a guy named Sid Gould, who is eight-two years old. Harvey Korman and I visit him in the Motion Picture Home and he has us falling on the ground with laughter. He's very sweet and dear to us. I think laughter is one of the most important emotions we own. Everyday, I hope two things happen to me: I want to think of my father, who died in 1946, and I want to get a belly laugh. If either of those things don't happen, it's an empty feeling I get. Jesus, if you could put this to some damned music . . !**

INTERVIEW WITH EVERETT GREENBAUM

Writer for *The Andy Griffith Show*
1961–64

The name Everett Greenbaum is quite familiar to those who love classic TV episodes. Greenbaum, in collaboration with his late writing partner Jim Fritzell, wrote many of the best episodes of *The Andy Griffith Show* and *M*A*S*H*, as well as several successful feature films for Don Knotts. Together, these two helped define the Mayberry that fans came to know and love, beginning with the series' second season. Among their most popular episodes were "Convicts at Large," "Barney's First Car," "Dogs, Dogs, Dogs," "Citizen's Arrest," "Barney's Sidecar," and "Man in a Hurry"—(generally regarded as the one that best exemplifies the charm of the show). Greenbaum has concentrated on voice-over work and acting in recent years, and he appears occasionally as Judge Katz on *Matlock*. He also cowrote *Return to Mayberry* with Harvey Bullock.

Evy (right) joins Andy and director Bob Sweeney in some musical high jinks between takes.

When in Southern California visit Universal City Studios

G-G-GUARANTEED!
YOU'LL BE SCARED UNTIL YOU LAUGH YOURSELF SILLY!

DON KNOTTS
The GHOST and MR. CHICKEN

TECHNICOLOR
CO-STARRING JOAN STALEY · LIAM REDMOND · DICK SARGENT
Written by JAMES FRITZELL and EVERETT GREENBAUM · Directed by ALAN RAFKIN
Produced by EDWARD J. MONTAGNE · A UNIVERSAL PICTURE

The Ghost and Mr. Chicken was Don Knotts's first film for Universal following his departure from *The Andy Griffith Show*. Written by Evy and Jim Fritzell, the movie was a box-office smash.

Q: How did you become teamed with your longtime partner, Jim Fritzell? **EG: We both wanted to write for the** *Mr. Peepers* **program. I was thrown into a room with him and told to write with him. It was supposed to last two weeks, and it went on for thirty years. Both of our cultures were middle Americana. We knew what most Americans talked like, whereas the guys from New York and Chicago were too sophisticated for middle America and the South. Jim knew all about sports—he lived for them. He also knew a lot about booze and card playing. I knew everything else!** (*laughs*). **He had an unhappy marriage at the time with a Swedish model.** Q: How can any marriage to a Swedish model be unhappy? **EG:** (*laughs*) **Right! Well, this one was. She eventually left him for the man who created** *Mr. Peepers*. **Anyway, after three years of writing forty shows a year, we were really tired of each other's voices. He was going through a bad period, and I had the offer to write for the** *George Gobel Show*, **so I came out to the West Coast. When I was writing for Gobel, I had a fight with a sponsor after my second year. There was a joke about a grandmother putting her false teeth in water and a sponsor wanted her to put them in condensed milk!** Q: Sounds like a pretty emotional issue. **EG:** (*laughs*) **It was! It got me fired! I was later writing for Eve Arden by myself. Jim eventually came out to the Coast to write a show called** *The Brothers* **with Bob Sweeney. That failed and he started writing a show called** *Mr. Adams and Eve* **for Ida Lupino and Howard Duff. One day he called me and said he was just stuck on writing this script. He offered me seven hundred dollars to write a few pages with him, and we ended up writing a whole act. I still wanted to be independent, however. Later, we cowrote a pilot for a show for Paddy Chayefsky. It was like magic working together, so we con-**

tinued to do so. We then wrote *The Real McCoys*. **Neither one of us had any great ambition. It wasn't a wonderful show. The plots were limited and it was cheaply done. Then we eventually got the offer to do** *The Andy Griffith Show*. Q: *The Andy Griffith Show* was already on the air for a season by that time. **EG: Yes, it had been on the air a full year. I hadn't been paying any attention to the show, to tell the truth. When I did see it, I saw little bits of off-beat, shaggy humor that I liked. When I got on the set, I realized that Andy loved that kind of stuff. For some reason, Jim and I always had a feel for small-town Americana. The show proved to be a love match right from the start, especially with Andy and Don. They're both such very talented guys.** Q: What do you recall about the script conferences on the show? **EG: In those days, the Writers Guild would let the writers have a preparatory week wherein they would meet every day without pay and suggest story ideas. At the end of the week, we would decide who would do certain stories. We would start out with notions for three stories. Once those were assigned, we would write the script. As the season went on, each writer—or writing team—would meet with Aaron Ruben and sometimes Sheldon Leonard, and as the years went on Andy would turn up. Andy has great humor and charm and loves to work. Andy, Jim and Don and I vibrated the same harmonics. I always had too much fun. Andy used to say, "Evy doesn't talk about the job the first day!" That was his motto for me.** Q: Andy tells me you always had the ability to crack him up. **EG: Well, when we were doing [the film]** *Angel in My Pocket* **we had a bungalow we were working in. One day I got him laughing so hard, he punched his hand through the wall and it came out the other side! I can still do that to him once in a while.** Q: A great

He's an ASTRO-KNOTT turned ASTRONAUT in the Maddest Mixup in Space History !!

UNIVERSAL presents

DON KNOTTS

The RELUCTANT ASTRONAUT

TECHNICOLOR

CO-STARRING Leslie NIELSEN · Joan FREEMAN · Jeanette NOLAN and Arthur O'CONNELL

...FRANK McGRATH · ROBERT PICKERING Written by JIM FRITZELL and EVERETT GREENBAUM Directed and Produced by EDWARD J. MONTAGNE A UNIVERSAL PICTURE

Evy and Jim also cowrote *The Reluctant Astronaut*, Don's follow-up feature to *The Ghost and Mr. Chicken*. It too proved to be a hit with audiences.

deal of credit for the quality of the early episodes must go to the late director Bob Sweeney. Did you have a good working relationship with him? **EG: We were very close because Jim and Sweeney went to high school together. Sweeney was Jim's idol because he was in the Sweeney and March comedy team [on radio]. It's a real shame that he died recently. It's also a tragedy that Jim died so young. He was only fifty-nine. Unfortunately, he was very self-destructive.** Q: Let's discuss some of the other alumni from the show and your recollections of them: Don Knotts. **EG: I always thought of Don as a naughty younger brother. We were on the road a lot to make his features for Universal. When we were doing *The Reluctant Astronaut* we went to Cape Canaveral and actually had lunch with some German scientists. Don said, "I'm getting to the other end of the table. You're Jewish and these guys were Nazis!" He's a very shy man but wonderfully talented.** Q: Frances Bavier. **EG: In all truthfulness, we never got along. It was probably because we had absolutely nothing in common and she was often critical of the writing. But I can't really say I knew her because I wasn't on the set all that much.** Ron Howard. **EG: Marvelous kid and marvelous man from a wonderful family. He's one of the few success stories among child actors. I've seen almost all his films as actor and director and he's very good.** Q: Howard McNear. **EG: He was closest to his character on the show out of everyone. I loved writing scripts with him. He once told me that when he was very young and trying to get parts, the studio sent him to a place on Hollywood Boulevard to take ballet lessons! He was very embarrassed to have to wear tights and stretch his legs. One day a guy showed up at the studio to fix the radiator. He stood and stared as Howard was raising his leg and pointing his toes. After** a while, all he could say was "Jesus Christ!!!" **(*laughs*)** Q: Can you recall how the characters of Goober and Gomer were created? **EG: Well, in the show where we introduced Gomer he says his cousin Goober was in town. He talked about Goober, but we never saw him. Do you know how we arrived at the name Goober? [At this point, Greenbaum relates a hysterically funny but off-color anecdote. Suffice it to say that his wife, Deane, grew up in a small town where the term "Goober" referred to something other than a garage mechanic.] You know, I got an awful lot of material from Deane for *The Andy Griffith Show* and *The Real McCoys* . . . Now as for the creation of Gomer Pyle, we did a show called *Man in a Hurry* and we were trying to create the new character of the garage owner named Wally. As it turned out, that didn't work, but a minor character did. He worked at the gas station and we got his first name from Gomer Cool, who was a writer in town and the last name was from Denver Pyle, who was Briscoe Darling on the show. We had not seen Jim Nabors at that time, so when we wrote it, I was thinking of the voice of Percy Kilbride, who played Pa Kettle. You know, he would always say something like "Good news, Mr. Fuller—we struck mud!" Later, Andy Griffith saw Jim Nabors at a nightclub called The Horn and gave him the part. He was just magic. The character of Gomer was inspired by a real-life incident where I ran into a gas station attendant who couldn't think of anything that could possibly be wrong with your car other than it needed more gas.** Q: Were you involved with the *Gomer Pyle, U.S.M.C.* TV show? **EG: I wasn't at all. It was a complete surprise to me. I thought Gomer was too dumb on that show. It was a shallower kind of humor. For me, It was too commercial, but it was certainly successful.** Q: Why did

you leave *The Andy Griffith Show* in 1964? EG: We had movie offers, and everyone would rather write for pictures than for TV. My first film after the show was *Good Neighbor Sam* [1964] with Jack Lemmon. It was very successful. Then I went onto *The Ghost and Mr. Chicken*, *The Reluctant Astronaut*, and *The Shakiest Gun in the West*, all with Don Knotts. We started to do a picture for Don and Andy together, and we still have the script—it's never been shot. It's called "Me and My Shadow," about two guys hiking across the country during the Depression. About that time, however, [Griffith's manager] Dick Linke decided that Andy would be better off making a picture on his own—*Angel in My Pocket*. It was clichéd—a *Romeo and Juliet* story twisted around a little bit, but it worked. Every known actor in town seemed to be in that! Getting back to *The Ghost and Mr. Chicken*, Andy would visit us in our bungalow on the set a lot. At the first screening, Andy fell down in the aisle laughing when Don says that line, "I'd rather have good food than bad food any day!" The music by Vic Mizzy was very helpful to that movie. It was a runaway hit which cost very little to make. By the way, I did the voice of the guy who keeps yelling, "Atta boy, Luther!" [Greenbaum then proves it by bellowing the incomparable yell which has become music to the ears of Knotts fans.] The scene where Don has to read his speech before the crowd was even funnier on the first take, but a musician laughed and we had to do another take. Q: Why were you not involved with Don's last film for Universal, *The Love God?* EG: I was, but only in a very small way as Jim and I were not available due to our writing *Angel in My Pocket*. You know the credits scene where it says "Don Knotts is 'The Love God?" Someone shouts out "WHATTTT???" That was my voice.

We could have gone on forever making those Don Knotts comedies because they were very profitable. But Don wanted to do a one-hour variety show each week. He offered us a fortune to do it with him, but we knew it would be nothing but frustrations and heart attacks, so we stayed with Universal. Q: You went on to write *M*A*S*H*—what are your memories of that show? EG: It was an immediate love match with [producer] Larry Gelbart. The whole ten years were wonderful because they trusted us so much that we sometimes didn't even have to go to the studio. They would mail us the ingredients they wanted for a show, and we would write the script and send it in. If we wrote too much, Larry would say, "I'm not going to waste this. I'll add twenty pages and we'll do two shows. That's how the tradition started of having the first and last episode of each season run for an hour. One of the best-known episodes we wrote involved McLean Stevenson's last appearance as Colonel Blake. We didn't even let the cast know how it was going to end, so they acted well. If they had known that McLean was going to die, they would have acted differently. I got thousands of letters about that show—half liked it, half didn't. Q: You cowrote *Return to Mayberry* in 1986 with veteran *Griffith Show* writer Harvey Bullock. Had you ever collaborated with him before? EG: We did work on either *Love, American Style* or *The Love Boat* Harvey had been the story editor. Of course, we would both attend those mass meetings for the *Griffith Show* years before. Working with him on the *Return to Mayberry* film was a very good experience. Harvey is a religious constructionist. He won't allow anything in the script unless it furthers the plot. Whereas, Jim and I could take little side ventures without anyone seeming to notice. The movie was quite a success. Q: What were your feelings about coming back to characters you had left over twenty years before? **EG: They were older now, so that made it even more interesting. I didn't have much to do with the cast other than Andy. I did visit the set, of course, and it was fun to see everyone. I had been seeing Ronny during the** *M*A*S*H* **days. I don't know what he was doing there [at the studio], but I didn't think he remembered me so I didn't talk to him. When I saw him on** *Return to Mayberry*, **he said, "Why didn't you talk to me?" He was very upset. He's still the same innocent person he was as a kid.** Q: How did you enter the field of acting? **EG: After** *The Andy Griffith Show*, **there was** *The New Andy Griffith Show*, **which lasted about six months. Jim had said the only way we would do it is if Everett got to play a small role in each one. I was so bad in two of them that they had to cut me out completely. Later, after I had sort of retired, I entered a musical comedy workshop just for fun and became quite good. Then I wrote an autobiography (***The Goldenberg [sic] Who Doesn't Dance***) which sold about three copies. Anyway, I was being interviewed on the radio and Larry Gelbart heard it and suggested I go into voice-over work. I wrote about ten funny commercials and recorded them and sent them out to all the agents. Eventually, I landed an AT&T commercial.** Q: How did this lead to your appearances as Judge Katz on *Matlock*? **EG: I had been on the writing staff when it first started. I had a disagreement with a producer about the development of the character Don Knotts was to play, so I left. A year later, I ran into the same man and he complimented me on a United Airlines commercial I had done. So I threw him up against the wall and said, "You go upstairs and put me on that show as an** *actor*!" **So he did. Of course, it wouldn't have been allowed if it wasn't for Andy. When**

I got on the stage, Andy had rewritten what they had written for me, as he has a pretty good ear for my voice. He was nervous as hell, but it was very easy and natural for me. We got a lot of laughs right there during the rehearsals. He was so happy, I can't tell you how pleased he was. I'm flying out next week to do another episode. Q: Do you have a favorite episode of *The Andy Griffith Show*? **EG: "Man in a Hurry" affected a lot of people. I have grown men who write to me and say they cry when they watch it. For funniness, I liked all those with Ernest T. Bass and the Darling family. I especially liked the one about superstitions where Barney rode a white horse east to west across the town [episode 120, "Divorce, Mountain Style"—Ed.]. The other one I really liked was "Mountain Wedding" [episode 94—Ed.] where we tricked Ernest T. into marrying Barney.** Q: Can you sum up your feelings about your involvement with *The Andy Griffith Show*? **EG: Well, I was a part of it and it was a part of me. It always will be. The people involved are still my friends. I think the fact that I was raised in a small town during the Depression allowed me to contribute to the atmosphere of the show. When we were writing the show I would say to Jim, "Maybe they'll rerun this three or four times." I never could have known that the scripts we were writing would contribute certain words to the national vocabulary. For instance, "Gomer" in the military means a droopy kind of guy. I remember going to see Stanley Kubrick's** *Full Metal Jacket*, **where they called one of the characters "Gomer Pyle." The word "Mayberry" is also listed in some dictionaries as representing small-town values. I had no idea this show would become part of America's folklore, and it just seems to get more popular every year.**

No book about The Andy Griffith Show would be complete without honoring the contributions of several prominent individuals who played such important roles in the series' success.

FRANCES BAVIER

"Aunt Bee"

Born in New York City on December 14, 1902, Frances Bavier seemed to be destined for show business from her earliest days. A graduate of the Academy of Dramatic Art, she began her career in vaudeville, and later starred on Broadway in *The Poor Nut; Native Son; The Strings, My Lord, Are False; Point of No Return*; and *Kiss and Tell*, acting with such luminaries as Orson Welles, Ruth Gordon, and a young Richard Widmark. Her credits also included roles in such diverse projects as *The Lone Ranger* on TV and *The Day the Earth Stood Still* (1951) in films. Her Henrietta Perkins, the daffy widow in the pilot episode of *The Andy Griffith Show* on *The Danny Thomas Show* led to her being cast as Aunt Bee in the series.

Frances's portrayal of Aunt Bee was the result of one of those miraculous casting decisions that makes it impossible to envision anyone else in the role. On the set, she was an intensely private person, and her costar's knew little about her personal life. Frances generally did not participate in the social activities and practical jokes which often took place after the day's shooting, although by all accounts she was generally affable to all, and always the ultimate professional. Following *The Andy Griffith Show*, Frances continued as Aunt Bee on the *Mayberry R.F.D.* series providing a vital link between the two. When she left the spin-off show, Alice Ghostley took over the role of the housekeeper. Frances Bavier retired to Siler City, North Carolina—a charming hamlet she fell in love with several years before. Here, she lived alone, but by all accounts, very happily. She was lured out of retirement in 1974 for a brief role in *Benji* and for several local commercials. She generally refused requests for interviews, and maintained a quiet presence in Siler City. The locals treated her as just another neighbor. After Frances Bavier passed away on December 8, 1989, fans made contributions to several charities in her name, in accordance with her wishes. Frances had also instructed that her estate be auctioned off for the benefit of the University of North Carolina Center for Public Broadcasting.

Hundreds of her admirers traveled to Siler City to tour her home and bid on her mementos. Over $120,000 was raised in one day. For generations to come, viewers young and old will enjoy Frances's work as one of the beloved character actresses in TV history.

HOWARD MCNEAR

"Floyd the Barber"

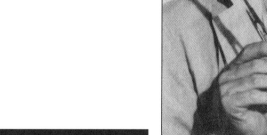

When fans compare their favorite moments from *The Andy Griffith Show*, the name of Howard McNear figures prominently. While Howard's work as Floyd the Barber was a major element in the success of the series, in recent years, he has become a cult hero. (Floyd T-shirts are selling faster than witch hazel at the barbershop!) The character of Floyd Lawson is among the most endearing on any sitcom. While much of the credit must go to the writers, even they conceded that it was Howard McNear's unique comic timing that made Floyd the larger-than-life comic presence he would become. As with other members of the cast, however, Howard did not seem destined for a career in comedy.

Born on January 27, 1905, in Los Angeles, Howard was the shyest of the four McNear brothers. Perhaps to compensate, he embarked upon a career in acting, performed with the acclaimed Savoy Players in San Diego, and received special acclaim for his performance as Renfield in *Dracula*. In 1935, he married model Helen Spats, who had recently gained a modicum of fame herself as Miss Santa Monica and Miss Venice. Howard served in the army during World War Two, and in 1944, he and Helen adopted their son, Christopher (known to all as "Kit"). McNear landed numerous roles in radio shows, and hit paydirt when he was cast as Doc in the radio version of *Gunsmoke* (1952–61). Throughout these years, he also worked steadily in television, with guest shots on everything from *I Love Lucy* to *The Twilight Zone*. His feature films included *Escape From Fort Bravo* and *Picnic*, both with William Holden, *The Long, Long Trailer* with Lucy and Desi, and *Anatomy of a Murder* with Jimmy Stewart all in the 1950s; then in the early sixties, *Voyage to the Bottom of the Sea*, "Good Day for a Hanging" (one of Robert Vaughn's first films) and three Elvis pictures: *Follow That Dream, Blue Hawaii*, and *Viva Las Vegas*. In fact, "The King" was quite fond of Howard, who must have

suppressed his "Floydian instincts" to go to town on Elvis's pompadour! Howard joined the cast of *The Andy Griffith Show* in its first season, replacing actor Walter Baldwin, who portrayed the barber in one episode. From the start, Howard managed to steal scenes from Andy Griffith and Don Knotts, both of whom had trouble keeping a straight face when Howard went to work. He endeared himself to the entire cast and crew, and is generally cited by all as the person most like their character in real life. According to Kit McNear, his dad was a loving and generous man, but all too prone to the kind of mishaps Floyd would encounter. A severe stroke in 1963 forced Howard off the show, and presumably into permanent retirement. However, Howard's work was his life, and it was evident he needed to get in front of a camera again, even though he was limited in his movements, and had lost the use of his left arm. Out of *The Andy Griffith Show* for a season and a half, Howard's talents were greatly missed on the set. Finally, Andy convinced him to return to work for "Barney's Bloodhound" (episode 133) in late 1964. Griffith accomodated Howard's physical needs, having a special brace constructed that allowed him to stand at the barber chair. While sentiment obviously played a role in Howard's return to the show, he quickly proved that he could carry his own weight. While his mobility was limited, his comic timing was as sharp as ever. By all accounts, he was a new man back on the set. Kit McNear told *The Andy Griffith Show* fan club journal, *The Bullet*, "I don't think that any other cast or individuals had the guts that Andy Griffith did. I think it is really unusual, virtually unheard of, for a production company to look after one of its members like that. I really, really have to praise Andy Griffith."

Sadly, Howard's physical condition deteriorated and he made his last appearance as Floyd in "Goober's Contest" (episode 219) on April 10, 1967. Howard McNear passed away on January 3, 1969. His

(Left) Frances in the premiere episode of the series, "The New Housekeeper."

"Lookin' a little shaggy around back!"

wake was a bittersweet affair, with many laughs and recollections of Howard's more amusing moments offsetting the deep sadness his friends and family felt at his loss. The eulogy was delivered by Parley Baer, his best friend and acting cohort from *Gunsmoke* and *The Andy Griffith Show* days. Fittingly, Howard McNear's contributions to the field of comedy continue to be appreciated. His work will be so honored for as long as people relish brilliant comedy.

several Don Knotts films and the golden years of *M*A*S*H*. Each of these individuals deserves the gratitude of fans for bringing their professionalism to *The Andy Griffith Show* and helping ensure the show's continuing popularity.

Other "Hall of Fame" Members

It would be virtually impossible to pay homage to all the talents and craftspeople in front of and behind the cameras for *The Andy Griffith Show* who are no longer with us today. Special recognition, of course, should be given to Danny Thomas, for playing such an integral role in the creation, and ultimate success of the series; Bob Sweeney, the multitalented director-actor-producer, whose steady hand as director helped create some of the most memorable episodes of the show (Bob's list of credits pertaining to other TV classics would take an entire volume!); Paul Hartman, who helped fill the gap left by Howard McNear's departure, joining the cast as Emmett the handyman (a role he would continue in the *Mayberry R.F.D.* years); Dick Elliott, the fussbudget Mayor Pike who often caused Andy more problems than the lawbreakers; Hope Summers, the wonderfully eccentric Clara Edwards; and writer Jim Fritzell, who, with his collaborator, Everett Greenbaum, created many of the best scripts of the series—in addition to writing the screenplays for

Magazines and periodicals from the show's original run are highly sought by collectors. (courtesy Dennis Hasty Collection)

Throughout the original run of *The Andy Griffith Show*, there was a surprising lack of licensed collectibles pertaining to the series. At that time, Andy Griffith closely guarded the merchandising rights, and never felt tempted to cash in to make a windfall from products related to the series. This is not to say that collecting was not a major pastime of *Griffith Show* fans. They simply had to be more creative. Many aficionados of the show concentrated on newspapers and magazines which featured the cast and crew. *TV Guide*, naturally, ran numerous cover stories with behind-the-scenes anecdotes. Today, these issues—which originally sold for 15 cents—have appreciated about one hundred times their cover price and routinely command $15 to $20 on the collectors circuit. *Griffith Show* fans began to expand their memorabilia to include the other achievements of the cast.

While researching this book, one of my editors, Al Marill, came up with a priceless find from his own archives: a complete run of all the original Andy Griffith comedy records, as well as the mint cast album of *Destry Rides Again* on Decca. Other album titles include *Just for Laughs, Andy Griffith Shouts the Blues and Old Timey Songs,* and *Andy and Cleopatra*. All of these were released on the Capitol label, along with a 1961 album called *The Andy Griffith Show*, which features Andy singing the lyrics to the show's jaunty theme song, "The Fishin' Hole." In 1992, Capitol released a compilation cassette and CD of many of the classic routines found on these records, including Andy's hit comedy recording "What It Was Was Football," and other gems like "Romeo and Juliet" and "Hamlet," told with Andy's special down-home twang. For traditionalists, there's also the vocal and instrumental versions of "The Fishin' Hole." While it's doubtful that MTV is bidding for the rights to these songs, what is undeniable is that their popularity will endure long after people ask, "2 Live Who?"

There are other avenues down which fans of the series pursue

Griffith memorabilia. In the early 1970s, I was friendly with a gentleman who specialized in selling movie posters to collectors. He said, "I can say for a fact that the biggest star we have today is Don Knotts." Apparently, demand for Don's movie posters was so great he could not keep up with it. This writer does not find it hard to believe. I've long argued with my wife that the poster for *The Reluctant Astronaut* should be framed and displayed in our living room. For a real conversation starter, there's no substitute for the sight of Don Knotts in a space suit hanging on your wall!

Memorabilia from Andy Griffith's big-screen achievements are also popular with collectors, particularly stills, pressbooks, lobby cards, and posters. Quite naturally, videos of any Griffith/Knotts features are a "must" among collectors, and most of their cinematic excursions are readily available. Strangely, however, most of the Don Knotts films for Universal are not. To date, only *The Shakiest Gun in the West* is in video release. The film was recently released on laser disc in deluxe letterbox format, so we can all enjoy the sweeping grandeur of Don wreaking havoc way out west.

Ironically, while the sixties produced little in the way of collectibles from *The Andy Griffith Show*, the 1990s are proving to be a bonanza for fans, with Viacom representing licensed products from the show. Andy, though, still has final say over every licensed item. As expected, the initial lineup of collectibles is tastefully done and very well made. The largest single license holder is Hometown TV, Inc., which produces *The Mayberry Collection* catalog—a slick, colorful encyclopedia of varying products relating to the show. The enterprise was started by Greg Akers and his partner, Mendy Abrahamson, longtime afficionados of the show. Frustrated by their inability to get collectibles from their favorite series, they did the only logical thing: hooked their life savings to create and market a

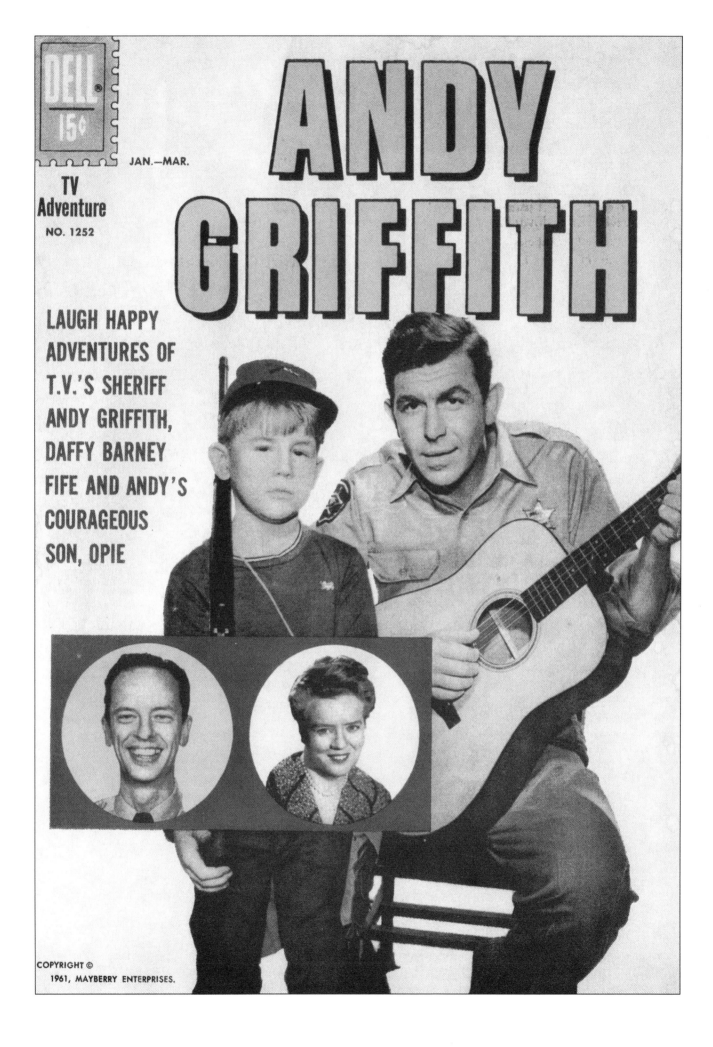

Above and right: The two *Andy Griffith Show* comic books
licensed in the 1960s can be worth up to $150 each.
(courtesy Dennis Hasty Collection)

Opposite: One of two comic books issued for *The Andy Griffith Show*,
both of which are valued collector's items today.
(courtesy Jim Clark Collection)

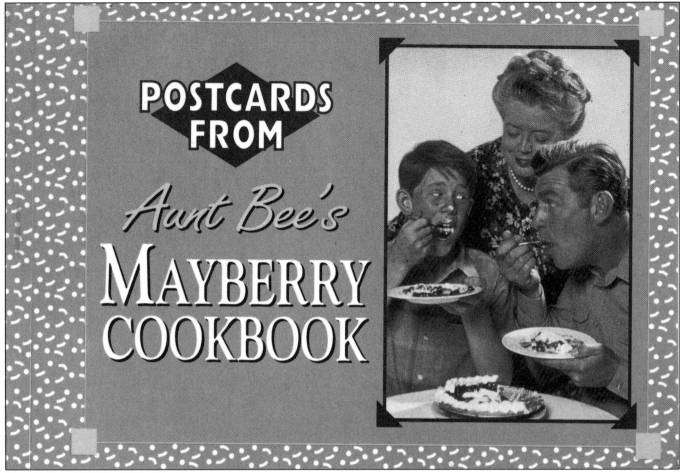

"Postcards From Aunt Bee's Mayberry Cookbook" (Rutledge Hill Press) was a spin-off of the original bestseller.

Pacific's series of enormously successful Andy Griffith trading cards.

That's right, pardner, it's Floyd himself—Howard McNear—in this rare theater lobby card from the 1950s. (courtesy Jim Clark Collection)

There's nothing fishy about the popularity of memorabilia from Don Knotts's films, such as this comic book from *The Incredible Mr. Limpet.* (1964)

Cover of *The Andy Griffith Show* writing tablet from 1960s. (courtesy Dennis Hasty Collection)

United American Video's series of tapes restore many of the epilogues which are traditionally edited from most reruns.

This coloring book sold for ten cents in 1967. Today, it goes for $50 and above. (courtesy Dennis Hasty Collection)

The Hamilton Collection's series of beautifully rendered plates grace many a wall in the houses of fans.

Dennis Hasty and Golden Richards, hosts of the weekly radio show *Good Morning, Mayberry*, proudly display Dennis's prize can of Andy Griffith beans and the elusive corn flakes box.

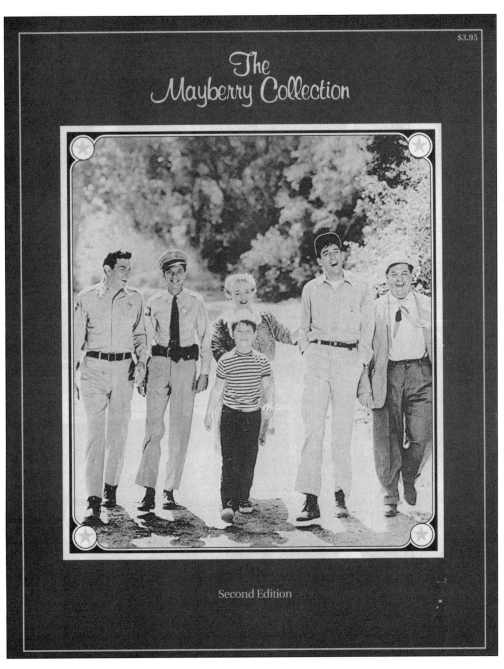

The
Mayberry Collection

$3.95

Second Edition

"The Mayberry Collection" is the highly successful catalog featuring dozens of exclusive, licensed collectibles from *The Andy Griffith Show*. (courtesy Hometown TV, Inc.)

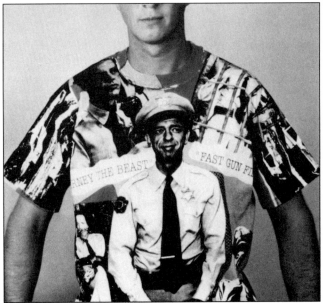

Hallmark's Father's Day card commemorating the Opie/Andy Relationship.

lineup of merchandise second to none.

The Mayberry Collection features such diverse "must-haves" as some of the most creative T-shirts imaginable; genuine replicas of Sheriff Taylor's badge and shirt; Barney boxer shorts (wonder what "the Fun Girls" would have thought of those!); collectors mugs; posters, pennants, and watches with Andy and Barney depicted on the faces (proof positive that "Mayberry's Finest" are legends in their own time)! The top-of-the-line item is an exact reproduction of the Mayberry High stadium jacket—the same one the men of Mayberry sported in the 1993 CBS reunion show. (Sorry, folks, but the Hometown TV group has not yet reproduced that septic tank Barney bought for his parent's anniversary!). The profusely illustrated catalog can be obtained through writing to: Hometown TV, Inc., 347 Stanley Ave., Cincinnati, Ohio 45226.

Aside from this book, there have been three others produced over the years which commemorate *The Andy Griffith Show* in their own ways. *The Andy Griffith Show* by Dr. Richard Kelly (John F. Blair Publisher) was first published in 1981. It is considered to be the landmark work about the show, as it gives excellent insights into behind-the-scenes production of *The Andy Griffith Show. The Andy Griffith Show Book* by Ken Beck and Jim Clark (St. Martins' Press (1985) is a fun-filled look at the fictional town of Mayberry, complete with amusing biographies of fictitious characters and maps of important locations. (This should settle for all time the burning question of how far Morelli's Restaurant is from Old Man Kelsey's Woods!) *Mayberry, My Hometown* by Stephen J. Spignesi (Popular Culture, Ink) is a massive 1986 encyclopedia of everything Mayberrian, with an "A to Z" dictionary of relevant facts and figure that is so detailed, one suspects Howard Sprague may have ghostwritten this essential volume!

Other hot items in recent years include the enormously popular Andy Griffith Show Trading Card Sets from Pacific. For fans of the show, the appearance of these cards in 1990 was like manna from heaven. Skeptics thought the idea of trying to sell cards based on a thirty-year-old show as foolhardy, but Pacific proved that you don't have to wear a bat mask and tight underwear to appeal to card collectors. The 110-card set, combining color and black-and-white shots from the show with some occasional original artwork, was a phenomenon that spawned two follow-up sets.

Quite naturally, every collector of *The Andy Griffith Show* rejoiced when the episodes became available on prerecorded video. Several companies have marketed various episodes, the most successful in terms of packaging design and insistence upon showing the complete programs has been United American video in Charlotte, North Carolina. Every attempt has been made to find and restore the master prints, which included the original epilogues. These short segments have traditionally been edited out of most broadcasts to allow for more commercials. The segments are very precious, and often contribute significantly to the plot. It is estimated that the equivalent of twenty full episodes are routinely edited out of the syndication broadcasts of the show. Therefore, these videos represent a sought-after way to see footage most fans have not experienced in many years.

What lies ahead on the collectors market for fans of *The Andy Griffith Show*? We'll just have to wait, but with interest in the series at an all-time high, you can bet the product line won' be nipped in the bud. All of you big-spending gents out there might someday be able to replicate Barney's birthday gift for Thelma Lou by obtaining an official pineapple skinner for *your* girl! As for myself, I'm eagerly waiting for an exact replica of Barney's famed "salt 'n' pepper" suit. We all know it can endure everything short of a nuclear disaster, and besides, I need it to do "the dips" when I take the wife out dancing. (We'll go "Dutch" of course, just to keep in the spirit of things!)

MAYBERRY MANIA!

"Barney's" J. T. Garrett and Edward Scott cavort with "Andy"'s Mark Hicks and Sterling White at the 1991 "Mayberry Days" Festival in Mount Airy, N.C. (courtesy Jim Clark Collection)

Public enthusiasm for nostalgic TV series is not always limited to classic shows. (Witness the renewed interest in *The Brady Bunch*!) However, the level of enthusiasm is generally in proportion to the quality of the series itself. Therefore, it comes a no surprise that there are fan clubs for outstanding programs like *Star Trek, The Man From U.N.C.L.E,* and *The Prisoner.* Several years ago the fan club for *The Honeymooners*—R.A.L.P.H (The Royal Association for the Longevity and Preservation of *The Honeymooners*) filled Madison Square Garden's Felt Forum with would-be Kramdens and Nortons. Aficionados of *The Andy Griffith Show* are no less dedicated, and indeed, rival any of the major fan movements in terms of the diverse methods they employ to honor their favorite program.

The common link for many of the fans is *The Andy Griffith Show* Rerun Watchers Club. In existence since the late 1970s, TAGSRWC has thousands of members. *The Bullet*, its quarterly newsletter, provides fun-loving analysis of favorite episodes, and shares the latest news on cast and crew members. Upon joining, a member is assigned to a chapter in his or her geographic area. Chapter names are based on references from *The Andy Griffith Show*, some obvious even to novices ("The Barney Chapter," "The Mayberry Sheriff's Department Chapter"), while other would tax even the most dedicated fan's ability to discern the relevance to *The Andy Griffith Show* ("The Ebum, Shoobum, Shoobum, Shoobum Chapter," "The 'Hit Her With a Leg of Lamb' Chapter").

Chapters agree to meet periodically to watch *Griffith* reruns and debate such earthshaking trivia questions as how many hatfuls of water it takes for Briscoe Darling to fill his radiator (A: Eleven) and "What is the number of the lane in which Howard Sprague bowls his perfect game?" (A: Ten) The Phoenix-based "Mayberry Says Thanks and Happy Motoring Chapter" succeeded in getting Don Knotts to

attend a local meeting. Well, at least Don W. Knotts—nephew of the beloved actor—who watched reruns with the club and related family anecdotes that had the members tied up in "Knotts" with laughter. Other social engagements held by chapters include "look-alike" contests in which members dress up as their favorite character in a sort of "Rocky Horror Picture Show Comes to Mayberry" scenario. These events are among the most creative and popular activities hosted by chapters, although the sight of an army of Floyd clones marching toward you is bound to be a "hair-raising' experience! The club is located at 42 Music Square West, Suite 146, Nashville, Tenn. 37203-3234.

Among the more ambitious activities created by *The Andy Griffith Show* aficionados are large-scale events celebrating the show, and often reuniting cast members. Each September *Griffith* diehards descend on Andy's hometown of Mt. Airy, North Carolina, for "Mayberry Day." With an array of fans wandering the streets of the small hamlet for that weekend, there's so much excitement that—in the words of Barney—it's doubtful anyone's head hits the pillow before quarter till eleven! Events have traditionally included a parade featuring look-alikes from the show (some strikingly good, while others seem less convincing than Deputy Fife's impersonation of a cleaning lady!); displays of memorabilia from the show and the infamous Aunt Bee's Kerosene Pickle Toss! (Pregnant women and those with weak hearts may find the excitement a bit much to take!)

A frequent and popular entertainer at the Mayberry Day celebration is David Browning, an actor from the bustling metropolis of Big Stone Gap, Virginia, who bares a resemblance to Deputy Fife and is called upon to entertain with his hilarious tribute to the inept lawman. For Browning, a career highlight was being told by Don Knotts

Don Knotts poses with Phyllis Rollins (left) and other enthused members of the Nashville-based "Barney Chapter" of *The Andy Griffith Show* Rerun Watchers Club." (courtesy Phyllis Rollins)

Bill Williams is president of the Omaha chapter "Tough Talk's Just Talk!" It was predestined, as evidenced by the chapter's address on Mayberry Street! (courtesy Bill Williams)

The author and wife Janet prepare daughter Nicole for "A little off the top," courtesy of Floyd at the Squad Car reunion in Ohio, 1993.

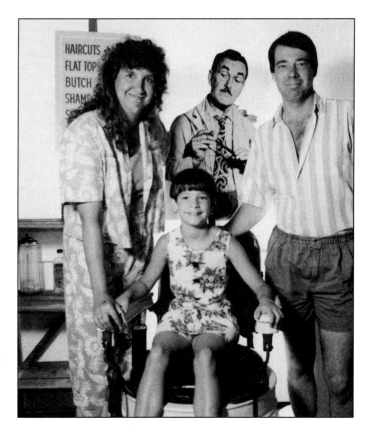

It's all in the family: Dick Stout pays homage to Floyd Lawson, while son Jeff emulates a certain Mayberry deputy (right down to the ol' "Roscoe"!).

Don't panic, it's not really Maude the Gun Moll from "Convicts at Large," just fan Sue Rauf of Fort Mitchell, Kentucky.

how much he enjoyed his work. Mayberry Day is good, clean fun, and attendees confess they find the annual event as addictive as Colonel Harvey's Elixier (For you novices, see episode 87). "Must-see" destinations in town include Floyd's Barber Shop, ("Two chairs—no waiting!") And the Snappy Lunch restaurant, which is informal enough to make the Blue Bird Diner look like Tavern on the Green, but can boast that Andy used to enjoy an occasional meal there as a youth. The famed pork chop sandwiches enticed Oprah Winfrey to dine there when she broadcast a show from Mt. Airy, which she labeled one of the most desirable towns in the United States in which to live.

The cast has come together on several occasions, aside from the reunion specials for television. In September 1991, the most ambitious gathering to date of alumni from *The Andy Griffith Show* took place at Opryland in Nashville. Here, fans could revel in anecdotes provided by the cream of Mayberry citizenry, headed by Don Knotts himself, in his first convention appearance. Other veterans of the classic sitcom present for the historic 1991 get-together were George Lindsey, Betty Lynn, Maggie Peterson, Hal Smith, Jack Prince, and the Dillards. It was Nirvana in Nashville when the cast members stepped back into character to perform a number of skits—thus allowing George Lindsey to let Goober favor the audience with his "eerily lifelike" imitations of Cary Grant, Edward G. Robinson, and Chester from *Gunsmoke*. In short, it was the hottest time south of the Mason-Dixon line since Sherman's march! As usual, the cast members graciously signed autographs—even Don Knotts, who risked getting writer's cramp in his "trigger finger."

As Barney would say, "Lose that, and I might as well leave the business!" The preceding September found many cast members reunited for another illustrious bash—this time in Charlotte, North

Carolina. There a packed house of fans felt privileged to listen to the jokes and anecdote of cast members at a celebration of the thirtieth anniversary of *The Andy Griffith Show*. In attendance: Betty Lynn, Howard Morris, Jack Prince, Hal Smith, Maggie Peterson, Aneta Corsaut, Jack Dodson, George Lindsey, and Clint Howard (sporting "Leon"'s trademark cowboy outfit and peanut butter and jelly sandwich). Predictably, the day provided more chaos and laughs than any ten visits to Mayberry by "the Fun Girls."

There is no limit to the creative ways Rerun Watchers pay tribute to their favorite show. Take Neal Brower, who, in addition to cosponsoring the Charlotte cast reunion, pontificates upon the significance of *The Andy Griffith Show* through an accredited college course that he brings to various southern universities. Brower, a Methodist minister, wants potential attendees to know that his course is not all fun and games. Although episodes are screened regularly, there follow some provocative discussions about everything from the social significance of the script to actual filmmaking techniques employed. (Imagine telling your parents you flunked a college course because you couldn't recall what Floyd's Latin teacher in barber college used to say?")

Not to be outdone is Bob Scheib, of Bradford, Ohio, a regular guy who dotes on his wife and kids. But Bob has gone well beyond any collector's call of duty—he purchased a 1965 Custom Ford and had it restored as an exact replica of Andy Taylor's squad car. He then went one better by turning his barn into an equally precise reproduction of Wally's Service Station, complete with original gas pumps, vintage soda pop and cigarette machines, and other period artifacts. Now, building a gas station to house your car may seem a little like buying a suit to match a new pair of socks. For Bob, however, it was a labor of love. He's even constructed an extensive showcase for his memorabilia collection inside the "Service Station," and has a Floyd-like barber chair on display as well. In July of 1993, Bob's "grand opening" drew fans from around the country, not to mention other owners of squad-car replicas—and George Lindsey himself. Assuming his wife Diana can withstand the commotion, Bob hopes to hold such get-togethers on an annual basis.

Another Ohio resident with a penchant for memorabilia from *The Andy Griffith Show* is Dennis Hasty, who cohosts (with Golden Richards) a weekly radio program called *Good Morning, Mayberry* on WMOH 1450 AM in Hamilton. Here, anyone within broadcast range can revel in discussions of Mayberry lore and listen to guests related to the series. Dennis's private collection of Griffith memorabilia is regarded as one of the most extensive anywhere. Dennis not only concentrates on collectibles from *The Andy Griffith Show*, but also has an impressive number of items from other career achievements of Andy Griffith and Don Knotts. Can anyone else boast of having an original can of "Andy Griffith Navy Beans" ("With Pork and a 'Smidge of Sugar. Just Heat and Eat!"), the early sixties Post Grape-Nuts Flakes cereal box featuring Andy on the back presenting the recipe for "Aunt Bee's Frozen Lemon Pie" or a rare coloring book for *The Reluctant Astronaut*?

Mayberry Mania has its share of celebrities, as well. Among those who have gone on the record as being diehard fans of the show are such diverse talents as Oprah Winfrey, George Bush, Randy Travis, Waylon Jennings, Bob Keeshan ("Captain Kangaroo"), Amy Grant, California "shock jocks" Mark and Brian, Burt Reynolds, Bob Uecker, Roy Clark, Emmylou Harris, George Jones, Ted Turner, Merle Haggard, Senator Jesse Helms, and the hard-rock group R.E.M. (Even the faintest possibility of seeing the latter two bump into each other at a Mayberry Day celebration is worth the trip! Seeing Jesse boppin' to "Losing My Religion" is as unlikely as Ben Weaver playing the jug with the Dillards!) Another unabashed Mayberryite is political consultant James Carville, who masterminded President Clinton's election campaign. In between such "inconsequential" activities as getting presidents and governors elected, Jim finds the time to watch nightly reruns of *The Andy Griffith Show*, and is quite active in his chapter of the fan club.

Mayberry Mania remains alive and well decades after the premiere of the pilot. It stands to reason that long after the present generations are gone, folks will be reveling in the antics of Andy, Barney, Gomer, Goober, Opie, Aunt Bee, and those other inimitable citizens of America's most popular fictional town. Will *The Andy Griffith Show* live forever? Probably only as long as people value brilliant comedy.

David Browning keeps fans in hysterics with his impersonation of Deputy Barney Fife.

Members of the "Dusty Gun and Rusty Knife Fite" chapter of Glen Alpine, N.C., during a typical, low-key meeting. (courtesy Jim Clark)

The following is a complete guide with significant episodes critiqued. Some might argue that it is ludicrous to subject individual episodes of *The Andy Griffith Show* to such critical scrutiny. Indeed, the phrase "Goober says 'Hey'" is unlikely to rank up there with "Rosebud" in terms of cinematic significance. However, *The Andy Griffith Show* represents television comedy at its best. Any objective critical analysis would certainly find that the writing, acting, and direction of most episodes not only were major achievements in their day, but have stood up remarkably well. Why shouldn't these talented people have their work examined in detail? Three decades later, their creative contributions to TV are being enjoyed by millions of viewers on a daily basis. How many people, in contrast, even remember, let alone watch on a regular basis, some of the most acclaimed films of our time.

The episodes were not without flaws, and in any body of work extending over an eight-year period, there are bound to be some peaks and valleys. What is amazing about the series is that the overall quality never faultered. From beginning to end, quality control was paramount in the minds of the cast and crew. Certain individual episodes may not have lived up to potential, but there is exceptional consistency throughout, especially when one considers the number of writers and directors associated with the show.

The following ratings system is based on "Barney Bullets," instead of "stars" commonly used to rate motion pictures. Ratings can be interpreted as follows:

•••• BARNEY BULLETS—EXCEPTIONAL. An episode that goes beyond the call of duty, like Barney when he orchestrated the rescue of Andy and Helen during that cave-in in episode 108!

•••1/2 BARNEY BULLETS—ABOVE AVERAGE. An episode which goes beyond expectations and wears better over the years than Barney's old salt 'n' pepper suit. (Although you still need the "threads" if you want to do those "dips"!)

••• BARNEY BULLETS—GOOD. A solid, successful show that is as reliable as ol' Barney when he testified on Andy's behalf at that job competency hearing in "Andy on Trial," episode 61.

•• 1/2 BARNEY BULLETS—AVERAGE OR SLIGHTLY UNDER PAR. The equivalent of Barney's date with his old flame, movie star Teena Andrews. In other words, it promises a bit more than it delivers.

•• BARNEY BULLETS—FAIR. Episode that is under par when compared with other in the series. The video equivalent of Barney's singing, which is generally out of sync with others.

In the cast listings for individual episodes, I have tried to include every actor who received screen credit. However, complete cast listings were unavailable for several shows and several players may have been overlooked. If readers can fill in any gaps, the revised credits will be used in future editions of this book. While everyone who worked on the series deserves a mention, for reasons of space this is not possible to do here. It should be noted, however, that the series had two producers who were instrumental in the success of *The Andy Griffith Show*: Aaron Ruben, who helped create the show and was with it from its first episode through September 1965, and Bob Ross, the producer from that point on. The executive producer was Sheldon Leonard, and the musical score was composed by Earle Hagen (who also whistled the main theme, titled "The Fishin' Hole").

Original CBS telop slide.

Pilot Episode: "The Danny Thomas Show" (2/15/60) ••••
PRODUCER and DIRECTOR: Sheldon Leonard; **WRITER:** Arthur Stander **CAST:** Danny Thomas, Marjorie Lord, Andy Griffith, Ron Howard, Frances Bavier, Frank Cady, Will Wright, Bill Baldwin, Rance Howard **SYNOPSIS:** TV personality Danny Williams and his wife Kathy are driving through Mayberry when they are given a summons by Sheriff Andy Taylor for running a stop sign. When Danny becomes belligerent, Andy (who is also justice of the peace and the editor of the town newspaper) fines him $1,000 or ten days in jail. Convinced he is being taken advantage of by a hayseed sheriff, Danny opts for jail time and brings his TV crew in to expose Andy as corrupt. However, Danny comes to regard Andy as a decent man and apologizes on camera. This does not stop the amiable sheriff though, from prorating Danny's fine for partial jail time served, and hitting him for the $70 difference. **CRITIQUE:** Fans of *The Andy Griffith Show* who have viewed this rarely seen episode can revel in the origins of the Mayberry we all came to know and love (as well as note the many differences between the pilot and the actual series). Sharply written, directed, and acted, the show does its best to allow Andy Griffith to have a field day with his country-bumpkin persona. Since the concept of Deputy Barney Fife had not been envisioned this early, the focus was on making Andy the main source of comedy, and he gets off a good many one-liners. Although Danny Thomas gives a hilarious, manic performance as the frustrated urbanite at odds with life in Mayberry, all the key scenes are stolen by Andy. Interestingly, Frances Bavier shows up, not as Aunt Bee but as a widow who is going broke from paying "rent" on the tuxedo in which her deceased husband was buried. So strong is her identification with the role of Aunt Bee, that it is jarring to see her in a different part. The episode also introduces young Ronny Howard as Opie in a winning performance that would only become even more impressive over time. Frank Cady, who would become a favorite as Mr. Drucker on *Petticoat Junction* and *Green Acres*, plays the town drunk here—a role later immortalized by Hal Smith. This episode is more than an outstanding comedic showcase for Andy Griffith, who previously had starred on TV in *No Time for Sergeants* and as a stand-up comedian. It can truthfully be called a classic TV moment. **FAVORITE DIALOGUE:** Andy draws an analogy between the death of Opie's beloved turtle to the passing away of Opie's mother, to which the boy replies: "Who stepped on Ma?"

Episode 1: "The New Housekeeper" (10/3/60) ••••
DIRECTOR: Sheldon Leonard; **WRITERS:** Jack Elinson and Charles Stewart **CAST:** Andy Griffith, Ron Howard, Frances Bavier, Don Knotts, Mary Treen, Frank Ferguson, Cheerio Meredith **SYNOPSIS:** When Andy Taylor's longtime housekeeper, Rose, moves away, depressing Opie, his Aunt Bee agrees to move into the Taylor household and raise Opie as she did Andy. Despite her efforts, she has trouble being accepted by Opie. Her attempts to "bond" with him by fishing and playing baseball end in disaster as the very elegant Bee has no talent for sports, and accidentally allows Opie's pet bird to fly away. Feeling things aren't working out, Aunt Bee prepares to leave. Opie, though, rushes to her side and begs her to stay. His change of heart has been motivated by his belief that Aunt Bee is so untalented in the things that young boys find important, that she cannot possibly survive in the world. Opie has found his mission: to teach Aunt Bee how to play ball, fish, and do "boy" things. **CRITIQUE:** This landmark episode in TV comedy history set the style for all *The Andy Griffith Show* stories to follow: low key, leisurely moving,

On the set of "The Jinx." (episode 49)

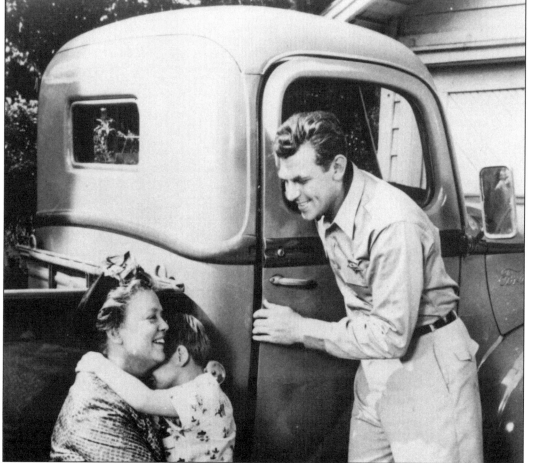

and irresistibly charming. Andy's gentle and dignified support allows his fellow actors to flourish. Frances Bavier is truly wonderful, embellishing Aunt Bee with the kind of traits that would make her character one of the most beloved in all of television. As for little Ronny Howard, it is safe to say there has never been a more talented, naturally appealing child star on any sitcom. This episode also introduces the character of Barney Fife, who is a bit out of control even by Mayberry standards. (In future episodes, Barney would be somewhat less hyper, but equally incompetent). There is the first of several brief references to Andy and Barney being cousins. **FAVORITE DIALOGUE:** Opie, explaining why he now wants Aunt Bee to stay: "If she goes, what'll happen to her? She can't do anything—play ball, catch fish or frogs. She'll be helpless! That's why she's gotta say, so I can teach them to her!"

Episode 2: "The Manhunt" (10/10/60)   ●●●1/2

DIRECTOR: Don Weis; **WRITERS:** Jack Elinson and Charles Stewart **CAST:** Andy Griffith, Don Knotts, Ron Howard, Frances Bavier, Hall Smith, Cheerio Meredith, Dick Elliott, Ken Lynch, Mike Steen, Lillian Culver **SYNOPSIS:** When an escaped convict heads toward Mayberry, Andy and Barney find themselves slighted by the state police who disregarding their small-town strategies. The police captain (Ken Lynch) is particularly abrasive and orders Andy off the case when the con surprises Barney and takes his gun. On their own, Andy and Barney track the con to a lake and induce him to make a getaway in Andy's dilapidated rowboat. The boat begins to sink, forcing the criminal to swim into the arms of the police. The state police leave with renewed respect for Mayberry's sheriff and deputy. **CRITIQUE:** Griffith and Knotts were still in their "over the top" characterizations of country bumpkins in this episode. However, their cultural differences with the big-city police officials make for some delightful moments of high comedy. Barney is particularly helpless here, proving to be more of a menace than the criminal he is stalking. In time, Knotts would make Barney at least semicompetent. While this episode remains a highlight of the early shows, one can see why Knotts and Griffith would have to tone down the character quirks of their on-screen alter egos, for fear they would lose all believability. Incidentally, this episode again mentions that Andy and Barney are cousins. **FAVORITE DIALOGUE:** Aunt Bee, warning the police captain of Andy's mood if denied his lunch: "He's meaner than a bear backed into a beehive!"

Episode 3: "Guitar Player" (10/17/60)   ●●●

DIRECTOR: Don Weis; **WRITERS:** Jack Elinson and Charles Stewart **CAST:** Andy Griffith, Don Knotts, Frances Bavier, Henry Slate, Jonathan Hole, Dub Taylor, Connie Van

Episode 4: "Ellie Comes to Town" (10/24/60)   ●●●1/2

DIRECTOR: Don Weis; **WRITERS:** Jack Elinson and Charles Stewart **CAST:** Andy Griffith, Don Knotts, Frances Bavier, Ron Howard, Cheerio Meredith **SYNOPSIS:** When pharmacist Fred Walker falls ill, his attractive niece Ellie (Elinor Donahue) comes to Mayberry to run the drugstore. Ellie, a registered pharmacist, is reluctant to accept the informal way of doing business in Mayberry. She locks horns with Emma Brand, hypochondriac, refusing Emma her daily pills because she lacks a prescription. Emma immediately takes to her "death" bed but Ellie softens her ways when she discovers the pills to be harmless placebos, and she delivers them personally, fitting in with the community. **CRITIQUE:**

This particularly nice episode allows the unique world of Mayberry to be viewed from the eyes of a newcomer, an assertive, independent woman whose philosophies initially put her at odds with town residents. Elinor Donahue, wonderful in the part, would contribute a great deal to the show's first season. Also delightful is Cheerio Meredith as the cranky Emma Brand (later named Emma Watson). Don Knotts has two hilarious scenes: getting stuck between the squad-car door and a mailbox, and his classic "memorization" of the sheriff's rule book. **FAVORITE DIALOGUE:** Emma, threatening Ellie with an economic boycott of the store: "Come next Christmastime, don't expect me to buy my cotton balls from you!"

Episode 5: "Irresistible Andy" (10/31/60) ●●●1/2
DIRECTOR: Don Weis; **WRITER:** David Adler **CAST:** Andy Griffith, Don Knotts, Ron Howard, Frances Bavier, Elinor Donahue, Harry Antrim, Robert Easton, Bill Mulliken, Ray Lanier

Episode 6: "Runaway Kid" (11/7/60) ●●●
DIRECTOR: Don Weis; **WRITER:** Arthur Stander **CAST:** Andy Griffith, Don Knotts, Ron Howard, Frances Bavier, Dennis Holmes, Donald Losby, Pat Rosson

Episode 7: "Andy, the Matchmaker" (11/14/60) ●●●
DIRECTOR: Don Weis; **WRITER:** Arthur Stander **CAST:** Andy Griffith, Don Knotts, Ron Howard, Elinor Donahue, Amzie Strickland, Jack Mann

Episode 8: "Opie's Charity" (11/28/60) ●●●●
DIRECTOR: Don Weis; **WRITER:** Arthur Stander **CAST:** Andy Griffith, Ron Howard, Frances Bavier, Stuart Erwin, Lurene Tuttle **SYNOPSIS:** Andy faces two separate problems: Opie's refusal to give more than three cents to the school charity drive, preferring to save his money for a gift for his girlfriend, and the return of the "late" Tom Silby (veteran actor Stuart Erwin) although wife Anna Belle (Lurene Tuttle) pronounced him dead years ago. Learning that it was Anna Belle's nagging that drove Tom out, and that she invented his "death" to avoid the scandal, he successfully reunites the couple, but he still has to cope with Opie's pennypinching. After scolding the boy, Andy finds he has misjudged his son, discovering that Opie was saving to buy his puppy love girlfriend a new coat, as her family is too poor to afford one. **CRITIQUE:** A charming dual storyline makes this a highly watchable episode. The plot about Tom Silby's return from the dead is just so much fluff, as the heart of the story centers on Andy learning to give the benefit of the doubt to Opie. The dialogue between Opie and Andy about giving to charity is a joy, and the rapport between Griffith and Howard in scenes like this makes clear there was never a father-son TV team with more genuine chemistry between them. **FAVORITE DIALOGUE:** Andy, humiliated after learning he has misjudged his son, is asked by Opie what is being served for dinner: "Well, you and Aunt Bee are having fried chicken and I'm having crow."

Episode 9: "A Feud Is a Feud" (12/5/60) ●●●
DIRECTOR: Don Weis; **WRITER:** David Adler **CAST:** Andy Griffith, Ron Howard, Frances Bavier, Arthur Hunnicutt, Chubby Johnson, Claude Johnson, Tammy Windsor

No rest for the weary lawmen of Mayberry, as they plot a roadblock.

Episode 10: "Ellie for Council" (12/12/60)   ••1/2
DIRECTOR: Bob Sweeney; **WRITERS:** Jack Elinson and Charles Stewart **CAST:** Andy Griffith, Don Knotts, Ron Howard, Frances Bavier, Hal Smith, Florence MacMichael, Frank Ferguson, Mary Treen, Forrest Lewis, Dorothy Neumann

Episode 11: "Christmas Story" (12/19/60)   •••1/2
DIRECTOR: Bob Sweeney; **WRITER:** David Adler **CAST:** Andy Griffith, Don Knotts, Ron Howard, Frances Bavier, Elinor Donahue, Will Wright, Sam Edwards, Margaret Kerry **SYNOPSIS:** On Christmas Day, curmudgeonly store owner Ben Weaver (Will Wright) arrests Sam (Sam Edwards), a local family man, for manufacturing moonshine. Despite Andy's pleas for leniency, Ben insists Sam be jailed. So that Sam can have the day spent with his family, Andy brings them into the jail and arranges for a Christmas party involving Aunt Bee, Ellie, Opie, and Barney. Wishing he too could be part of the celebration, Ben finds pride won't allow him to ask, so he manages to get arrested for trespassing. Once inside the jail, he produces gifts for all. **CRITIQUE:** This early episode was *The Andy Griffith Show*'s contribution to the traditional sitcom Christmas saga. It's all rather corny, and Andy was still laying on the accent a bit thick in those days, but there is so much goodwill on display, one would have to be a bigger Scrooge than Ben Weaver not to be moved by many memorable moments: Ellie's singing of "Away in a Manger," Barney's impersonation of an underfed Santa Claus, Aunt Bee's home-cooked feast, and Andy's genuine love for the folks in his life. And, of course Scrooge-like Ben Weaver turns out to be a good guy after all. **FAVORITE DIALOGUE:** Barney sheepishly telling Andy what a Christmas card from a female admirer reads: "Merry Christmas, Barney-Pooh!"

Episode 12: "Stranger in Town" (12/26/60)   ••1/2
DIRECTOR: Don Weis; **WRITERS:** Arthur Stander **CAST:** Andy Griffith, Don Knotts, Ron Howard, William Lanteau, Walter Baldwin, George Dunn, William Erwin, Sara Seegar, Phil Chambers, Marlene Willis, Pat Colby

Episode 13: "Mayberry Goes Hollywood" (1/2/61)   ••••
DIRECTOR: Bob Sweeney; **WRITER:** Benedict Freedman and John Fenton Murray **CAST:** Andy Griffith, Don Knotts, Ron Howard, Frances Bavier, Howard McNear, Dick Elliott, Josie Lloyd, Dan Frazer **SYNOPSIS:** Enchanted by Mayberry's simple pleasures, a movie producer announces he will shoot his next film there. This prompts the populace to undergo a complete change in their personalities, as they try to "Hollywood-ize" the town. Horrified by the development, the producer chastises the Mayberrians for destroying the lifestyle that lured him there. Embarrassed, the locals resume their normal lives and the film proceeds on schedule. **CRITIQUE:** There's nonstop laughter as the residents of Mayberry become enamored with show biz and try to emulate Tinseltown society. Even Floyd (inexplicably named "Colby" instead of "Lawson" here) repaints his sign to read "Tonsorial Parlor" and plays up "Cary Grant Haircuts." We also get to meet Orville, an amusing character who operates a TV repair shop in his funeral parlor. And wait till you hear the (then) contemporary references to Hollywood's hottest stars, including Gary Cooper, Gabby Hayes, and Rock Hudson! **FAVORITE DIALOGUE:** Andy introducing Floyd to the producer: "Floyd used to practice on cats. We had the baldest cats in the county!"

"Andy and Opie, Housekeepers." (episode 23)

Episode 14: "The Horse Trader" (1/9/61)   ●●●
DIRECTOR: Bob Sweeney; **WRITERS:** Jack Elinson and Charles Stewart **CAST:** Andy Griffith, Don Knotts, Ron Howard, Elinor Donahue, Dick Elliott, Casey Adams, Pearl Cooper, Spec O'DonnellGriffith-19

Episode 15: "Those Gossipin' Men" (1/16/61)   ●●●●
DIRECTOR: Bob Sweeney; **WRITERS:** Jack Elinson and Charles Stewart **CAST:** Andy Griffith, Don Knotts, Ron Howard, Frances Bavier, Howard McNear, Cheerio Meredith, Jack Finch, Jonathan Hole, Mary Treen, Phil Chambers, Harry Antrian, Sara Seegar **SYNOPSIS:** After she and her friends are criticized by Andy for rumor mongering, Aunt Bee decides to prove that Mayberry's men are also guilty of gossip. She leads Andy and Barney to think that a timid traveling shoe salesman is actually a TV producer searching for talent in town. Before the day is out, the salesman is besieged by citizens auditioning their musical skills for him, all the while pretending they want to buy shoes. On leaving town, he thanks the men of Mayberry for revitalizing his sagging career, and dumbfounded, they realize Aunt Bee has more than proven her point. **CRITIQUE:** A very funny script makes this one of the best of the early episodes. Guest star Jack Finch plays a wimpy salesman so down and out he makes Willy Loman look successful. His puzzlement at the sudden "siege" of clients to his hotel room makes for a hilarious sequence. Wait until you see Floyd, who inexplicably has a son in this episode, instructing his offspring to play some of that "Sax-o-mania" for the salesman while getting fitted for a pair of shoes. **FAVORITE DIALOGUE:** Barney, contemplating a minor scratch on his finger: "That's my trigger finger. I lose that, I might as well leave the business!"

Episode 16: "The Beauty Contest" (1/23/61)   ●●●●
DIRECTOR: Bob Sweeney; **WRITERS:** Jack Elinson and Charles Stewart **CAST:** Andy Griffith, Frances Bavier, Elinor Donahue, Howard McNear, Dick Elliott, Frank Ferguson, Lillian Bronson, Josie Lloyd, Elvia Allman, Gail Lucas, Yvonne Adrian **SYNOPSIS:** As part of the annual tribute to the local heritage, the town council elects Andy to judge a "Miss Mayberry" beauty contest, an honor that quickly becomes a nightmare, as virtually everyone in town pressures him to choose one of their relatives. Andy unexpectedly names an elderly woman named Erma Bishop as the winner. His basis? That the contest should honor inner as well as outer beauty, and Erma had selflessly given so much of herself in arranging the pageant that she should be titled "Miss Mayberry." **CRITIQUE:** Laughs abound as Andy must endure the local residents' overbearing attempts to bribe him into fixing the beauty contest. The "twist" ending is telegraphed early on, but it still doesn't dilute the hilarity of seeing Andy's frustrations at being the center of Mayberry's battle of egos. The comic highlight: Floyd's juvenile song "Miss Mayberry"—although it is still a notch better than the real-life "Here She Comes, Miss America"! **FAVORITE DIALOGUE:** Floyd's witty new advertisement for the barbershop: "Best Clip Joint in Town."

Episode 17: "Alcohol and Old Lace" (1/30/61)   ●●●1/2
DIRECTOR: Gene Reynolds; **WRITERS:** Jack Elinson and Charles Stewart **CAST:** Andy Griffith, Don Knotts, Hal Smith, Charity Grace, Gladys Hurlbut, Jack Prince, Thom Carney

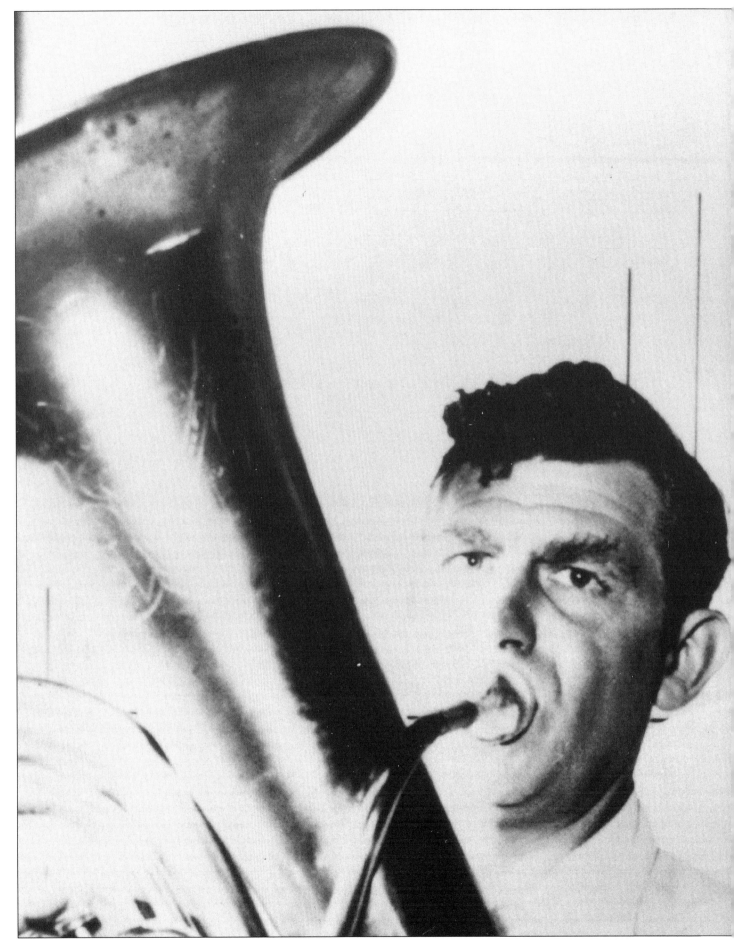

Come blow your horn, Mayberry style. Andy's skills as a sheriff do not extend to his tuba playing, if Barney and Gomer's reactions are any indication, in "The Sermon for Today." (episode 99)

Ron, brother Clint, and dad Rance during a rain delay on the set of "A Black Day for Mayberry." (courtesy Rance Howard)

Episode 18: "Andy, the Marriage Counselor" (1/30/61) •••
DIRECTOR: Gene Reynolds; **WRITER:** David Adler **CAST:** Andy Griffith, Don Knotts, Ron Howard, Frances Bavier, Jesse White, Claudia Bryer, Forrest Lewis, Norman Leavitt, Tim Stevenson

Episode 19: "Mayberry on Record" (2/13/61) •••1/2
DIRECTOR: Gene Reynolds; **WRITERS:** Benedict Freedman and John Fenton Murray **CAST:** Andy Griffith, Don Knotts, Ron Howard, Elinor Donahue, Howard McNear, Hugh Marlowe, George Dunn, William Erwin and the Country Boys **SYNOPSIS:** Arriving in Mayberry to search for local singing talent, Maxwell (Hugh Marlowe), a big city scout, finds an abundance of outstanding warblers and records them with the idea of creating an album. However, when he agrees to let the townspeople invest their money in the venture, Andy denounces him as a crook, especially when Maxwell leaves town suddenly. As Andy orchestrates efforts to have him arrested, the "wanted man" returns bearing a record contract with a major label and the first dividend payment for the stockholders. Andy's usually-sound instincts are wrong for once. **CRITIQUE:** "Know-it-all" Andy puts his foot in his mouth in this highly amusing show that sets him up for the kind of embarrassing fall Barney usually is apt to take. Indeed, this is one episode where Barney's intuition is proven to be much sounder than old Andy's. Best scene: Andy proving to Barney how gullible he is by selling him a "rare" nickel with the buffalo facing the wrong way. The resulting interaction makes for some memorable laughs. **FAVORITE DIALOGUE:** Barney complaining to Andy about deductions from his paycheck when the latter reminds him he can't take it with him: "If they keep nibblin' at me like this, I'll be lucky to go myself!"

Episode 20: "Andy Saves Barney's Morale" (2/20/61) •••1/2
DIRECTOR: Bob Sweeney; **WRITER:** David Adler **CAST:** Andy Griffith, Don Knotts, Ron Howard, Frances Bavier, Howard McNear, Hal Smith, Burt Mustin, Joseph Chester

Episode 21: "Andy and the Gentleman Crook" (2/27/61) •••
DIRECTOR: Bob Sweeney; **WRITERS:** Ben Gershman and Leo Solomon **CAST:** Andy Griffith, Don Knotts, Ron Howard, Frances Bavier, Hal Smith, Mike Steen

Episode 22: "Cyrano Andy" (3/6/61) •••
DIRECTOR: Bob Sweeney; **WRITERS:** Jack Elinson and Charles Stewart **CAST:** Andy Griffith, Don Knotts, Elinor Donahue, Betty Lynn

Episode 23: "Andy and Opie: Housekeepers" (3/13/61) •••1/2
DIRECTOR: Bob Sweeney; **WRITER:** David Adler **CAST:** Andy Griffith, Ron Howard, Frances Bavier, Hope Summers, Rory Stevens

Episode 24: "The New Doctor" (3/27/61) •••
DIRECTOR: Bob Sweeney; **WRITERS:** Charles Stewart and Jack Elinson **CAST:** Andy Griffith, Don Knotts, Ron Howard, Frances Bavier, Elinor Donahue, George Nader

Episode 25: "A Plaque for Mayberry" (4/3/61) •••1/2

DIRECTOR: Bob Sweeney; **WRITERS:** Ben Gershman and Leo Solomon **CAST:** Andy Griffith, Don Knotts, Hall Smith, Dick Elliott, Isabel Randolph, Dorothy Neumann, Carol Veazie, Burt Mustin, Joseph Hamilton, Joseph Crehan **SYNOPSIS:** A historical society announces it has found that a Revolutionary War hero resided in Mayberry and plans to present a plaque to his living descendent. The town goes from enthusiasm to panic when it is discovered that Otis is to be the recipient of the honor. Barney and the mayor urge Andy to get someone else to accept the award, fearing Otis will arrive drunk. Andy insists that Otis receive the plaque, however. When the big day arrives, Andy's instincts are proven correct when Otis shows up sober and makes a moving thank-you speech. **CRITIQUE:** This episode allows another of those wonderful sequences in which Barney attempts to use scientific methods to "cure" Otis of drinking. The tables turn when Otis proves more adept at the tests than Barney. Hal Smith, a fine actor, gives a wonderful performance in the final scene, wherein a proud and distinguished Otis—in the presence of his wife—makes a humble speech upon receiving the plaque. **FAVORITE DIALOGUE:** Barney: "Andy, you know we couldn't give a sobriety test to Otis last night—he was too drunk!"

Episode 26: "The Inspector" (4/10/61) ●●●1/2
DIRECTOR: Bob Sweeney; **WRITERS:** Jack Elinson and Charles Stewart **CAST:** Andy Griffith, Don Knotts, Hall Smith, Tod Andrews, Willis Bouchey, Jack Prince, Ray Lanier

Episode 27: "Ellie Saves a Female" (4/10/61) ●●●
DIRECTOR: Bob Sweeney; **WRITERS:** Jack Elinson and Charles Stewart **CAST:** Andy Griffith, Don Knotts, Ron Howard, Elinor Donahue, R. G. Armstrong, Edris March, Bob McQuain

Episode 28: "Andy Forecloses" (4/24/61) ●●●1/2
DIRECTOR: Bob Sweeney; **WRITERS:** Ben Gershman and Leo Solomon **CAST:** Andy Griffith, Don Knotts, Ron Howard, Frances Bavier, Margaret Kerry, Hope Summers, Bob McQuain

Episode 29: "Quiet Sam" (5/1/61) ●●●1/2
DIRECTOR: Bob Sweeney; **WRITERS:** Jim Fritzell and Everett Greenbaum **CAST:** Andy Griffith, Don Knotts, Ron Howard, Frances Bavier, William Schallert, Howard McNear, Hal Smith **SYNOPSIS:** Barney becomes obsessed with wondering why farmer Sam Becker (William Schallert) is so reclusive. Spying on him, Barney becomes convinced Becker is hiding criminal activities. When Andy is summoned to Becker's house in the middle of a storm, Barney breaks in to "rescue" Andy, who he thinks is a hostage. Instead, he finds Andy is there to help deliver a baby. At the last moment, Floyd arrives with a "posse" wielding a deadly weapon: a rock. (His wife wouldn't allow him to take a stick!) **CRITIQUE:** There is some genuine hilarity here, especially in Barney's ill-fated spying excursions. The episode illustrates what a closed society Mayberry actually is, with one of their own falling under suspicion simply because he lacks social graces. William Schallert gives an engaging performance as Becker, and there is an especially amusing scene in which Andy must comfort the childlike Otis during a lightning storm. **FAVORITE DIALOGUE:** Barney, criticizing Andy's lack of observation as they spy on Becker's farm: "You wouldn't notice a dirty elephant in

Back to the same old grind—or at least rind—for Andy and Ron in this early publicity photo.

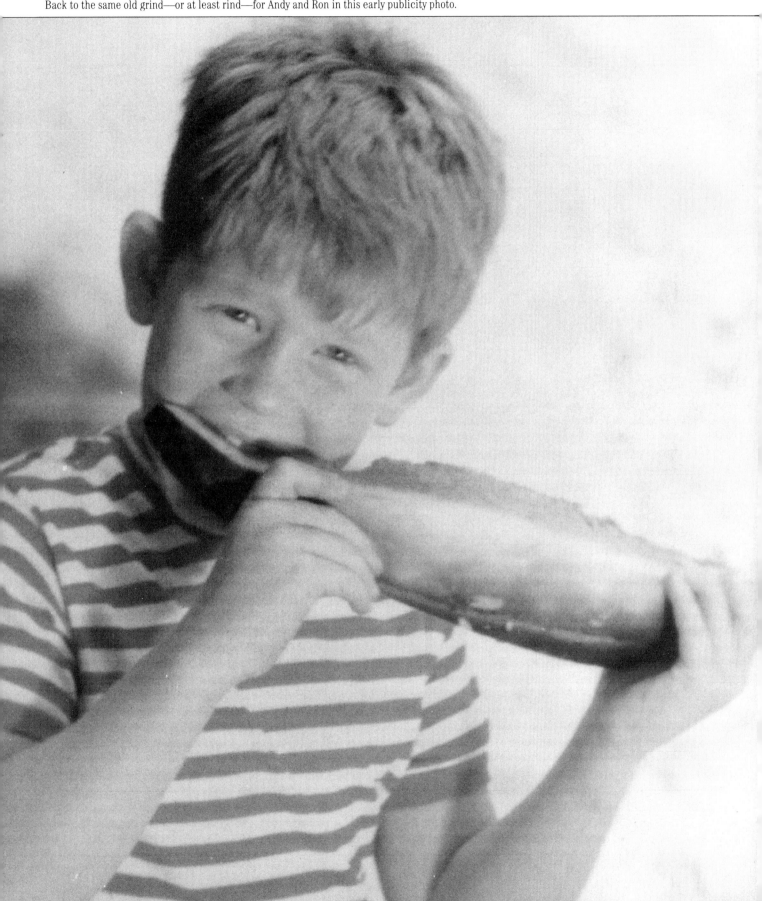

Right: Andy demonstrates the use of firearms to the "banjo-playing deputy" (Jerry Van Dyke). (episode 159)

the snow!" Andy: "You tryin' to tell me Sam Becker's got a dirty elephant up at his place?"

Episode 30: "Barney Gets His Man" (5/8/61) ••••
DIRECTOR: Bob Sweeney; **WRITERS:** Ben Gershman and Leo Solomon **CAST:** Andy Griffith, Don Knotts, Ron Howard, Frances Bavier, Betty Lynn, Barney Phillips, Mike Steen, Bob McQuain, Burt Mustin, Joseph Hamilton, Norman Leavitt **SYNOPSIS:** Barney inadvertently captures an escaped convict and becomes a town hero. However, when the convict gets away, Barney learns he plans on returning to Mayberry to seek revenge. An extremely nervous Barney joins a manhunt in the woods where the convict was sighted. Andy discovers the con hiding in a barn, and through some clever planning, ensures that Barney is able to recapture him. Again, Barney emerges a hero, although it is not through his own doing. **CRITIQUE:** Vintage Don Knotts/Barney Fife humor highlights this outstanding episode that shows the paradox in the deputy's personality: although he is clearly terrified at the prospect of the convict hunting him, he still has (barely) enough self respect to carry out his professional duties. The episode lets Don Knotts fully display his comedic genius as he struts about town lecturing on his prowess at defeating crooks in hand-to-hand combat. **FAVORITE DIALOGUE:** Barney, ego in full bloom: "I never thought our town would come to this: Mayberry, gateway to danger!"

Episode 31: "The Guitar Player Returns" (5/15/61) •••
DIRECTOR: Bob Sweeney; **WRITERS:** Jack Elinson and Charles Stewart **CAST:** Andy Griffith, Don Knotts, James Best, Howard McNear, Henry Slate, Tom Browne, Herb Ellis, Phil Chambers

Episode 32: "Bringing Up Opie" (5/22/61) •••
DIRECTOR: Bob Sweeney; **WRITERS:** Jack Elinson and Charles Stewart **CAST:** Andy Griffith, Don Knotts, Ron Howard, Frances Bavier, Hal Smith, Mike Brent

Episode 33: "Opie and the Bully" (10/2/61) ••••
DIRECTOR: Bob Sweeney; **WRITER:** David Adler **CAST:** Andy Griffith, Don Knotts, Ron Howard, Frances Bavier, Terry Dickinson **SYNOPSIS:** Opie has suddenly begun lying about extra milk money he supposedly needs for school, and Barney later discovers that Opie is "paying off" a bully named Sheldon who threatens him with a beating. Rather than humiliate Opie, Andy contrives a tale about how he handled a bully in his own past, and convinces his son that a black eye hurts far less than being a coward. Opie nervously confronts his nemesis, and indeed gets a black eye. But he gives as good as he takes, and ultimately restores his pride. **CRITIQUE:** The secret of the show's success is often said to have been the scripts that so captured small-town America. As this script illustrates, the various writers also succeeded in examining the world from a child's viewpoint when stories centered on Opie, and this tale strikes a chord with everyone who has ever been confronted by a bully. You'll share Andy and Barney's concern as they eagerly await the results of Opie's first fight. The chemistry between Griffith and Howard has never been better, and it's tough to keep a dry eye when Andy has to send his son out into "battle." **FAVORITE DIALOGUE:** Opie, explaining why his father should give him additional milk money: "You wouldn't want my bones to get soft, wouldya, Pa?"

Episode 34: "Barney's Replacement" (10/9/61) •••
DIRECTOR: Bob Sweeney; **WRITERS:** Jack Elinson and Charles Stewart **CAST:** Andy Griffith, Don Knotts, Ron Howard, Mark Miller, Betty Lynn, Hope Summers, Cheerio Meredith

Episode 35: "Andy and the Woman Speeder" (10/16/61) •••
DIRECTOR: Bob Sweeney; **WRITERS:** Jack Elinson and Charles Stewart **CAST:** Andy Griffith, Don Knotts, Ron Howard, Frances Bavier, Howard McNear, Jean Hagen, Dick Elliott, Helen Thurston, Pete Cooey

Episode 36: "Mayberry Goes Bankrupt" (10/23/61) •••
DIRECTOR: Bob Sweeney; **WRITERS:** Jack Elinson and Charles Stewart **CAST:** Andy Griffith, Ron Howard, Frances Bavier, Andy Clyde, Dick Elliott, Warren Parker, Phil Chambers, Jason Johnson, Hal Torey

Episode 37: "Barney on the Rebound" (10/30/61) •••
DIRECTOR: Bob Sweeney; **WRITERS:** Jack Elinson and Charles Stewart **CAST:** Andy Griffith, Don Knotts, Betty Lynn, Jackie Coogan, Beverly Tyler

Episode 38: "Opie's Hobo Friend" (11/13/61) •••
DIRECTOR: Bob Sweeney; **WRITER:** Harvey Bullock **CAST:** Andy Griffith, Don Knotts, Ron Howard, Frances Bavier, Buddy Ebsen

Episode 39: "Crime-Free Mayberry" (11/20/61) •••1/2
DIRECTOR: Bob Sweeney; **WRITER:** Paul Henning **CAST:** Andy Griffith, Don Knotts, Frances Bavier, Howard McNear, Dick Elliott **SYNOPSIS:** Two con men pose as FBI agents and inform Mayberry the town is to get an award for having the lowest crime rate in the nation. The scheme is to use the resulting celebration as a distraction while they rob the bank. However, they slip up when they pose for a photo with Andy—something FBI special agents are not allowed to do. Andy catches on to the scheme and is waiting to arrest them when the bank vault is broken into. **CRITIQUE:** Big-city crooks never seem to learn that the surest way to arrest is to underestimate Mayberry's sheriff, although, admittedly, Barney is like putty in the hands of the bad guys. The show's best moment comes when one of the crooks finally breaks into the vault only to find Andy already in there, waiting for him with a warm greeting—and a pair of handcuffs. **FAVORITE DIALOGUE:** Barney, impressing tourists with his prowess: "I do have a nickname I'm stuck with and can't seem to lose—'Fast Gun Fife.'"

Episode 40: "The Perfect Female" 11/27/61) •••1/2
DIRECTOR: Bob Sweeney; **WRITERS:** Jack Elinson and Charles Stewart **CAST:** Andy Griffith, Don Knotts, Ron Howard, Frances Bavier, Betty Lynn, Alfred Hopson

Episode 41: "Aunt Bee's Brief Encounter" (12/4/61) •••1/2
DIRECTOR: Bob Sweeney; **WRITERS:** Ben Gershman and Leo Solomon **CAST:** Andy Griffith, Ron Howard, Frances Bavier, Edgar Buchanan, Doodles Weaver, George Cisar, Sherwood Keith **SYNOPSIS:** Aunt Bee becomes enamored of a traveling handyman named Mr. Wheeler, whom

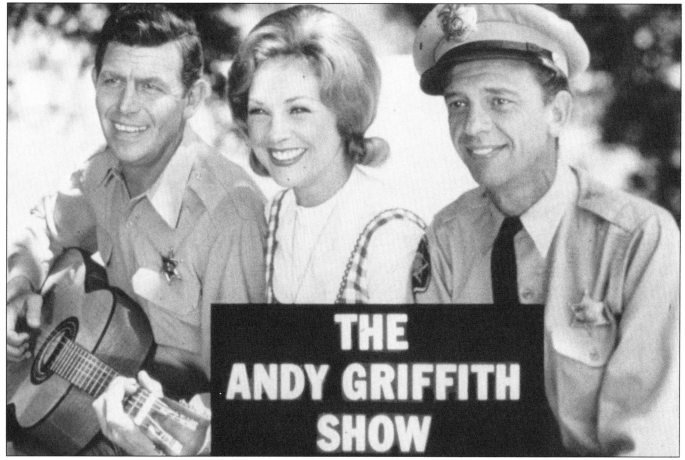

Telop slide featuring Andy, Joanna Moore (Peggy McMillan), and Don.

she invites to stay at the house, inventing small chores to justify his presence. Andy soon learns that the charismatic gentleman is a notorious loafer with a police record from preying on hospitable spinsters. Andy tells Wheeler he insists he marry Aunt Bee, and reinforces his opinion with a shotgun. Predictably, Wheeler runs away, and Andy spares Bee's feelings by telling her Wheeler was a decent man who could not resist the life of a wanderer. **CRITIQUE:** Edgar Buchanan, seen here in his preUncle Joe of *Petticoat Junction* persona, is well cast as a W. C. Fieldstype con man who takes advantage of the Taylors' hospitality. It's rather tough to dislike him, as he brings real joy to Aunt Bee. This is a memorable episode that does not water down the story by having Buchanan emerge as a nice guy. At the finale, one can only sympathize with Aunt Bee as she stands on the porch feeling the pain of her rejection. **FAVORITE DIALOGUE:** Andy 'coincidentally' holds a shotgun while he informs Mr. Wheeler: "I don't know what I'd do to anyone who'd want my Aunt Bee!"

Episode 42: "The Clubmen" (12/11/61) ●●●1/2
DIRECTOR: Bob Sweeney; **WRITERS:** Fred S. Fox and Iz Elinson **CAST:** Andy Griffith, Don Knotts, Ron Howard, Frances Bavier, Howard McNear, Burt Mustin **SYNOPSIS:** When Andy is asked by an influential friend and member to visit the exclusive Esquire Club, he makes the mistake of inviting Barney along. Overly eager to be voted into the club on an exclusive basis, Barney spends the evening bragging about his wealth and importance—tactics which alienate rather than impress his hosts. The next day, Andy is advised he has been accepted for membership, but Barney was not. Andy politely rejects the offer and informs Barney of the bad news that only one of them had been offered membership. Such is Barney's ego that he presumes Andy is the "odd man out" and refuses to join because of the slight to his friend. **CRITIQUE:** A surefire formula for laughs is to mingle Mayberry's Finest with big-city sophisticates, as this episode amply demonstrates. The sequence of Barney trying to impress his hosts is funny to watch, but you can't help feeling Andy's embarrassment at seeing his friend humiliate himself by talking about everything from stocks and bonds to golf advice. **FAVORITE DIALOGUE:** Barney explaining the origins of Baked Alaska to Andy: "It's that new dessert that's come out since it's become a state!"

Episode 43: "The Pickle Story" (12/18/61) ●●●●
DIRECTOR: Bob Sweeney; **WRITER:** Harvey Bullock **CAST:** Andy Griffith, Don Knotts, Ron Howard, Frances Bavier, Hope Summers, Lee Kreiger, Stanley Farrar, Warren Parker **SYNOPSIS:** Aunt Bee's decision to enter the annual pickle contest has one slight hitch: her pickles taste like kerosene, and Barney and Andy have replaced the homemade versions with store-bought ones. Since Andy can't have "professionally made" pickles entered by Aunt Bee, he, Barney, and Opie must devour them all and ask Bee to fill the jars with a batch of new homemade pickles. When the judges taste Aunt Bee's batch, they, too, are reminded of kerosene and award Clara with the coveted prize. Meanwhile, Bee is so happy that the boys like her pickles that she promptly whips up yet another batch. **CRITIQUE:** "The Pickle Story" is a popular episode with fans and cast alike, with Don Knotts citing it as his favorite show of the series. The script certainly defies logic, even by Mayberry standards, as it's hard to fathom why Andy and Barney can't just bury the dreaded pickles rather than give them away or actually eat them. But this is being picky, as the countless laughs more than compensate for lack of logic. It's also fun to see that Aunt Bee is not totally invincible in her kitchen

"Hello, Sarah? Get me the diner."

domain. A fun episode from start to finish. **FAVORITE DIALOGUE:** Barney: "I don't know how I can face the future when I know there's eight quarts of pickles in it!"

Episode 44: "Sheriff Barney" (12/25/61) ●●●1/2
DIRECTOR: Bob Sweeney; **WRITERS:** Ben Gershman and Leo Solomon **CAST:** Andy Griffith, Don Knotts, Ron Howard, Howard McNear, Jack Prince, Hal Smith, Dabbs Greer, Ralph Dumke, Paul Bryar, Orville Sherman, Frank Warren, Joseph Hamilton, Jack Teagarden **SYNOPSIS:** Convinced that Barney is a tough-as-nails lawman, the neighboring town of Greendale offers him the position of sheriff. Andy cautions Barney that he is not seasoned enough for the spot, but Barney arrogantly insists he is. He agrees to switch jobs with Andy for a day to prove he can handle being sheriff. The results are predictably disastrous, with Barney failing to adequately resolve any crisis. Ultimately, Andy convinces notorious moonshiner Rafe Hollister to surrender to Deputy Fife. Barney uses this "coup" to refuse the sheriff's position in Greendale on the basis that his crime-fighting skills are needed in Mayberry. **CRITIQUE:** This episode was the first to have Jack Prince as Rafe Hollister, although the actor played similar roles in previous episodes. The scene in which he tries to surrender to a disinterested Barney is very funny, as is the sequence in which Otis makes a mockery of Barney's psychological methods of finding the source for moonshine. **FAVORITE DIALOGUE:** Barney, reacting to Andy's practical joke: "Why don't we go up the hospital some night and take the bolts off the wheelchairs—that'd be funny too!"

Episode 45: "The Farmer Takes a Wife" (1/1/62) ●●●
DIRECTOR: Bob Sweeney; **WRITERS:** Jack Elinson and Charles Stewart **CAST:** Andy Griffith, Don Knotts, Ron Howard, Frances Bavier, Alan Hale, Jr., Betty Lynn, Adoree Evans, Bob McQuain

Episode 46: "Keeper of the Flame" (1/8/62) ●●●1/2
DIRECTOR: Bob Sweeney; **WRITERS:** Jack Elinson and Charles Stewart **CAST:** Andy Griffith, Don Knotts, Ron Howard, Frances Bavier, Everett Sloane, Flip Mark

Episode 47: "Bailey's Bad Boy" (1/12/62) ●●●●
DIRECTOR: Bob Sweeney; **WRITERS:** Ben Gershman and Leo Solomon **CAST:** Andy Griffith, Don Knotts, Ron Howard, Frances Bavier, Hal Smith, Bill Bixby, Jon Lormer, John Graham **SYNOPSIS:** Young Ron Bailey (Bill Bixby) is a rich hotshot who lives off his prominent father's money and influence. Driving through Mayberry, he is arrested for speeding and sentenced to several days in jail. At first, Bailey ridicules small-town life, but when he observed Andy teaching Opie a lesson about personal responsibility, he turns over a new leaf. When his father's attorney fixes it so Ron can be freed, the young man opts to do his time instead. His visit to Mayberry has taught him to stand on his own two feet. **CRITIQUE:** Bill Bixby gives a vigorous performance as the obnoxious Bailey who looks down his nose at rural life. His transformation, after hearing Andy's discussion with Opie, seems reasonable and moving. Like the popular "Man in a Hurry" episode which would follow, this one allows viewers to sample the simple pleasures of Mayberry life through the eyes of a big-city cynic. After hearing Barney describe the joy of whipping up homemade ice cream, you'll want to do it too. There is also a great deal of dignity in the way Andy and Barney treat their prisoner,

Andy and Opie in a classic image from a classic show.

despite his initial contempt for them. **FAVORITE DIALOGUE:** Barney, missing the point when Bailey asks him if the town "swings" at night: "Of course we got swings! We just don't use 'em at night!"

Episode 48: "The Manicurist" (1/22/62) •••1/2

DIRECTOR: Bob Sweeney; **WRITERS:** Jack Elinson and Charles Stewart **CAST:** Andy Griffith, Don Knotts, Barbara Eden, Howard McNear, Dick Elliott, Sherwood Keith, Cheerio Meredith, Frank Warren **SYNOPSIS:** Ellen Brown (Barbara Eden), a vivacious young manicurist, arrives in town and sets up her business at Floyd's Barber Shop. At first the men of Mayberry are too intimidated to go near her, but before long, they're all lining up for manicures, much to the chagrin of their wives. Andy gently tries to tell Ellen that she should move away because the men are too henpecked to patronize her any longer. She interprets Andy's concern as a marriage proposal, but inadvertently solves the problem by announcing she is returning to the city to marry her old beau. **CRITIQUE:** The men of Mayberry have never been known for their womanizing ways. During the sexual revolution, one suspects they served as hostages! This is never more apparent than in this very funny episode in which the locals are alternately obsessed and intimated by shapely manicurist Barbara Eden, the future *I Dream of Jeannie* star. When she turns up in town, they literally run and hide. The initial pandemonium she causes in Floyd's shop is hilarious (pay close attention to Floyd, who becomes so flustered that he begins cutting the air above Andy's head!). **FAVORITE DIALOGUE:** Andy, explaining to Ellen why he never had a manicure: "I generally cut 'em myself. My Aunt Bee's got a good size pair of dress shears."

Episode 49: "The Jinx" (1/29/62) •••1/2

DIRECTOR: Bob Sweeney; **WRITERS:** Jack Elinson and Charles Stewart **CAST:** Andy Griffith, Don Knotts, Ron Howard, Frances Bavier, John Qualen, Howard McNear, Sherwood Keith, Frank Warren, Sherman Sanders **SYNOPSIS:** Barney spreads a cruel rumor that elderly resident Henry Bennett (John Qualen) is a jinx who should be avoided. Andy tries to counter the claim by teaming with Henry in a fishing tournament, only to have the boat sink. As evidence mounts of his bad luck, Henry announces he will move away rather than offend his neighbors. Out of guilt, the locals attempt to rig a lottery so Henry will win, but even this plan goes awry. Henry, however, is so moved that his friends thought enough of him to develop the scheme that he agrees to stay in Mayberry. **CRITIQUE:** John Qualen, who played lovable old coots in numerous John Ford films (notably *The Searchers*), gives a very endearing performance as the victim of Barney's accusation. Although the script effectively denounces rumormongering and mob hysteria, it does so in a comedic way. Funniest moments have superstitious Barney attempting to negate Henry's jinx by constantly rubbing Opie's red hair. **FAVORITE DIALOGUE:** Barney, responding to Andy's ridicule of his belief in superstitions: "You're funny, you are! Why don't you put a flower in your lapel and squirt water?"

Episode 50: "Jailbreak" (2/5/62) •••1/2

DIRECTOR: Bob Sweeney; **WRITER:** Harry Bullock **CAST:** Andy Griffith, Don Knotts, Allan Melvin, Ken Lynch, Fred Sherman, Frank Warren, Bob McQuain, Sally Mills, Rita Kenaston **SYNOPSIS:** While left to guard an important "guest," Barney tries to learn more about the man's criminal operation by posing as a fellow inmate in the Mayberry jail. The man catches onto the ruse and tricks Barney into allowing him to escape.

Andy is the reluctant recipient of Charlene's attentions in "The Darlings Are Coming." (episode 88)

Barney and Andy are chastised by a state law official and warned to keep out of the case. However, the disgraced Andy and Barney track the crook and his girlfriend to a trailer camp where they are holding the state law officer hostage. Barney succeeds in a daring plan and drives the trailer to the courthouse, thus delivering the criminals back to jail and redeeming Andy's reputation. **CRITIQUE:** Here we see Barney at his best and worst. The worst comes with a ludicrous plan to pass himself off as a hardened criminal—a ruse the real crook can see through partly because Barney fails to remove a photo of himself in his deputy uniform from the wall! One cringes with embarrassment as the state lawman dismisses Mayberry's Finest as two incompetent hicks. This is Don Knotts at his best—running the gamut of emotions from pathos to pride, and as usual, there's no one who can present such a range so successfully. **FAVORITE DIALOGUE:** Barney trying to pass himself off as a hardened criminal: "I been called plenty—everything from 'Chopper' to 'Mad Dog.' One name they never called me—'Tattletale'!

Episode 51: "A Medal for Opie" (2/12/62) ••••

DIRECTOR: Bob Sweeney; **WRITER:** David Adler **CAST:** Andy Griffith, Don Knotts, Ron Howard, Frances Bavier, Bob McQuain, Ralph Leabow, Joan Carey, Pat Coghlan **SYNOPSIS:** Opie is determined to win the fifty-yard dash in an annual competition. Inspired by a pep talk and a dubious training course initiated by Barney, Opie never lets the possibility of a loss enter his mind. When he comes in last, he becomes angry with himself and shuts out those around him from his life. He is also crushed by his father's criticism that he has disappointed him by acting spoiled. Opie sees the errors of his ways, and apologizes. He then sets a goal of doing better in next year's race. **CRITIQUE:** Like many episodes of the series, this one would seem like much ado about nothing on paper. Due to the talented cast, though, it remains one of the most touching shows of all. Don Knotts provides some very amusing moments as he begins an ill-fated training course for Opie that results in the boy outperforming his mentor. David Adler's script and Bob Sweeney's direction are both first rate. However, the lion's share of the credit must still go to Griffith and Howard, who somehow make their on-screen personas overshadow the fact that they are actors. **FAVORITE DIALOGUE:** Opie, praying to God to allow him to win a medal: "If you let me win one, I promise I'll take it off to take a bath—once in a while!"

Episode 52: "Barney and the Choir" (2/19/62) ••••

DIRECTOR: Bob Sweeney; **WRITERS:** Jack Elinson and Charles Stewart **CAST:** Andy Griffith, Don Knotts, Frances Bavier, Olan Soulé, Betty Lynn **SYNOPSIS:** When a member of the choir drops out a couple of weeks before an important contest, Barney volunteers his voice. The only problem is, he cannot sing. Everyone realizes this immediately except Barney, who feels he is superb. To spare his feelings, Andy arranges for him to do solos during the contest. What Barney doesn't know, however, is that his microphone is dead and another choir member's voice is being substituted. Oblivious to the ruse, Barney blithely sings away and all ends well. **CRITIQUE:** Barney's ego and bullheadedness are in full bloom in this very funny tale. Hilarity ensues when he recognizes "someone" is out of key and mingles throughout the choir to find the culprit. The biggest laughs occur during the contest when Barney's voice is replaced by a deep baritone. The sight of a Pavarotti-type sound coming from the skinny lawman is a vision to behold. **FAVORITE DIALOGUE:** Andy, musing about how to keep Barney out of the contest: "Maybe he'll fall down and break his mouth!"

Opie the Entrepreneur in
"A Deal Is a Deal."
(episode 121)

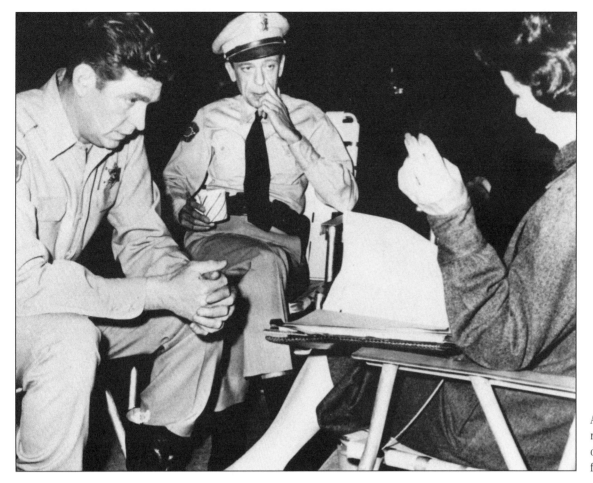

Andy and Don review the script during a break in filming.

Episode 53: "Guest of Honor" (2/26/62) ●●●1/2
DIRECTOR: Bob Sweeney; **WRITERS:** Jack Elinson and Charles Stewart **CAST:** Andy Griffith, Don Knotts, Ron Howard, Howard McNear, Jay Novello, Frank Warren, Bill Hickman

Episode 54: "The Merchant of Mayberry" (3/5/62) ●●●1/2
DIRECTOR: Bob Sweeney; **WRITERS:** Ben Gershman and Leo Solomon **CAST:** Andy Griffith, Don Knotts, Ron Howard, Frances Bavier, Sterling Holloway, Will Wright, Sara Seegar, Mary Lansing, Bob McQuain

Episode 55: "Aunt Bee, the Warden" (3/12/62) ●●●1/2
DIRECTOR: Bob Sweeney; **WRITERS:** Jack Elinson and Charles Stewart **CAST:** Andy Griffith, Don Knotts, Frances Bavier, Hal Smith, Orville Sherman, Bob McQuain, Paul Bakanas, Mary Lansing, Hope Summers **SYNOPSIS:** When the Mayberry jail becomes filled with moonshiners, Andy makes Otis serve his time for drunkenness at the Taylor home. At first, Otis welcomes the news, expecting to be pampered as he is in his cell. However, when Aunt Bee takes on the role of drill instructor, she puts Otis to work on an unending series of physically demanding chores. It's hard not to feel sorry for them, indeed, he begins to refer to the Taylor house as "The Rock." In desperation, Otis makes several attempts to escape, but Bee thwarts all of them. Eventually, Otis adopts a new image and swears off the booze—all out of fear of Aunt Bee. **CRITIQUE:** Hal Smith and Frances Bavier dominate this episode with some highly amusing banter. Don Knotts does have a scene-stealing segment to his credit, as he pursues an ill-fated plan to rehabilitate the incarcerated moonshiners by giving them children's arts-and-crafts kits, which the prisoners use to make passkeys. **FAVORITE DIALOGUE:** Gruff, hard-edged criminal responding to Barney's order to choose an arts-and-crafts kit: "I'll take the Mr. Potato set!"

Episode 56: "The County Nurse" (3/19/62) ●●●
DIRECTOR: Bob Sweeney; **WRITERS:** Jack Elinson and Charles Stewart **CAST:** Andy Griffith, Don Knotts, Julie Adams, Jack Prince

Episode 57: "Andy and Barney in the Big City" (3/26/62) ●●●1/2
DIRECTOR: Bob Sweeney; **WRITER:** Harvey Bullock **CAST:** Andy Griffith, Don Knotts, Ron Howard, Frances Bavier, Allan Melvin, Les Tremayne, Peter Leeds, Arte Johnson, Robert S. Carson, Ohola Nesmith, Thomas Myers, Roger Til **SYNOPSIS:** Traveling to Raleigh with Andy to attend a police function, Barney, eager to get some attention for Mayberry's Finest, is convinced the hotel house detective is a jewel thief who is planning to rob a rich guest. Ironically, Barney enlists the aid of a real jewel thief to thwart the nonexistent caper. The crook dupes him into letting him steal the jewels, but Andy foils the plot at the last minute and makes it appear that Barney's detective work was responsible for nabbing the culprit. **CRITIQUE:** Lest Mayberry become claustrophobic, this episode "opens up" and allows Andy and Barney a refreshing change of pace. It's fun to see the two rural lawmen cope with the pace of "civilization": Andy is astonished that rooms at the hotel average $7 per night, and there is a priceless scene in which Barney's attempt to bluff his way through a French menu ends up with him requesting snails and brains. Allan Melvin, who would make so many guest appearances on this show he might well be considered a regular, is the shady-looking

The only difference between "Barney's First Car" and the *Titanic*, is that the *Titanic* had a band! Ellen Corby is the little old lady hustler. (episode 90)

house detective whom Barney confuses with a thief. Keep an eye out for future *Laugh-In* star Arte Johnson as the hotel clerk. **FAVORITE DIALOGUE:** Barney to Andy, upon arrival in Raleigh: "You know, Andy, this is where I belong. Barney Fife in the asphalt jungle!"

Episode 58: "Wedding Bells for Aunt Bee" (4/2/62) ●●●1/2

DIRECTOR: Bob Sweeney; **WRITER:** Harvey Bullock **CAST:** Andy Griffith, Ron Howard, Frances Bavier, Fred Sherman, Hope Summers, Hal Smith **SYNOPSIS:** Clara Edwards convinces Aunt Bee that she is standing in the way of Andy's finding a wife. Guilt-ridden, Bee begins dating Mr. Goss, the humorless, pennypinching owner of the local dry cleaners. Andy disapproves, but pretends he supports the relationship, thinking it's what Aunt Bee desires. Eventually, however, both confess they do not care for Mr. Goss. Reassured by Andy that she is in no way interfering with his life, a relieved Aunt Bee terminates her "love affair" with Mr. Goss. **CRITIQUE:** This episode tackles the issue of elderly relatives becoming burdens on their families. Aunt Bee's interaction with the unpleasant Goss is almost too painful to watch. Indeed, Goss would only make good companionship for those in dire need of a two-hour lecture on how to remove butter stains from clothing. The heartwarming conclusion is the show's highlight, as Andy reassures Aunt Bee that his love for her is so strong she could never be perceived as a burden. (This episode was virtually remade as "Aunt Bee's Invisible Beau" in 1965. Episode #154) **FAVORITE DIALOGUE:** Otis to Andy: "I'm dead sober, but I expect I'll get over it!"

Episode 59: "Three's a Crowd" (4/9/62) ●●●1/2

DIRECTOR: Bob Sweeney; **WRITERS:** Jack Elinson and Charles Stewart **CAST:** Andy Griffith, Don Knotts, Betty Lynn, Sue Ane Langdon **SYNOPSIS:** Andy is frustrated by constant interruptions in his romantic evenings with county nurse Mary Simpson. Among the most annoying problems is the presence of Barney, who never seems to get the hint that he is becoming a nuisance. Finally, Barney spreads a rumor that Andy wants to be alone with Mary so that he can propose to her. Before long, Barney has a caravan of cars headed toward Mary's house to celebrate the "good news," only to find that once again jumping the gun has made him appear foolish. **CRITIQUE:** In this winning episode with Barney at his most annoying, one can feel for Andy. When Barney isn't on the phone, he's at the front door, and you haven't lived till you hear him pound out "La Cucuracha" on his bongo drums! In fairness, however, Mary doesn't seem overly disposed to Andy's overtures. As played by Sue Ane Langdon, the role is an example of an unsuccessful early attempt at finding a romantic interest for Andy—although it has always been felt that Elinor Donahue was a fine choice. Langdon has a high-pitched voice and a schoolgirl manner that makes her appear to be a very well developed fourteen. Still, there are a great number of laughs courtesy of Barney's unending intrusions and Andy's famous "slow-burn" reaction. **FAVORITE DIALOGUE:** Barney comforting a sobbing Aunt Bee about Andy's secret "engagement," while holding back his own tears: "Now, don't you get started, Aunt Bee. If you do, I'm a goner!"

Episode 60: "The Bookie Barber" (4/16/62) ●●●●

DIRECTOR: Bob Sweeney; **WRITERS:** Harvey Bullock and Ray Allen Saffian **CAST:** Andy Griffith, Don Knotts, Ron Howard, Frances Bavier, Howard McNear, Herb Vigran, Taggart Casey, Harry Swoger; Tom Monroe, Joe Stannard **SYNOPSIS:** Eager to fulfill his dream of owning "a two-

Goober tutors Malcolm Merriweather for a fight with Ernest T. Bass in "Malcolm at the Crossroads."

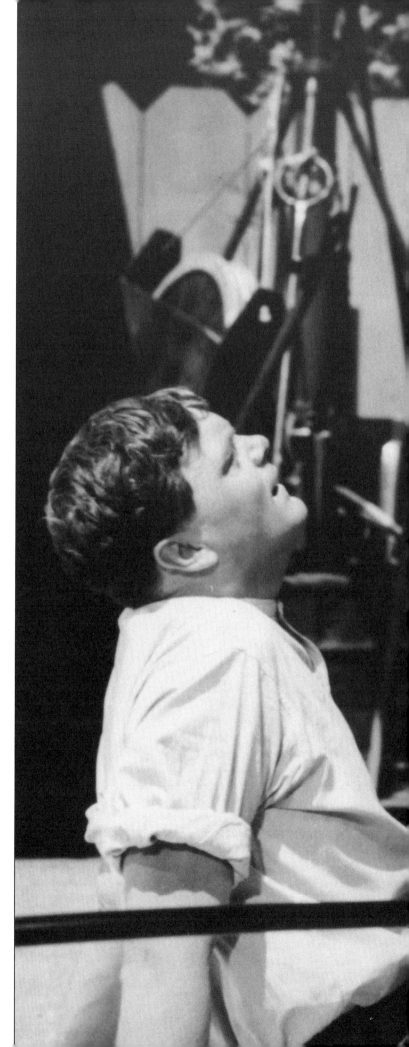

OOOOPPPS! Barney allows the bad guys to lock him and two federal agents in one of the Mayberry jail's "maximum security cells" in "The Big House." (episode 95)

chair shop," Floyd naively allows an aggressive big-city barber (Herb Vigran) to operate in his shop on a commission basis, and a steady stream of new customers appears immediately. Andy and Barney soon learn that the barber is using the shop as a front for a bookie operation and the customers are, in fact, his "runners." To bust the ring, Barney dresses as an eccentric old lady who wants to place a bet. The plan nearly goes awry when Opie recognizes him, but Barney succeeds—in his own bumbling way—in cracking the case. **CRITIQUE:** A top-notch episode featuring Barney in one of his classic "undercover" missions. As usual, the bad guys are easily identified as big-city types who look like they just stepped over from *The Untouchables* set. Howard McNear is as funny as ever in the episode's earlier sequences, but one wishes he was given more interaction with the crooks, who carry on their scheme right under his nose. **FAVORITE DIALOGUE:** Floyd, pondering the expansion of his business: "A two-chair shop! And I've got the magazines to swing it!"

Episode 61: "Andy on Trial" (4/23/62) ••••
DIRECTOR: Bob Sweeney; **WRITERS:** Jack Elinson and Charles Stewart **CAST:** Andy Griffith, Don Knotts, Ruta Lee, Roy Roberts, Robert Brubaker, Sally Mansfield, Byron Morrow, Richard Vath **SYNOPSIS:** Andy angers powerful publishing magnate J. Howard Jackson (Roy Roberts) by hauling him into court for a speeding ticket. In return, Jackson sends a beautiful female reporter (Ruta Lee) to Mayberry in the guise of a college student preparing a thesis on local government. She tricks Barney into making unflattering remarks about Andy that are taken out of context in a newspaper story about the lack of law in Mayberry. Andy is subjected to a hearing which will determine whether he keeps his job, and the key prosecution witness is Barney, whose own words are used to damning effect. However, the deputy makes an impassioned speech on behalf of Andy that cites his many attributes. Moved, the hearing officer declares Andy fit for the job and Jackson loses the fight to have Andy removed. **CRITIQUE:** An unusually dramatic episode, heightened by the look of pain and incredulousness on Andy's face as he has to hear Barney's accusations taken out of context at the hearing. Barney's desperate—and successful—testimony on behalf of his best friend is both moving and memorable, perhaps because it mirrors the real-life relationship of Knotts and Griffith. Note: Hal Smith's name appears in the credits, but he is not in this episode. **FAVORITE DIALOGUE:** Barney's impassioned plea to the hearing officer on Andy's behalf: "You got to understand this is a small town. The sheriff is more than just a sheriff—he's a friend. And the people in this town, they ain't got a better friend than Andy Taylor."

Episode 62: "Cousin Virgil" (4/30/62) •••
DIRECTOR: Bob Sweeney; **WRITERS:** Philip Shuker and Johnny Greene **CAST:** Andy Griffith, Don Knotts, Ron Howard, Frances Bavier, Michael J. Pollard, Hal Smith

Episode 63: "Deputy Otis" (5/7/62) •••1/2
DIRECTOR: Bob Sweeney; **WRITERS:** Fred S. Fox and Iz Elinson **CAST:** Andy Griffith, Don Knotts, Ron Howard, Frances Bavier, Hal Smith, Stanley Adams, Amzie Strickland, Dorothy Neumann **SYNOPSIS:** Otis Campbell panics at the news that his older brother Ralph and is wife are coming to Mayberry. It seems he has told his family that he is a deputy sheriff. To spare Otis embarrassment, Andy temporarily deputizes him.

Brando in *The Wild One*?
No, just Deputy Fife preparing Sheriff Taylor for take-off in "Barney's Sidecar"...
(episode 111)

Although Ralph is initially suspicious, Otis manages to stay sober and the charade works. However, Ralph staggers into the courthouse dead drunk one night and makes a startling confession: he is not the success story he has led Otis to believe he is. In fact, he is his own town's resident drunk. Inspired by Otis's achievement as a lawman, he forsakes the bottle and promises to straighten out his life. **CRITIQUE:** This episode is unique in that it represents the only time that Otis's alcoholism is presented as something other than a joke. The laughs about being drunk are still there in abundance, but there are some sensitive moments as well. The best comes when Hal Smith speaks movingly about the pain and shame his drunkenness has caused him. When he sobers up and puts on his police uniform, one can almost feel his pride, though Otis would resume his drunken ways in weeks to come. Here, however, Hal Smith gets to deliver a great performance. **FAVORITE DIALOGUE:** Andy, on Otis's favorite pastime: "In a way, that drinking does a good service for the town. Otis laps it up so fast, other folks can't get to it!"

Episode 64: "Mr. McBeevee" (10/1/62) ●●●●
DIRECTOR: Bob Sweeney; **WRITERS:** Harvey Bullock and Ray Allen Saffian **CAST:** Andy Griffith, Don Knotts, Ron Howard, Frances Bavier, Karl Swenson, Earl Holmes **SYNOPSIS:** Andy becomes concerned when Opie continues to bring home gifts from a Mr. McBeevee, who Andy has assumed was an imaginary playmate. Opie's description of McBeevee as a man capable of walking through trees is too improbable to believe. Against Barney's advice, Andy gives Opie the benefit of the doubt, but is privately worried the boy is lying. Later, Andy learns to his relief that McBeevee does indeed exist and Opie's description is technically correct: he does "walk" in trees (with the aid of a safety harness), as he is a lineman for the local power company. **CRITIQUE:** This gentle episode is beloved by virtually all fans of *The Andy Griffith Show*. The message, well stated by Andy, is that when doubt rears its head the most, you must stand by the people in whom you have faith. In many previous episodes, Andy's knee-jerk reactions to Opie's apparent transgressions have left him ashamed. Here, he refreshingly shows he has learned from those mistakes, and his faith is rewarded by his son's honesty. A charming, poignant episode, wonderfully enacted by Andy and Ron Howard, with special kudos to veteran radio actor Karl Swenson as Mr. McBeevee. **FAVORITE DIALOGUE:** Opie, describing Mr. McBeevee during Barney's hilarious interrogation: "He can make smoke come out of his ears. He learned that from the cannibals."

Episode 65: "Andy's Rich Girlfriend" (10/8/62) ●●●1/2
DIRECTOR: Bob Sweeney; **WRITERS:** Jim Fritzell and Everett Greenbaum **CAST:** Andy Griffith, Don Knotts, Frances Bavier, Joanna Moore, Betty Lynn, Donald Lawton, Warner Jones **SYNOPSIS:** Andy begins to date nurse Peggy McMillan but, learning she comes from wealth, is self-conscious about his ability to treat her in the manner to which he assumes she has become accustomed. Just about convinced by Barney, who assures Andy she is not his type, Andy begins to avoid seeing Peggy—a strategy that leads to her being hurt and angered. Eventually, she convinces Andy that she is a simple person despite her family's wealth, and that she enjoys the same things he does. His confidence renewed, Andy resumes his relationship with her. **CRITIQUE:** Although Andy Griffith has maintained he never quite felt comfortable as a romantic lead until Aneta Corsaut joined the series, this insecurity is never evident on-screen and he enjoys a good chemistry with stunning Joanna Moore as Peggy McMillan. Moore, who is a very competent actress, provides a good foil for Andy, particularly in a memorable scene where he feels very

. . . as Andy discovers the new crime-stopping vehicle has just one "minor" shortcoming.

much out of place in an exclusive French restaurant. However, the character of Peggy is never fully explored in any depth. **FAVORITE DIALOGUE:** At dinner, Andy responds to Peggy's question about whether he has ever dined on escargot (snails): "I've stepped on quite a few in my time, but I've never eaten one!"

Episode 66: "Andy and the New Mayor" (10/15/62) ●●●1/2

DIRECTOR: Bob Sweeney; **WRITER:** Harvey Bullock **CAST:** Andy Griffith, Don Knotts, Ron Howard, Parley Baer, Roy Engel, Helen Kleeb, Janet Stewart **SYNOPSIS:** Mayor Stoner begins his term by admonishing Andy and Barney for running a lax jail. He orders them to tighten up procedures and stop doing personal favors for local citizens. He is enraged further when touring the jail, he discovers Andy and Barney babysitting an infant and allowing a prisoner time off to tend his crops. When the prisoner does not appear as scheduled, an outraged Stoner accompanies Andy and Barney to the man's farm to arrest him. Here Stoner learns why the prisoner has been delayed—he's trapped in a tree by a bear, who soon forces Stoner into an identical situation! **CRITIQUE:** On the heels of the indecisive, self-serving Mayor Pike comes Mayor Stoner. He's decisive, all right—but more resembles a dictator than a public servant. Parley Baer was cast in the unsympathetic role, and his performances over the years would make the perfect foil for Andy Griffith's laid-back charm. Baer, an accomplished actor with the ability to play "heavies" and broad comedy, gets a chance to show the range of those talents in this highly watchable episode. The "Baer vs. bear" finale is a riot. **FAVORITE DIALOGUE:** Andy, upon noticing Barney's new cologne: "What's that smell? You been painting?"

Episode 67: "Andy and Opie: Bachelors" (10/22/62) ●●●

DIRECTOR: Bob Sweeney; **WRITERS:** Jim Fritzell and Everett Greenbaum **CAST:** Andy Griffith, Ron Howard, Frances Bavier, Joanna Moore, Howard McNear, Ray Lanier

Episode 68: "The Cow Thief" (10/29/62) ●●●

DIRECTOR: Bob Sweeney; **WRITERS:** Harvey Bullock and Ray Allen Saffian **CAST:** Andy Griffith, Don Knotts, Malcolm Atterbury, Parley Baer, Ralph Bell, Jon Lormer

Episode 69: "Barney Mends a Broken Heart" (11/5/62) ●●●1/2

DIRECTOR: Bob Sweeney; **WRITER:** Aaron Ruben **CAST:** Andy Griffith, Don Knotts, Frances Bavier, Joanna Moore, Betty Lynn, Jean Carson, Joyce Jameson, Josie Lloyd, Fred Beir, Michael Ross **SYNOPSIS:** Andy breaks up with Peggy when he finds her in the company of an old flame, and Barney attempts to lift Andy's spirits by introducing him to Thelma Lou's friend Lydia, who proves to be as exciting as watching paint dry. Barney moves to "Plan B"—duping Andy into meeting "the Fun Girls," Skippy and Daphne, at the Mt. Pilot diner. Here, Andy becomes embroiled in a fight with Skippy's former boyfriend, which leads to his sporting a black eye. Peggy, however, takes pity on him and the two apologize to each other and make up. **CRITIQUE:** This episode has relevance beyond its high quota of laughs—it's the first appearance of Skippy and Daphne, heretofore known as "the Fun Girls." Played by Jean Carson ("Hello, doll.") and Joyce Jameson ("Oh, Bernie, you're a scream!"), they would bring Mayberry as close as possible to the sexual revolution. The episode has many other delights, aside from these ladies—one was

the debut of Josie Lloyd as the ever-boring Lydia, who seems allergic to fun. **FAVORITE DIALOGUE:** Lydia, throwing cold water on yet another suggestion for social activities: "When I go out into the sun, I get the herpes."

Episode 70: "Lawman Barney" (11/12/62)   ●●●1/2
DIRECTOR: Bob Sweeney; **WRITER:** Aaron Ruben **CAST:** Andy Griffith, Don Knotts, Howard McNear, Allan Melvin, Orville Sherman, Norman Leavitt, Bob McQuain **SYNOPSIS:** Barney allows himself to be scared off by two unlicensed peddlers who humiliate him. Andy orders him to return to run the men off, but does not tell him that he has secretly informed the men that Barney is a real "killer." This time, the peddlers leave, and Barney believes he strikes fear into the hearts of lawbreakers. However, the men learn of Andy's ruse and return to pick a fight with Barney. Andy offers to help his deputy, but Barney summons his courage and stands up to the wiseguys. He succeeds in running them off, and in doing so, restores his pride. **CRITIQUE:** "Lawman Barney" delves deeply into the psyche of Barney Fife. While he is a coward on the surface, he manages to be heroic when the chips are down. To do otherwise would make his character a pathetic, incompetent fraud. While the episode has a great many laughs in displaying Barney's desperate initial attempts to avoid a confrontation, the highlight is clearly his heroic stance against the bullies. In this show, Barney has rarely looked so helpless, but rarely has he stood so tall. **FAVORITE DIALOGUE:** Andy, informing the wiseguys of Barney's nicknames: "Barney the Beast; Fife the Fierce; and Crazy Gun Barney."

Episode 71: "The Mayberry Band" (11/19/62)   ●●●●
DIRECTOR: Bob Sweeney; **WRITERS:** Jim Fritzell and Everett Greenbaum **CAST:** Andy Griffith, Don Knotts, Parley Baer, Howard McNear **SYNOPSIS:** Mayor Stoner refuses to have the town pay for the expenses of the Mayberry Band on their annual trip to the capital for a music competition. He maintains the band is horrendous and brings disgrace to the town. Andy's arguments fall on deaf ears, so he devises a plan wherein the visiting Freddy Fleet Band of jazz musicians intermingle with the regulars in the Mayberry Band. Stoner is amazed by the dramatic "improvement" and agrees to allow the band to go on their outing. **CRITIQUE** A top-notch episode which allows Parley Baer to get plenty of laughs as the sourpuss Mayor Stoner. One can't blame Stoner for chastising the band, as it really is beyond horrible. The scene in which he is subjected to an audition fully justifies his strategy of listening to the music *before* lunch. Other funny tidbits include Barney's incessant playing of the cymbals and his fascination with jazz jargon. (He refers to everyone as "Chicky, baby.") The final sequence of Stoner realizing he's been "had" as the bus drives away with the band playing in its usual manner is extremely funny. **FAVORITE DIALOGUE:** Andy to Mayor Stoner: "We're a walkin' band. We've got to keep movin'." Stoner: "After hearing you play, I can believe that!"

Episode 72: "Floyd, The Gay Deceiver" (11/26/62)   ●●●●
DIRECTOR: Bob Sweeney; **WRITER:** Aaron Ruben **CAST:** Andy Griffith, Ron Howard, Frances Bavier, Howard McNear, Doris Dowling **SYNOPSIS:** Floyd receives the devastating news of the impending visit of vivacious pen pal Madeline (Doris Dowling), to whom he has misrepresented himself as a millionaire. To spare him humiliation, Andy allows Floyd to use the stately home of a vacationing family as his own "residence"— with Andy posing as Floyd's son and Aunt Bee as the maid. When Madeline announces she wants to stay for a week, Andy prepares to confess

Telop slide depicting Andy and Deputy Warren Ferguson (Jack Burns).

Parley Baer as the less-than-lovable Mayor Stoner.

the charade. However, he exposes Madeline as a con woman looking to exploit rich older men. She agrees to leave town, and Andy refrains from telling Floyd that his would-be love was actually a greater deceiver than he was. **CRITIQUE:** An all-around classic episode, with Howard McNear's comedic talents used to full advantage. Seldom have we seen Floyd so confused and bewildered. The highlight of the show is when Andy and Opie pose as Floyd's sons. Andy explains that, as an only child, he was lonely and needed a companion—despite the obvious thirty-year age difference between him and Opie! The rapport between Griffith and McNear is superb. Refreshingly, the script allows Andy to have a big share of the laughs instead of playing the usual straight man. **FAVORITE DIALOGUE:** Floyd (pondering having to confess his deception to Madeline): "'Time heals everything.' Know who said that? My Latin teacher at barber college!"

Episode 73: "Opie's Rival" (12/3/62) •••
DIRECTOR: Bob Sweeney; **WRITER:** Sid Morse **CAST:** Andy Griffith, Ron Howard, Frances Bavier, Joanna Moore

Episode 74: "Convicts at Large" (12/10/62) ••••
DIRECTOR: Bob Sweeney; **WRITERS:** Jim Fritzell and Everett Greenbaum **CAST:** Andy Griffith, Don Knotts, Howard McNear, Reta Shaw, Jean Carson, Jane Dulo, Willis Bouchey **SYNOPSIS:** Three dangerous gun molls led by Big Maud (Reta Shaw) take refuge in a remote, deserted cabin on the outskirts of Mayberry. Coincidentally, Barney and Floyd seek help at the cabin when their car runs out of gas while on a fishing trip. They are taken hostage and alternately charmed and menaced by the cons. While Barney tries to escape, he gets no help from Floyd, who seems oblivious to the danger and begins to enjoy the situation. Eventually, Andy learns of their predicament, and with the help of the cabin's owner, succeeds in capturing two of the molls. The third is outwitted by Barney when he literally dances her into Andy's custody. Throughout, Floyd remains only concerned about the status of some eggs the women were cooking. **CRITIQUE:** For many fans, this is arguably the funniest episode of the series, a true classic. Everything jells perfectly, including the casting of the cons. Amply built Reta Shaw (who later would make a name for herself as the maid in *The Ghost and Mrs. Muir*) is wonderful as Big Maud, and Jean Carson is equally good as Naomi, the con who confuses Barney with a former boyfriend and constantly refers to him as "Al"—a trait the impressionable Floyd eventually picks up! The chemistry between Don Knotts and Howard McNear is an example of two comic talents at work. Knotts's attempts to charm the women into submission are unforgettable, and McNear's immediate submission to the "Stockholm syndrome" (captives befriending their captors) is simply hilarious. Indeed, when Barney gives Floyd the opportunity to disarm Big Maud while he dances with her, Floyd merely sits on the sofa keeping time to the music and munching on a banana! **FAVORITE DIALOGUE:** Floyd, returning from a trip to town for provisions while Barney's life has been hanging in the balance: "We're home!!!"

Episode 75: "The Bed Jacket" (12/17/62) ••••
DIRECTOR: Bob Sweeney; **WRITERS:** Harvey Bullock and Ray Allen Saffian **CAST:** Andy Griffith, Frances Bavier, Hope Summers, Parley Baer, Dabbs Greer, Mary Lansing **SYNOPSIS:** Aunt Bee has a guilty pleasure: she has fallen in love with an expensive bed jacket she spotted in the window of a local shop and throws hints to Andy that she would like it for her birthday. Andy misses the point and buys Bee sets of canning

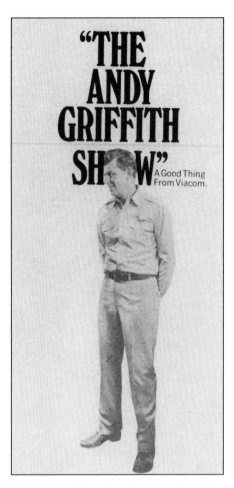

Promotional brochure from Viacom, circa 1970.

jars instead. Heartbroken, Bee bursts into tears. Andy then learns from Clara about the bed jacket. However, it has since been purchased by Mayor Stoner for a surprise present for his wife. Stoner refuses to relinquish the jacket, but ultimately offers to trade it for Andy's most prized possession—his favorite fishing rod, "Ol' Eagle-Eye Annie." Andy makes the swap and feels he got the better deal when Bee becomes overjoyed at the gift. **CRITIQUE:** This episode features touching performances by Andy Griffith and Frances Bavier, and their chemistry has never seemed more sincere. Bee's all-too-human side manifests itself for the first time in a materialistic way. But both Andy and Bee are treated tenderly here, Mayor Stoner is represented in a completely unsympathetic light, and he is not even given the customary opportunity to redeem himself by the episode's end. The sequence when Andy observes Bee reveling in her gift and proclaiming this "the best birthday I've ever had" is among the most moving moments in the series. (Note: the little-seen epilogue has Mayor Stoner reluctantly returning the fishing rod to Andy in return for Andy's assuring his wife that he did not give the bed jacket to another woman.) **FAVORITE DIALOGUE:** Andy explains to Opie why he traded his beloved fishing pole for the bed jacket: "I kinda swapped it for another kind of pleasure. So "Ol' Eagle-Eye Annie" is doing what she's always done. Even now she's givin' me pleasure." He looks at Aunt Bee happily bragging on the phone about her jacket—"real heart-warming pleasure."

Episode 76: "The Bank Job" (12/24/62) ●●●●
DIRECTOR: Bob Sweeney; **WRITERS:** Jim Fritzell and Everett Greenbaum **CAST:** Andy Griffith, Don Knotts, Jim Nabors, Lee Kreiger, Frances Osborn, Charles Thompson, Warren Parker, Al Checco, Mary Lansing, Clint Howard **SYNOPSIS:** When Barney's warnings of lax security at the bank are ignored, he dresses as a cleaning woman to "rob" the place, but only succeeds in locking himself in the vault. While the townspeople work frantically to get him out, he smashes through the wall into a beauty salon—another sign, he warns, of how crooks could make a getaway. Later, when thieves do hit the bank and get the drop on its owner and Andy, Barney manages to overcome the bad guys. Once more, Barney Fife's instincts have been proven correct and he emerges with the respect of the Mayberrians. **CRITIQUE:** There are more laughs than you can count in this episode that gives Don Knotts the opportunity to steal the whole show. And steal it he does, with a classic impersonation of a cleaning lady that fools absolutely no one. Other highlights are Barney's chastising of the bank's guard, Asa, who is older than Methuselah. The episode also features a welcome appearance by little Clint Howard, Ronny's brother, as the silent, but ever-watchful peanut-butter king, Leon. **FAVORITE DIALOGUE:** Barney to Asa, the bank guard, "What are those green things in your cartridge belt?" ASA: "Bullets!"

Episode 77: "One-Punch Opie" (12/31/62) ●●●1/2
DIRECTOR: Bob Sweeney; **WRITER:** Harvey Bullock **CAST:** Andy Griffith, Don Knotts, Ron Howard, Scott McCartor, Kim Tyler, Richard Keith, Stanley Ferrar, Clint Howard **SYNOPSIS:** Steve, a new boy in Mayberry, disrupts Opie's circle of friends by bullying the boys into doing illegal activities like breaking street lamps and stealing apples. Initially intimidated, Opie goes along with some of Steve's mischief, but ultimately decides to stand up to him. When confronted with a fight, Steve runs away, leaving Opie proclaimed a hero to his friends. **CRITIQUE:** This slice-of-life episode should ring a bell with everyone who ever had a run-in with a bully. Barney tries to intimidate the boys with a tour of

Don Knotts returned for "Barney Hosts a Summit Meeting," the worst Cold War crisis since the building of the Berlin Wall.

Jean Hagen works her charms on Sheriff Taylor in "Andy and the Woman Speeder." (episode 35)

Mayberry's "maximum security" cells where he accidentally locks himself in. You can't help feeling pride for Opie's courage in this moving story, and as always, the character benefits from a wonderfully sincere performance by Ronny Howard. **FAVORITE DIALOGUE:** Barney, warning Andy that Opie and his friends are heading toward juvenile delinquency: "Next thing you know, they'll be on motorcycles with leather jackets, zooming around.. It'll be a reign of terror! Nip it! Nip it in the bud!"

Episode 78: "Barney and the Governor" (1/7/63) •••1/2

DIRECTOR: Bob Sweeney; **WRITERS:** Bill Freedman and Henry Sharp **CAST:** Andy Griffith, Don Knotts, Parley Baer, Hal Smith, Carl Benton Reid, Joe Hamilton, Bob McGuain, Rance Howard, Burt Mustin **SYNOPSIS:** When Barney tickets the car of the governor (Carl Benton Reid) for illegal parking, Mayor Stoner informs him the governor is coming to Mayberry presumably to fire him. In the meantime, Otis spikes the office water barrel with gin, and Barney inadvertently becomes drunk. He is sobered up in the nick of time by Andy, who informs him that the governor's purpose in coming is to congratulate him for not showing favoritism under the law. Unfortunately, by this time Mayberry has another drunken victim of Otis's scheme: Mayor Stoner. **CRITIQUE:** This comedy of errors is built around numerous misunderstandings, and the result is a first-rate episode. Watching a depressed Barney accidentally fall victim to Otis's spiked water supply is quite funny, particularly since Don Knotts can hold his own against Hal Smith when it comes to acting inebriated. Parley Baer also gets to "let down his hair" when even the stony Mayor Stoner can't stay away from that enticing water barrel. Ron Howard's dad Rance appears as the governor's chauffeur. **FAVORITE DIALOGUE:** A drunken Barney reacting to the threat of the governor's visit: "Tell the governor to put that in his smipe and poke it!"

Episode 79: "Man in a Hurry" (1/14/63) ••••

DIRECTOR: Bob Sweeney; **WRITERS:** Jim Fritzell and Everett Greenbaum **CAST:** Andy Griffith, Don Knotts, Ron Howard, Frances Bavier, Jim Nabors, Robert Emhardt, William Keene, Norman Leavitt **SYNOPSIS:** Big-city businessman Malcolm Tucker (Robert Emhardt) is stranded in Mayberry when his car breaks down on the eve of an important meeting in Charlotte. Blowhard Tucker finds it infuriating when the town's slow pace on Sunday precludes rapid repair of his car. Gradually, however, the low-key atmosphere of Mayberry makes an impression and he begins to revel in the charm of the town and its citizens. Although Gomer Pyle manages to get Tucker's car repaired, the businessman makes an excuse for staying the night—and enjoys his most relaxing evening in memory. **CRITIQUE:** Of all the episodes of the series, this poignant and sentimental story is the one most often cited by fans as the best of the series. Robert Emhardt is the city slicker who initially fails to see Mayberry's simple pleasures in trying to peel an apple with the skin intact, Aunt Bee's home cooking, and just plain taking it easy on a Sunday afternoon. He bellows that the residents are living in another world, but by the episode's end, that's less an insult than a compliment. The final scene shows the usually-harried businessman sleeping soundly in a rocker—an apple, waiting to be peeled, displayed in his hand. Everett Greenbaum and Jim Fritzell's script is charming in its understatement, and Bob Sweeney's direction is equally inspired. A memorable show for the ages, and one whose message is even more timely today. **FAVORITE DIALOGUE:** Opie to Mr. Tucker, upon his departure: "Oh, rats! If you were staying, I'd get to sleep on the ironing board between two chairs—that's adventure sleeping!"

Living on the edge! Andy and Barney risk incurring the wrath of Mrs. Mendlebright by cooking in "Up in Barney's Room." (episode 105)

Episode 80: "High Noon in Mayberry" (1/21/63) •••1/2
DIRECTOR: Bob Sweeney; **WRITERS:** Jim Fritzell and Everett Greenbaum **CAST:** Andy Griffith, Don Knotts, Ron Howard, Frances Bavier, Hal Smith, Jim Nabors, Leo Gordon

Episode 81: "The Loaded Goat" (1/28/63)
DIRECTOR: Bob Sweeney; **WRITER:** Harvey Bullock **CAST:** Andy Griffith, Don Knotts, Hal Smith, Parley Baer, Forrest Lewis, Bing Russell
SYNOPSIS: When a local farmer's pet goat eats sticks of dynamite, Andy and Barney are at a loss as to what to do with the potentially explosive livestock. They place the goat in a jail cell, but Otis infuriates the animal when he tries to evict it. Ultimately, Barney plays the French harp to lull the goat into submission, and Andy and he remove the animal to the outskirts of town. **CRITIQUE:** The visual gags in this episode are many, as Andy, Barney, and Otis are alternately cornered by the "enraged" goat, who can explode at any moment. The icing on the cake is the epilogue in which Mayor Stoner mistakenly thinks the goat has been detonated and has taken the lawmen into the Great Beyond. Among the many laughs, however, consider that it is never satisfactorily explained just how the goat fares after this "dynamite" experience in Mayberry.
FAVORITE DIALOGUE: A drunken Otis coming face to face with the goat in his cell: "Uncle Nat, what are you doing here?"

Episode 82: "Class Reunion" (2/4/63) •••1/2
DIRECTOR: Bob Sweeney; **WRITERS:** Jim Fritzell and Everett Greenbaum **CAST:** Andy Griffith, Don Knotts, Barbara Perry, Don Haggerty, Frank Behrens, Mollie Dodd, Paul Smith **SYNOPSIS:** Andy and Barney organize a reunion of their high school class with mixed results. They cannot recognize many of their former classmates: Barney finds his former sweetheart does not even remember his name, and Andy's much-anticipated reunion with his former girlfriend, Sharon De Spain (Barbara Perry), proves to be bittersweet at best. It seems that as soon as the two make plans to become an item again, they are reminded of the differing lifestyle goals that parted them originally. **CRITIQUE:** This is one of the few episodes in which the drama is more plentiful than the laughs. Indeed, Andy and Sharon's reacquaintance is quite affecting, and ol' Andy acts more romantic than we've ever seen him. There are still plenty of comic highlights: we learn of Barney's high school activities, including serving on the board of directors of the tinfoil drive; the original senior prom band—Carl Benson's Wildcats—is reunited (now with Carl's mother on the sax), and Barney awaits his former love impatiently, only to have her mistake him for a bartender. **FAVORITE DIALOGUE:** Barney asking Andy about his involvement with the Philomathian Society in high school: "What was that Philomathian, Andy?" Andy: "It was a group that got together and cut out current events and pasted them in a book." Barney: "Sorry I didn't get in on that. Sounds like fun."

Episode 83: "Rafe Hollister Sings" (2/11/63) ••1/2
DIRECTOR: Charles Irving; **WRITER:** Harvey Bullock **CAST:** Andy Griffith, Don Knotts, Ron Howard, Frances Bavier, Jack Prince, Kay Stewart, Parley Baer, Olan Soulé

Episode 84: "Opie and the Spoiled Kid" (2/18/63) •••1/2
DIRECTOR: Bob Sweeney; **WRITERS:** Jim Fritzell and Everett Greenbaum **CAST:** Andy Griffith, Don Knotts, Ron Howard, Frances Bavier,

It's "The High and the Mighty" Mayberry style when Aunt Bee heads for the clouds in "Aunt Bee's Big Moment." (episode 242)

Opie finds himself a reluctant "father" in "Opie Finds a Baby." (episode 199)

Ronny Capo, Harlan Warde, Mary Lansing

Episode 85: "The Great Filling Station Robbery" (2/25/63) •••
DIRECTOR: Bob Sweeney; **WRITER:** Harvey Bullock **CAST:** Andy Griffith, Don Knotts, Ron Howard, Jim Nabors, Pat Colby, Jack Shea, Johnny Silver, Willis Bouchey

Episode 86: "Andy Discovers America" (3/4/63) •••1/2
DIRECTOR: Bob Sweeney; **WRITER:** John Whedon **CAST:** Andy Griffith, Don Knotts, Ron Howard, Frances Bavier, Aneta Corsaut, Joey Scott, Dennis Rush, David Keith **SYNOPSIS:** Andy gets into hot water with Opie's new teacher, Miss Crump, when the youngster tells her his dad thinks studying history is a waste of time. Before long, all the kids in the class use Andy's words as a reason for not doing homework. Annoyed, Helen Crump accuses Andy of being a terrible influence on children. To make amends, he uses psychology to encourage the boys to study history, and even forms an educational club called the Mayberry Minutemen. The boys' schoolwork improves accordingly, and Andy and Helen bury the hatchet. **CRITIQUE:** Generally unsuccessful in finding an actress with whom he shared a genuine chemistry, Andy Griffith struck paydirt with the casting of Aneta Corsaut in this, her first appearance on the show. Although the schoolboys refer to her as "Old Lady Crump," she is strikingly beautiful and her independent streak allows her to put Andy in his place when he makes careless remarks about education. There are other delights as well: Barney trying to bluff knowledge of the Emancipation Proclamation, and Andy's summary of the entire American Revolution in a five-minute monologue reminiscent of his early comedy routines. **FAVORITE DIALOGUE:** Andy to Barney, following Helen's chastisement: "See that foot? How could that great big foot—all of it—fit in my mouth?"

Episode 87: "Aunt Bee's Medicine Man" (3/11/63) •••1/2
DIRECTOR: Bob Sweeney; **WRITER:** John Whedon **CAST:** Andy Griffith, Don Knotts, Ron Howard, Frances Bavier, John Dehner, Mary Lansing, Ruth Packard, Kathryn Hart, Noreen Gammill, Jewel Rose **SYNOPSIS:** Aunt Bee and her friends find renewed vigor in life, courtesy of an elixir with a secret ingredient which they purchase from traveling medicine man Colonel Harvey. Before long, Bee and her friends are stumbling all over in a giddy state, and Andy and Barney discover that the "secret ingredient" in Harvey's elixir is pure alcohol. By this time, Bee and her friends must be arrested by Andy so they can sober up. Ironically, the neighboring cell is now occupied by their onetime hero Colonel Harvey. **CRITIQUE:** Guest star John Dehner almost steals the show with a larger-than-life performance as the lovable con man Colonel Harvey. Frances Bavier gives some unlikely competition to Hal Smith with an out-of-character display of pure silliness, courtesy of her beloved "elixir." As Andy ponders her behavior, he initially dismisses the idea of her being drunk because "she won't even allow fruit cake into the house!" **FAVORITE DIALOGUE:** A "giddy" Aunt Bee greeting Andy: "Look! It's Sheriff Matt Dillon! Where's Chester?"

Episode 88: "The Darlings are Coming" (3/18/63) ••••
DIRECTOR: Bob Sweeney; **WRITERS:** Jim Fritzell and Everett Greenbaum **CAST:** Andy Griffith, Don Knotts, Frances Bavier, Denver Pyle, Maggie Peterson, Olan Soulé, Hoke Howell, and The Dillards **SYNOPSIS:** Mayberry is thrown into a tizzy by the arrival of the Darlings, a back-

woods family consisting of patriarch Briscoe, teen-age daughter Charlene, and her brothers—a group of silent simpletons who come to life only when they play bluegrass music. Andy befriends the clan, finding their lack of civilized ways endearing. Charlene is in town to meet her fiancé who is returning from the army, but the flirtatious girl turns her eye on Andy, who outwits her and arranges for her to marry her betrothed. **CRITIQUE:** This is an important episode in *The Andy Griffith Show* canon, as it introduced the Darlings, a group that would appear periodically throughout the years to the delight of many fans. The culture clash that ensues is quite funny, and the Darlings make most of Mayberry's residents look like Park Avenue sophisticates. Denver Pyle is hilarious as the lovable Briscoe Darling, and Maggie Peterson is equally amusing as the love-starved Charlene. The Dillards became huge favorites with audiences as the zombielike Darling boys, who would become the influence for the characters of Larry, Darryl, and Darryl on *Bob Newhart*. **FAVORITE DIALOGUE:** Briscoe, leading the band: "Let's try 'Slimy River Bottom' and this time make it purty!" Charlene: "That one makes me cry!"

Episode 89: "Andy's English Valet" (3/25/63) ●●●1/2
DIRECTOR: Bob Sweeney; **WRITER:** Harvey Bullock **CAST:** Andy Griffith, Don Knotts, Ron Howard, Frances Bavier, Bernard Fox, Bob McQuain **SYNOPSIS:** Malcolm Merriweather, a "gentleman's gentleman" from Great Britain runs afoul of the law by driving recklessly while passing through Mayberry. Andy allows Malcolm to pay off his fine by working as a valet in Aunt Bee's absence, but while Malcolm proves to be efficient, his strict mannerisms and attention to detail drive Andy crazy. One night, Malcolm overhears Andy complaining to Barney about the situation and is so disheartened that he leaves town. Feeling guilty at having offended Malcolm, Andy "rearrests" him and acts as though he truly needs his services. Once again feeling needed, Malcolm gladly returns to the Taylor household. **CRITIQUE:** The first appearance of Malcolm Merriweather remains a favorite of fans, due in no small part to the performance of Bernard Fox as the lovable valet. He may be inept at many things, but certainly not his professional duties. However, the most memorable scenes are the quiet moments in which Malcolm transfixes Opie with his magic tricks. A winning episode in every way. **FAVORITE DIALOGUE:** Andy lures Malcolm back by pretending to need his services:"It's a terrible thing—the high sheriff having to tie his own tie!"

Episode 90: "Barney's First Car" (4/1/63) ●●●●
DIRECTOR: Bob Sweeney; **WRITERS:** Jim Fritzell and Everett Greenbaum **CAST:** Andy Griffith, Don Knotts, Ron Howard, Frances Bavier, Betty Lynn, Ellen Corby, Allan Melvin, Hallene Hill, Tom Allen **SYNOPSIS:** Despite Andy's reservations, Barney invests his life savings (all $300) in a used car owned by an elderly widow. No sooner does Barney take his friends out for a ride than the car begins to fall apart. On another ride, it finally dies, leaving Barney and Andy dozing in the back seat. They awaken to find themselves inside the hideout of a stolen-car ring—run by the "widow." Andy and Barney bide their time, then get the drop on the gang with some help from Barney's firearm—now loaded for action with his infamous bullet. **CRITIQUE:** Ellen Corby, later to find TV immortality as Grandma on *The Waltons*, gives a deliciously funny performance as the little old lady who gets the naive Barney to buy a clunker. Highlights of the episode include her moving speech about the car belonging to her dearly departed husband, as Barney fights to control the tears. Later, the look on Don Knotts's face as the car disinte-

"Howard the Bowler": Emmett, Goober, and Andy encourage the nervous Mr. Sprague as he nears his perfect game.

Bernard Fox as Malcolm Merriweather, proving to Opie that the Americans and the British are "two people separated by a common language."

grates around him is heartbreaking, though one can't help laughing at his misfortune. (Not even Chaplin can convey pathos like Knotts.) A first-rate episode. **FAVORITE DIALOGUE:** Barney: "Last big buy I made was my mom and dad's anniversary present." Andy: "What did you get 'em?" Barney: "A septic tank. They're really hard to buy for!" Andy: "You're a good son, Barn."

Episode 91: "The Rivals" (4/8/63) ●●●1/2
DIRECTOR: Bob Sweeney; **WRITER:** Harvey Bullock **CAST:** Andy Griffith, Don Knotts, Ron Howard, Betty Lynn, Ronda Jeter

Episode 92: "A Wife for Andy" (4/15/63) ●●●
DIRECTOR: Bob Sweeney; **WRITER:** Aaron Ruben **CAST:** Andy Griffith, Don Knotts, Ron Howard, Frances Bavier, Aneta Corsaut, Betty Lynn, Barbara Perry, Janet Waldo, Rachel Ames, Janet Stewart

Episode 93: "Dogs, Dogs, Dogs" (4/22/63) ●●●●
DIRECTOR: Bob Sweeney; **WRITERS:** Jim Fritzell and Everett Greenbaum **CAST:** Andy Griffith, Don Knotts, Ron Howard, Hal Smith, Roy Barcroft, Robert Cornthwaite **SYNOPSIS:** Andy and Barney are besieged by a group of stray dogs on the day a state inspector is coming to the courthouse to evaluate their request for additional funding. Barney transports the canines to a remote open field. Upon returning, however, he empathizes with Opie's concerns that the dogs are endangered by a furious lightning storm. Barney retrieves the pooches, and they "ambush" the inspector. The man proves to be a dog lover and looks so favorably on the animals that he grants all of Andy and Barney's funding requests. **CRITIQUE:** Don Knotts's superb monologue extolling the abilities of dogs to survive inclement weather makes this one of the best episodes. Watch him as he tries to assure Ronny Howard of the durability of the canines. As the lightning storm worsens, Knotts becomes more concerned with convincing himself than the child. Eventually he rambles into a hilarious and pointless comparison between dogs and giraffes, followed by his running to save the endangered mutts. Also watch Griffith and Howard allow Knotts the spotlight by underplaying their actions. **FAVORITE DIALOGUE:** Barney, crazily trying to blame giraffes for his guilt over leaving the dogs in the lightning storm: "Giraffes are selfish! Just running around looking after number one, getting hit by lightning!"

Episode 94: "Mountain Wedding" (4/29/63) ●●●1/2
DIRECTOR: Bob Sweeney; **WRITERS:** Jim Fritzell and Everett Greenbaum **CAST:** Andy Griffith, Don Knotts, Howard McNear, Howard Morris, Denver Pyle, The Dillards, Maggie Peterson, Hope Howell, Dub Taylor **SYNOPSIS:** Socially gauche backwoodsman Ernest T. Bass insists the marriage of Charlene Darling to Dud is not valid because it was a civil ceremony. He endlessly assaults the Darling cabin and threatens to kidnap Charlene, but instead nabs Barney who is made a decoy in a bride's dress. Andy uses the diversion to get Charlene and Dud remarried by a preacher. Frustrated, though satisfied that Charlene cannot be his, Ernest T. gives up his quest to "declare" for her. **CRITIQUE:** This episode has great importance as the first of Ernest T. Bass's five infamous appearances on the series. It's safe to say that, as played by Howard Morris, television had never seen, nor will ever see, a character quite so outrageous. Don Knotts manages to steal a scene from the equally hyperactive Morris, but he has to wear a wedding dress to do so. Lots of laughs, especially when Andy and Barney must contend with the Darlings' ear-split-

If you disagree with Sheriff Andy Taylor's decisions, you can always appeal—to Justice of the Peace Andy Taylor!

ting snoring habits. **FAVORITE DIALOGUE:** Dud suggests a tune to Briscoe Darling: "Hey, how about 'Never Hit Your Grandma With a Great Big Stick'?" Charlene: "Oh, Dud, that one always makes me cry!"

Episode 95: "The Big House" (5/6/63) ••••

DIRECTOR: Bob Sweeney; **WRITER:** Harvey Bullock **CAST:** Andy Griffith, Don Knotts, Ron Howard, Jim Nabors, George Kennedy, Lewis Charles, Billy Halop, Jack Lambert, Bob McQuain, Richard Angarola, Arthur Kendall **SYNOPSIS:** Detectives keep two hardened criminals in the Mayberry jail in hopes of luring their accomplices into a rescue attempt. Unfortunately, Barney and "temporary deputy" Gomer constantly let the two inmates escape, with only Andy's presence of mind allowing them to be recaptured. Eventually, Barney mistakes the detectives for the accomplices, and arrests them while letting the four criminals abscond. Through sheer luck, Gomer's incompetence results in Andy's arresting the whole gang. Characteristically, Andy spares Barney embarrassment by pretending the whole chain of events were part of a carefully orchestrated plan. **CRITIQUE:** A knee-slapping, laugh-out-loud episode with Don Knotts at his nervous best and Jim Nabors nothing short of hilarious in one of his most memorable appearances as Gomer Pyle. The best scene has Barney reading the rules of life at the Mayberry "Rock" to his manipulative prisoners. Future Oscar winner George Kennedy is among the hapless victims of Barney and Gomer's mayhem. **FAVORITE DIALOGUE:** Barney reads the rules to his prisoners: "Here at 'the Rock' we have two basic rules. The first rule is, obey all rules! Secondly, don't write on the walls as it takes a lot of work to erase writing off of walls!"

Episode 96: "Opie, the Birdman" (9/30/63) ••••

DIRECTOR: Richard Crenna; **WRITER:** Harvey Bullock **CAST:** Andy Griffith, Don Knotts, Ron Howard, Frances Bavier **SYNOPSIS:** Opie becomes careless with a new slingshot and inadvertently kills a mother bird. Driven by guilt, he rescues the bird's three babies and begins to raise them himself. As the days progress, he becomes emotionally attached to each of them and he devotes himself to keeping them safe and healthy. Ultimately, however, Opie heeds his father's advice to release the birds once they are self-sufficient. The pain Opie feels parting with his pets is outweighed by his pride at having done a very good deed. **CRITIQUE:** For series fans, this episode ranks in the top ten, a wonderful example of how the cast, writer, and director (here actor/director Richard Crenna) are capable of creating a full gamut of very emotional moments within a very short time frame. Ronny Howard is superb here, as Opie must first deal with the pain of knowing that his carelessness has cost an innocent bird its life. The second half of the story has Opie becoming increasingly proud of his caring for the birds. The moment when he realizes they must go free and the subsequent final shot of Andy and Opie listening to the happy sounds of the birds in the trees are among the sequences most cited as examples of why *The Andy Griffith Show* is such a beloved classic. **FAVORITE DIALOGUE:** Opie to Andy, after having just set the birds free: "The cage sure looks empty, don't it, Pa?" Andy: "Yes, son, it sure does. (Glancing up at the chirping birds) But don't the trees seem nice and full?"

Episode 97: "The Haunted House" (10/7/63) ••••

DIRECTOR: Earl Bellamy; **WRITER:** Harvey Bullock **CAST:** Andy Griffith, Don Knotts, Ron Howard, Jim Nabors, Hal Smith, Ronnie Dapo,

Opposite: *Return to Mayberry* was the ratings triumph of 1986.

"A beautiful piece of work," gushes Floyd, as Andy learns the danger of letting Mr. Pyle run the courthouse for a day, in "Goober Takes a Car Apart." (episode 144)

Jean Carson and Joyce Jameson as
Daphne and Skippy, "The Fun Girls,"
encounter a rather overwhelmed
Don Knotts and Andy Griffith.

Nestor Paiva, James Seay **SYNOPSIS:** Opie is too frightened to retrieve his baseball from inside a supposedly haunted house, so Andy sends a clearly reluctant Barney and Gomer to get it. Spooky noises, however, send them running back to Andy with stories of ghosts. Andy suggests they return with him to the house to investigate. Inside they find any number of seemingly psychic occurrances, which leads them to flee once again. However, Andy sneaks back into the house and finds the real cause: Otis and another moonshiner are using the old mansion as the site of a still and are scaring away all visitors by making the place appear haunted. **CRITIQUE:** Certainly another one of the top-ten episodes of the series, this show offers side-splitting hilarity from start to finish. The sight of the petrified Barney and Gomer inside the haunted mansion ranks with some of the most memorable images in any sitcom. Indeed, the episode proved so popular that it inspired Don's big screen hit *The Ghost and Mr. Chicken*. **FAVORITE DIALOGUE:** Barney reciting rhymes as he shows Otis how to skip rope for a sobriety test: "Call for the doctor; Call for the nurse; Call for the lady with the alligator purse."

Episode 98: "Ernest T. Bass Joins the Army" (10/14/63)　●●●1/2
DIRECTOR: Richard Crenna; **WRITERS:** Jim Fritzell and Everett Greenbaum **CAST:** Andy Griffith, Don Knotts, Howard Morris, Allan Melvin, Paul Smith, Alice Backes, Tom Myers, David Lipp **SYNOPSIS:** An army recruiting sergeant ignores Andy's advice and allows Ernest T. Bass to enlist. The result is instant havoc and Ernest T.'s quick dismissal from the service. In retaliation, Ernest T. wages war on Mayberry and begins breaking windows all over town. He repeatedly manages to escape from jail, and Andy is at his wits' end as to how to control him. Eventually, Andy finds out that Ernest T. simply wants a uniform to impress his girlfriend. Andy orders Barney to give Ernest T. his uniform, and the wild man returns to the mountains, leaving Mayberry in peace. **CRITIQUE:** Another welcome appearance by the scenery-chewing Howard Morris ensures this episode is fun from beginning to end. Ernest T. proves to be more of an enemy for the army than any foe they have faced on the battlefield, and his antics during a medical inspection provide a good number of laughs. Don Knotts is no slouch in these episodes, either, and he gets the biggest laugh of all when he accidentally breaks a window he has been warning Ernest T. to stay away from. **FAVORITE DIALOGUE:** Barney debating with Andy as to whether a local resident has false teeth: "You just offer him the first bite of an apple and watch him turn you down!"

Episode 99: "The Sermon for Today" (10/21/63)　●●●●
DIRECTOR: Richard Crenna; **WRITER:** John Whedon **CAST:** Andy Griffith, Don Knotts, Ron Howard, Frances Bavier, David Lewis, Hope Summers, Forrest Lewis, William Keene, Roy Engel, Joe Hamilton **SYNOPSIS:** A visiting preacher from New York convinces the residents of Mayberry that their lives are too hectic and chaotic. They attempt to slow down and relax by planning a spontaneous old-time band concert in the park. However, the preparations are so nerve-wracking that by the end of the day everyone is ill-tempered and worn out. Ironically, upon seeing the exhausted parishioners, the preacher thinks they have been relaxing all day and congratulates them on following his advice. **CRITIQUE:** Along with "Man in a Hurry," this great episode is most representative of the Mayberry lifestyle. The idea of the local residents needing to slow down and relax is, of course, absurd. However, their attempts to equate the stress of everyday life to that of New Yorkers provides for a

wealth of laughs. Next time, savor the richness of the dialogue and actions of Don Knotts and Andy Griffith as they emerge onto the front porch after one of Aunt Bee's home-cooked dinners. Their wry underplaying and endless discussion about who will go to the store for ice cream is as charming after a hundred viewings as it was on the first. **FAVORITE DIALOGUE:** Barney, explaining why stuffing himself during dinner doesn't have an ill effect on him: "That's a mark of us Fife's—everything we eat goes to muscle!"

Episode 100: "Briscoe Declares for Aunt Bee" (10/28/63) ••••

DIRECTOR: Earl Bellamy; **WRITERS:** Jim Fritzell and Everett Greenbaum **CAST:** Andy Griffith, Ron Howard, Frances Bavier, Denver Pyle, The Dillards **SYNOPSIS:** Briscoe Darling becomes enraptured with Aunt Bee and proposes marriage. When Bee refuses, he and his boys kidnap her and take her to their mountain cabin. Andy realizes the Darlings will continue to bother Aunt Bee unless Briscoe loses interest in marrying her. Bee pretends to accept Briscoe's proposal, but immediately takes on a bossy, demanding persona. The ruse works, as Briscoe rescinds his offer of marriage, complaining that Aunt Bee would work him to death. **CRITIQUE:** A highly amusing episode with Denver Pyle and Frances Bavier providing most of the laughs as the ne'er-to-be lovers. Most amusing is Briscoe's table manner, which consists of shouting "Bread!" or "Taters!" when he wants seconds. We also get to observe Aunt Bee reciting poetry, Ronny Howard singing a solo, and the Dillards performing "Dueling Banjos"—an irony since they have often been compared to the mountain men in *Deliverance*. **FAVORITE DIALOGUE:** Briscoe to Andy: "That haircut of yours may be city style, but your heart was shaped in a bowl!"

Episode 101: "Gomer, the Houseguest" (11/4/63) •••1/2

DIRECTOR: Earl Bellamy; **WRITERS:** Jim Fritzell and Everett Greenbaum **CAST:** Andy Griffith, Ron Howard, Frances Bavier, Jim Nabors, Howard McNear, Trevor Bardette, Lee Kreiger, Forrest Lewis, Roy Engel, Joe Hamilton

Episode 102: "A Black Day for Mayberry" (11/11/63) ••••

DIRECTOR: Jeffrey Hayden; **WRITER:** John Whedon **CAST:** Andy Griffith, Don Knotts, Ron Howard, Frances Bavier, Jim Nabors, Rance Howard, Clint Howard, Ken Lynch, Joe Hamilton, Roy Engel, Charles P. Thompson, Doodles Weaver, Phil Arnold, Alex Barringer, Leslie Barringer **SYNOPSIS:** Treasury agents alert Andy and Barney to a top-secret piece of information: a truck carrying $7 million in gold will be stopping in Mayberry en route to Fort Knox. It's Andy and Barney's job to keep the truck's presence unknown to the locals, and to provide security during the stopover. Within minutes, Barney spreads the word, and by the time the truck arrives there is a virtual parade of Mayberrians waiting to greet it. More trouble occurs when Barney discovers the truck contains sand, not gold, and is taken on a wild ride by the drivers, whom he accuses of being thieves. It is revealed that the truck was merely a decoy to divert attention from the real gold shipment which passed through another town. **CRITIQUE:** Once you have Barney deputizing Gomer, you know you're in for a riotous time, and this episode doesn't disappoint. Between Barney spreading the big secret about the gold, to Gomer filling the truck with gas—through the air slot(!)—this is a laugh-a-minute affair throughout. Incidentally, this episode features three of the prolific Howard clan: Ronny, brother Clint as the tight-lipped little Leon, and dad Rance as a treasury agent. **FAVORITE DIALOGUE:** Andy: "Op, is this something we can talk about later?"

robinson crusoe
ice spectacle

the monday night speci

ab

One of many TV roles Andy had in the years between *The Andy Griffith Show* and *Matlock*.

Andy spots some disheartening news in the *Mayberry Gazette* in "Aunt Bee, the Swinger." (episode 163)

Opie: "Well, if you give me a dime, we don't have to talk about it at all!"

Episode 103: "Opie's Ill-Gotten Gain" (11/18/63) ••••

DIRECTOR: Jeffrey Hayden; **WRITER:** John Whedon **CAST:** Andy Griffith, Don Knotts, Ron Howard, Frances Bavier, Aneta Corsaut **SYNOPSIS:** Never a remarkably good student, Opie stuns Andy and Aunt Bee when he brings home a report card consisting of straight A's. Carried away with pride, Andy lavishes praise and gifts on his son. The next day, however, Helen Crump apologetically tells Opie she has marked his report card incorrectly and, in fact, he has failed math. Humiliated, Opie runs away from home rather than disappoint his pa. When Andy finds him, he explains to Opie that as long as he tries his best, he will always be very proud of him. His confidence renewed, Opie achieves a B+ on his next math exam. **CRITIQUE:** Episodes with a "father-son" theme are always among the most touching of the series, and this one is no exception. Poor Opie. The one time his conservative father indulges him in praise and toys turns out to be the one time his report card is marked incorrectly. We share Opie's devastation when he hears the news. Like so many other shows centering on Andy and Opie, this one has a finale that will cause most viewers to wipe a tear away. When viewing the acting in episodes such as these, it makes it almost criminal that Griffith and Howard could have been ignored at Emmy time. **FAVORITE DIALOGUE:** Andy to Opie after learning of the report card error: "You're my son and I'm proud of you for that. You do the best you can and that's all I'll ever ask of you."

Episode 104: "A Date for Gomer" (11/25/63) •••1/2

DIRECTOR: Richard Crenna; **WRITERS:** Jim Fritzell and Everett Greenbaum **CAST:** Andy Griffith, Don Knotts, Ron Howard, Frances Bavier, Jim Nabors, Aneta Corsaut, Betty Lynn, Mary Grace Canfield, Howard McNear

Episode 105: "Up in Barney's Room" (12/2/63) •••1/2

DIRECTOR: Jeffrey Hayden; **WRITERS:** Jim Fritzell and Everett Greenbaum **CAST:** Andy Griffith, Don Knotts, Enid Markey, J. Pat O'Malley, Betty Lynn **SYNOPSIS:** Barney's longtime landlady Mrs. Mendlebright (Enid Markey) evicts him for cooking in his room and rents the apartment to a Mr. Fields (J. Pat O'Malley), a charming man who is new to town. Unable to find a suitable place to live, Barney sets up quarters in the back of the jail. This leads to problems when Andy and Opie interrupt an embarrassing romantic situation between Barney and Thelma Lou. Desperate to return to his former residence, Barney makes amends with Mrs. Mendlebright, but is informed that she and Mr. Fields are planning to be married and will be leaving town that day. However, Barney and Andy prove that Fields is a con man, and as a reward for helping her, Mrs. Mendlebright gives Barney back his apartment—and permission to cook in his room. **CRITIQUE:** This rare glance into the private world of Barney Fife does not disappoint—Barney's room is as sparse as one might imagine. Yet, to the deputy, it is virtually a Taj Mahal. Spartan existence would be pathetic to most; for the loner lawman, it's paradise. The funniest scene features Barney's ill-fated romantic liaison with Thelma Lou in the courthouse, and Opie's concern that the lipstick all over Barney's face might be blood. Special praise should go to Enid Markey's charming performance as the eccentric landlady. **FAVORITE DIALOGUE:** Andy perusing Barney's collection of *True Blue Detective* stories: " 'I Married a Fink,' 'How It Feels to Pull the Switch,' 'I Picked a Pocket and Paid' . All good stories!"

Catching up on the latest gossip in the "Mayberry After Midnight" column.

Episode 106: "Citizen's Arrest" (12/16/63)   ••1/2
DIRECTOR: Richard Crenna; **WRITERS:** Jim Fritzell and Everett Greenbaum **CAST:** Andy Griffith, Don Knotts, Ron Howard, Frances Bavier, Jim Nabors, Hal Smith, Roy Engel, Joe Hamilton

Episode 107: "Opie and His Merry Men" (12/30/63)   •••
DIRECTOR: Richard Crenna; **WRITER:** John Whedon **CAST:** Andy Griffith, Don Knotts, Ron Howard, Douglas Fowley, Richard Keith, Joey Scott, Dennis Rush

Episode 108: "Barney and the Cave Rescue" (1/6/64)   ••••
DIRECTOR: Richard Crenna; **WRITER:** Harvey Bullock **CAST:** Andy Griffith, Don Knotts, Ron Howard, Aneta Corsaut, Jim Nabors, Betty Lynn, Warren Parker, Roy Engel, Joe Hamilton **SYNOPSIS:** Barney has been made to look foolish when he mistakes the owner of the Mayberry bank for a robber. Rather than be subjected to ridicule, Barney and Thelma Lou join Andy and Helen for a picnic in the woods. While exploring an old cave, however, Andy and Helen are trapped by a rock slide. By the time they find a way out and get back to town, they learn that Barney has organized a massive rescue attempt. Rather than make Barney look foolish again, Andy and Helen reenter the cave and pretend to be on the verge of death. The ruse works and Barney is made a local hero, and his reputation is restored. **CRITIQUE:** This episode exemplifies the camaraderie between Andy and Barney. The latter does everything humanly possible to aid his friend when he thinks he is in danger, while the former goes to great lengths to protect his pal's ego. In actuality, Barney does a darn good job of organizing the rescue effort, and his desperate attempts to reach Andy and Helen speak volumes about the sentimental side of this character. There is also some wonderful comic relief as Barney trains Gomer to be deputy for a day. (The latter can't remember which is cell #1 and cell #2!) **FAVORITE DIALOGUE:** Barney, reinforcing the importance of acting as lawman: "Whoever sits in that chair is the only law west of Mt. Pilot!"

Episode 109: "Andy and Opie's Pal" (1/13/64)   •••1/2
DIRECTOR: Richard Crenna; **WRITER:** Harvey Bullock **CAST:** Andy Griffith, Don Knotts, Ron Howard, David A. Bailey, Richard Keith, Dennis Rush

Episode 110: "Aunt Bee, the Crusader" (1/20/64)   •••1/2
DIRECTOR: Coby Ruskin; **WRITER:** John Whedon **CAST:** Andy Griffith, Don Knotts, Ron Howard, Frances Bavier, Hal Smith, Charles Lane, Mary Lansing, Noreen Gammill

Episode 111: "Barney's Sidecar" (1/27/64)   ••••
DIRECTOR: Coby Ruskin; **WRITERS:** Jim Fritzell and Everett Greenbaum **CAST:** Andy Griffith, Don Knotts, Ron Howard, Frances Bavier, Virginia Sale, Rodney Bell, Joe Hamilton, Ray Kellogg, Hal Landon, Terry Brutsche **SYNOPSIS:** To crack down on speeders on the local thruway, Barney purchases an old army motorcycle and sidecar. He is so intent on keeping the trucks to the posted speed limit, they can no longer make it up a steep grade. The drivers then divert their route through the middle of Mayberry, causing a twenty-four-hour assault on peace and quiet. Andy convinces Barney that the motorcycle belonged to General Pershing, and the deputy reluctantly donates it to the town

Andy does some "duelin' guitars" with Mayberry's celebrated musician Jim Lindsey (James Best) . . .

as a museum piece. **CRITIQUE:** Always a favorite with fans, this episode provides an abundance of laughs. Chief among them is the sight of Don Knotts in leather jacket, helmet, and oversize goggles astride his beaten up "motorsickle," which he proudly races around town. In addition to looking like a deranged version of Brando in *The Wild One*, he wreaks havoc everywhere. The best scene is Barney's insistence that Andy sit in the sidecar and join him on a ride, only to have the sidecar detach as Barney speeds away. **FAVORITE DIALOGUE:** Barney, explaining the sensation of speeding about on his "'sickle": "You know something that I found out? If you're ridin' into the wind with your mouth open and you put your tongue on the roof of your mouth, it's impossible to pronounce a word that begins with *S*."

Episode 112: "My Fair Ernest T. Bass" (2/3/64)   •••1/2
DIRECTOR: Earl Bellamy; **WRITERS:** Jim Fritzell and Everett Greenbaum **CAST:** Andy Griffith, Don Knotts, Frances Bavier, Howard Morris, Doris Backer, Jackie Joseph **SYNOPSIS:** Lovesick Ernest T. Bass wreaks his usual havoc in Mayberry in his attempts to find a girlfriend. Andy engages him in an aggressive program designed to make him respectable. Ernest T. emerges both well dressed and well mannered. Andy takes him to Mrs. Wiley's dance for singles, and Mrs. Wiley actually thinks Ernest T. is an aristocrat. He becomes smitten by a wallflower named Ramona, and reacts violently when someone else wants to dance with her. Before long, he is back to his old disreputable self, horrifying Mrs. Wiley and her guests. Ramona, however, likes the excitement and runs off with Ernest T. **CRITIQUE:** This popular episode is a Mayberry version of *My Fair Lady*, with Andy playing Henry Higgins in his attempt to teach couth to Ernest T. As with all shows featuring this character, everyone else just steps back while Howard Morris caroms around the scenery with his over-the-top performance. This is probably his most memorable appearance on the series, as the script allows him to run a full gamut of personality changes. The scenes of him trying to bluff Mrs. Wiley into thinking he is a sophisticate are particularly funny. **FAVORITE DIALOGUE:** Barney, expressing doubt to Andy about Ernest T.'s transformation: "Oh, he's coming' right along! For a minute there I thought he was the Count of Monte Cristo!"

Episode 113: "Prisoner of Love" (2/10/64)•••
DIRECTOR: Earl Bellamy; **WRITER:** Harvey Bullock **CAST:** Andy Griffith, Don Knotts, Frances Bavier, Susan Oliver, Hal Smith

Episode 114: "Hot Rod Otis" (2/17/64)•••
DIRECTOR: Early Bellamy; **WRITER:** Harvey Bullock **CAST:** Andy Griffith, Don Knotts, Hal Smith

Episode 115: "The Songfesters" (2/24/64)   ••••
DIRECTOR: Earl Bellamy; **WRITERS:** Jim Fritzell and Everett Greenbaum **CAST:** Andy Griffith, Don Knotts, Frances Bavier, Jim Nabors, Olan Soulé, Reta Shaw, Barbara Griffith **SYNOPSIS:** Barney eagerly anticipates his solo in an upcoming choir performance, but choral director John Masters wants to replace him with a more talented tenor. He chooses Gomer Pyle, who stuns the choir by exhibiting an astonishing singing voice. Barney reacts to his "firing" by sulking, and Gomer, out of guilt, feigns hoarseness the night of the performance to ensure that Barney does the solo. When Gomer's ruse is discovered, he is pushed on stage to do the solo. When the big moment arrives, Andy has both Barney and Gomer perform the number. **CRITIQUE:** When this episode was first aired, many viewers thought Jim Nabors's singing voice was dubbed, as it

was so unlike his Gomer Pyle persona. When it became clear Jim had enormous talent as a crooner, it allowed him to develop the successful singing career he pursues to this day. The show itself is filled with comic gems, such as Reta Shaw's "Knute Rockne"–type speech to her voice student, Barney Fife, and the choir's nearly disastrous rendition of "Santa Lucia," wherein they must hold the same note indefinitely while Barney and Gomer decide who will sing the solo portion. Andy Griffith's first wife, Barbara, appears as one of the choir members. **FAVORITE DIALOGUE:** Barney's voice teacher inspires him by citing the success of one of her former students: "You're going to be another Leonard Blush! He just walked in here off the street one day. Two years later, he was singing 'The Star-Spangled Banner' at the opening of the County Insecticide Convention!"

Episode 116: "The Shoplifters" (3/2/64) ●●●●
DIRECTOR: Coby Ruskin; **WRITERS:** Bill Idelson and Sam Bobrick **CAST:** Andy Griffith, Don Knotts, Ron Howard, Frances Bavier, Tol Avery, Charles P. Thompson, Clint Howard, Lurene Tuttle, Jewel Rose, Elizabeth Harrower, Mary Lansing **SYNOPSIS:** When Ben Weaver reports a wave of shoplifting in his store, Barney goes into undercover action and poses as a dummy in the sporting goods department. He accuses a little old lady of being the culprit, but the woman's shopping bag does not contain any stolen goods, and she threatens to sue Weaver. Initially disgraced, Barney is redeemed when the woman steps outside and Andy arrests her and reveals she had concealed the merchandise under her coat. **CRITIQUE:** You won't find many episodes of the series that are as perfect as this one in every respect. Don Knotts has never been funnier than in his attempt to pose as a department-store dummy in order to nab a crook. Clad in an absurd hunting outfit, he provokes laughs from the townspeople who note the resemblance the dummy has to Barney Fife. Enter little Leon, who as usual blows Barney's cover in an hysterically funny sequence. **FAVORITE DIALOGUE:** Barney browses with Andy in Weaver's Department Store: "Hey, Andy, you ever see one of these? It's a beer-can opener with an umbrella on it. It'd make a nice gift." Andy: "Yeah, for Mother's Day. That way she could open the can without getting her fingers wet!"

Episode 117: "Andy's Vacation" (3/9/64) ●●●●
DIRECTOR: Jeffrey Hayden; **WRITERS:** Jim Fritzell and Everett Greenbaum **CAST:** Andy Griffith, Don Knotts, Frances Bavier, Jim Nabors, Allan Melvin, Dabbs Greer, James Seay, Molly Dodd **SYNOPSIS:** Andy's plans to spend a quiet vacation week at home go awry when Barney and temporary deputy Gomer constantly interrupt him with various crises. In desperation, Andy goes off to camp in the woods, while Barney and Gomer take custody of a convict from the state police. Within minutes, they allow him to escape. The con ends up by Myer's Lake, where Andy succeeds in arresting him and tying him to a tree while he goes for help. Barney and Gomer arrive and release the man by mistake. *Despite* the help of his deputies, Andy manages to get the drop on the convict again and arrest him once more. **CRITIQUE:** When, oh when, will Andy ever learn not to leave Barney and Gomer in charge of the courthouse? Once again, Andy's misfortunes are the viewers' gain, and the combined performances of Don Knotts and Jim Nabors should be required viewing for anyone interested in being a comedic actor. See if you can keep from laughing at the sight of the disheveled Gomer lining up for "inspection." **FAVORITE DIALOGUE:** Barney tells Gomer how they'll treat their

THE ANDY GRIFFITH SHOW

Andy and Don as depicted by the legendary Al Hirschfeld.

Gomer hasn't gone antiestablishment but is merely left holding the sign for a resident eccentric in "A Black Day for Mayberry." (episode 102)

Andy with Elinor Donahue, discussing a scene on the set.

prisoner: "We'll give him maximum security!" Gomer: "What's maximum security?" Barney: "Keys in the drawer!"

Episode 118: "Andy Saves Gomer" (3/16/64) ••••

DIRECTOR: Jeffrey Hayden; **WRITER:** Harvey Bullock **CAST:** Andy Griffith, Ron Howard, Frances Bavier, Jim Nabors, Howard McNear **SYNOPSIS:** When alerted by Andy to a small fire, a dozing Gomer becomes convinced Andy has saved his life. To repay the debt, he stays by Andy's side day and night doing odd jobs and chores. The resulting chaos exasperates the Taylors. Finally, Andy develops a ruse. Gomer is convinced he has now saved the sheriff's life from a gas leak. His debt repaid, Gomer now leaves Andy in peace. **CRITIQUE:** An outstanding episode with Gomer almost literally killing Andy, Opie, and Aunt Bee with kindness. Andy's scheme to make Gomer feel he has saved Andy's life is wonderfully played, as is the opening sequence in which Andy and Floyd try to explain to Opie what a peekaboo blouse is without blushing. **FAVORITE DIALOGUE:** Andy and Floyd read a letter from Barney, who is vacationing in Raleigh: "Having fun, but money sure doesn't last long here. Been here three days, and already have gone through $10!"

Episode 119: "Bargain Day" (3/23/64) •••1/2

DIRECTOR: Jeffrey Hayden; **WRITER:** John Whedon **CAST:** Andy Griffith, Ron Howard, Frances Bavier, Jim Nabors, Hope Summers, Frank Ferguson

Episode 120: "Divorce, Mountain Style" (3/30/64) •••

DIRECTOR: Jeffrey Hayden; **WRITERS:** Jim Fritzell and Everett Greenbaum **CAST:** Andy Griffith, Don Knotts, Maggie Peterson, Denver Pyle, The Dillards, Bob Denver

Episode 121: "A Deal Is a Deal" (4/6/64) ••••

DIRECTOR: Jeffrey Hayden; **WRITERS:** Bill Idelson and Sam Bobrick **CAST:** Andy Griffith, Don Knotts, Ron Howard, Frances Bavier, Jim Nabors, George Petrie, Lewis Charles, Dennis Rush, Richard Keith, Ronnie Dapo, David A. Bailey **SYNOPSIS:** When Opie and his friends become involved in selling a "miracle salve" in order to win a pony, it appears as though the distributor may be engaging in a scam. To expose the plot, Barney and Gomer go "under cover," using aliases to investigate. Their plan goes awry, however, and the end result is that Gomer is billed for 946 jars of the useless salve. **CRITIQUE:** The Don Knotts/Jim Nabors combination is a guarantee for laughs,and this episode proves no exception. The sequence in which they adopt aliases to investigate the salve scam is a gem, with Barney posing as U. T. Pendyke, D.V.M., and Gomer as Opie Taylor, Sr.! While it is a shame that Knotts and Nabors did not work together again with any consistency since this series, we can relish this episode as a prime example of both men at their best.

Episode 122: "Fun Girls" (4/13/64) ••••

DIRECTOR: Coby Ruskin; **WRITER:** Aaron Ruben **CAST:** Andy Griffith, Don Knotts, Ron Howard, Frances Bavier, Jim Nabors, George Lindsey, Joyce Jameson, Jean Carson, Dick Winslow **SYNOPSIS:** After canceling dates with Thelma Lou and Helen due to a heavy workload, Andy and Barney become saddled with the "Fun Girls": Skippy and Daphne—two out-of-town floozies who immediately try to entice the boys for a night of frivolity. To get rid of them, Andy and Barney drive them home to Mt. Pilot, not knowing they have been spotted by Thelma Lou and Helen, who immediately get the wrong idea. In retaliation, they stand up Andy and Barney for a big dance the following night, opting instead to go with Gomer and his cousin Goober. Through a twist of fate, Barney and Andy end up with the Fun Girls at the same dance. However, Andy and Barney explain to Helen and Thelma Lou that they are victims of circumstance, and the situation is resolved. Meanwhile, Skippy and Daphne find a new set of boyfriends: Gomer and Goober. **CRITIQUE:** It's not easy to steal a show from the likes of Andy Griffith and Don Knotts, but Joyce Jameson and Jean Carson manage to do just that with their hilarious interpretations of the "Fun Girls." Their characters represent the closest the series ever came to displaying overt sexuality. These are "easy" women who try everything to seduce Andy and Barney, and reactions from the lawmen provide a lot of laughs. Jameson is wonderful as the "brainy" Fun Girl, while Jean Carson's distinctive voice gurgles like a draining sink. The episode also features George Lindsey's first appearance as Goober, and he and Jim Nabors provide plenty of additional levity. **FAVORITE DIALOGUE:** Goober trying to impress with his Cary Grant imitation: "Judy, Judy, Judy."

Episode 123: "The Return of Malcolm Merriweather" (4/20/64) •••
DIRECTOR: Cory Ruskin; **WRITER:** Harvey Bullock **CAST:** Andy Griffith, Don Knotts, Ron Howard, Frances Bavier, Bernard Fox

Episode 124: "The Rumor" (4/27/64) •••1/2
DIRECTOR: Coby Ruskin; **WRITERS:** Jim Fritzell and Everett Greenbaum **CAST:** Andy Griffith, Don Knotts, Ron Howard, Frances Bavier, Jim Nabors, Aneta Corsaut, Betty Lynn, Howard McNear, Ronda Jeter, Molly Dodd, William Newell, Mary Lansing, Rance Howard

Episode 125: "Barney and Thelma Lou, Phfftt" (5/4/64) •••1/2
DIRECTOR: Coby Ruskin; **WRITERS:** Bill Idelson and Sam Bobrick **CAST:** Andy Griffith, Don Knotts, Betty Lynn, Jim Nabors **SYNOPSIS:** A careless remark by Barney about taking Thelma Lou for granted is repeated to her by Gomer. Thelma Lou decides to retaliate by making it appear that she is in love with Gomer. The ruse backfires when Gomer insists upon marrying her. Finally, Andy gets all the parties together and resolves everyone's differences, and Barney learns that he doesn't quite have Thelma Lou in his hip pocket. **CRITIQUE:** A comedy of errors—Mayberry style. The episode begins with an amusing but touching scene in which Barney and Thelma Lou begin to talk marriage, only to have him throw cold water on the idea. One can only sympathize with the long-suffering Thelma Lou. Barney takes his lumps, however, as Thelma Lou successfully plays her trump card—Gomer—to make him jealous. Jim Nabors is particularly funny, especially when he insists that mountain tradition mandates he and Thelma Lou must marry due to her kissing him on the jaw. **FAVORITE DIALOGUE:** Andy explaining Barney's jealousy to Gomer: "Barney's been bit by the green-eyed monster!" Gomer: "They got some stuff down the drugstore that'll keep 'em off ya!"

Episode 126: "Back to Nature" (5/11/64) •••1/2
DIRECTOR: Coby Ruskin; **WRITER:** Harvey Bullock **CAST:** Andy Griffith, Don Knotts, Ron Howard, Jim Nabors, Howard McNear, Willis Bouchey, David A. Bailey, Richard Keith, Dennis Rush **SYNOPSIS:** Andy, Barney, and Gomer lead a group of boys on an overnight camping trip. When Opie is missing, Barney and Gomer go in search of him. Opie, however, returns, but Barney and Gomer are hopelessly lost. Afraid Barney

Andy flirts with county nurse Mary Simpson (Sue Ane Langdon).

will be the subject of ridicule after he has bragged about his abilities in the great outdoors, Andy arranges it to appear as though Barney was in control at all times. With Andy's help, Barney convinces himself and the boys that he has trapped animals and started a fire. Not only is Barney spared ridicule, he becomes a hero to the kids. **CRITIQUE:** Once you begin to imagine the premise of Barney and Gomer lost in the woods, you don't have to be told there will be an unending string of belly laughs. To paraphrase Woody Allen, Barney is at two with nature, and the result is hilarity. **FAVORITE DIALOGUE:** Gomer tries to justify why he won't go on the camping trip: "There's this movie on TV tomorrow night with Preston Foster I really want to see!"

Episode 127: "Gomer Pyle, U.S.M.C." (5/19/64)   ●●●1/2

DIRECTOR and WRITER: Aaron Ruben **CAST:** Andy Griffith, Jim Nabors, Frank Sutton, Frank Albertson, Eddie Ryder, Karl Lukas, Alan Reed, Jr., Charles Myers **SYNOPSIS:** When Gomer advises Andy he has joined the United States Marine Corps (or "corpse" as Gomer pronounces it), the latter foresees disaster and accompanies his friend to his first day at boot camp. Here, Gomer meets his drill instructor, Sergeant Carter— and incurs his wrath at every turn. To keep Gomer from being tossed out of the Corps, Andy convinces the exasperated Carter that Pyle is the son of a famous general. Carter then gives Gomer a personal training course which results in his getting high grades on his first official inspection—but not before the sergeant is informed that the famed General Pyle had no son! **CRITIQUE:** Just as *The Andy Griffith Show* was spun off from *The Danny Thomas Show*, this episode served as a pilot for Jim Nabors's highly successful *Gomer Pyle, U.S.M.C.* There is an immediate and wonderful chemistry between Nabors and Frank Sutton, whose portrayal of the long-suffering Sergeant Carter would become a favorite with audiences. This predictable but amusing episode was important on two levels. First, it helped launch Jim Nabors on a career as a leading actor. Second, it proved that the character of Gomer could obtain at least a minimal amount of independence and (inadvertent) efficiency—a necessary transformation if one was to accept him as a U.S. Marine. **FAVORITE DIALOGUE:** Gomer, trying to impress Sergeant Carter by informing him that he knows the words to "The Halls of Montezuma": "Nelson's Funeral Parlor back home put out a calendar one year with all the words on it—that's how come I learned it!"

Episode 128: "Opie Loves Helen" (9/21/64)   ●●●●

DIRECTOR: Aaron Ruben; **WRITER:** Bob Ross **CAST:** Andy Griffith, Don Knotts, Ron Howard, Aneta Corsaut, Mary Lansing, Richard Keith, Betsy Hale, Ronda Jeter **SYNOPSIS:** Andy thinks it's cute that Opie has a crush on an older girl and encourages him to buy presents for her. When Andy discovers that the present consists of a pair of stockings, he learns that Opie's "betrothed" is none other than Helen Crump. Rather than embarrass Opie, Andy and Helen explain that they are a couple and that Opie is "moving in" on his dad. Not wanting to hurt his father, Opie agrees to withdraw from dating Helen and tells them he looks forward to the day they marry. **CRITIQUE:** In this cute and amusing tale, we can fully understand Opie's crush on Helen—how many of us have had a teacher so kind and lovely? The biggest laughs involve the scenes of Andy and Barney talking about their memories of their teacher, Mrs. Von Roder, "the beast of the fourth floor." In another hilarious scene, Barney prompts Opie to read romantic poetry to his girl over the phone, not realizing it is Helen. **FAVORITE DIALOGUE:** Barney: "I remember

I went overboard with Thelma Lou on her last birthday . . . Nicest present I ever gave her—took her out to dinner. You know, we usually go Dutch . . . Took her to Morelli's. Now there's a place to take a girl. Out on the highway like that. Nice and secluded. Red-checkered table cloth . . . You know, you can hold it down to a dollar eighty-five if you don't have the shrimp cocktail!"

Episode 129: "Barney's Physical" (9/28/64)   ••••

DIRECTOR: Howard Morris; **WRITER:** Bob Ross **CAST:** Andy Griffith, Don Knotts, Ron Howard, Frances Bavier, Betty Lynn, Howard McNear, Larry Thor, Charles Thompson, Richard Keith, Dennis Rush **SYNOPSIS:** Faced with the devastating news that new civil service physical requirements find him an inch too short and underweight, Barney embarks on an ambitious plan to retain his job as deputy. By hanging for hours from a neck harness, he manages to gain the inch, but a case of hiccups precludes him from attaining the required weight. Andy finds the solution: he attaches a heavy chain to Barney's police whistle, which he is required to wear during the weigh-in. **CRITIQUE:** A top-notch episode, directed by Howard (Ernest T. Bass) Morris, that allows Don Knotts to play a full range from comedy to pathos as the deputy on the verge of losing his job. The show does make a dramatic case against bureaucrats who view people as simply statistics, and the sequence in which Andy has to give Barney the news that his job is in jeopardy is superbly enacted by both Griffith and Knotts. Comedy is king here, however, and the crash course Barney and his friends embark on to save his career is filled with laughs. **FAVORITE DIALOGUE:** Floyd: "I always enjoy cutting Barney's hair. His ears kind of wing out and give you room to work."

Episode 130: "Family Visit" (10/5/64)   ••••

DIRECTOR: Howard Morris; **WRITERS:** Jim Fritzell and Everett Greenbaum **CAST:** Andy Griffith, Ron Howard, Frances Bavier, Howard McNear, James Westerfield, Maudie Prickett, Forrest Lewis, Billy Booth, Richard Keith, Kenneth Butts **SYNOPSIS:** Aunt Bee invites Andy's Uncle Ollie and his wife and kids to stay at the Taylor household for an overdue family reunion. It's a decision she and Andy soon regret, as Ollie proves to be an obnoxious, bossy blowhard who constantly argues with his wife. He also butts into police business, wreaks havoc on the Taylor home, and has a penchant for driving off in the squad car with siren blasting. Andy ensures that Ollie and his clan depart hastily, however, when he asks his cowardly uncle for help in tracking down some escaped criminals. **CRITIQUE:** "Be careful what you wish for, you just might get it." That's the moral of this rollicking tale of family relations gone sour. Uncle Ollie and kin are the strangest group of people to assemble under one roof since *The Addams Family*. James Westerfield is marvelous as the obnoxious Ollie, who is every bit "the relative from hell." A wonderfully enacted episode with all cast members in top form. **FAVORITE DIALOGUE:** Andy responding to Aunt Bee when she asks how his night of sharing a bed with Ollie went: "Half the night, he had his arm in my mouth. The other half, he dreamed he was riding a bicycle. All in all, I'd say it was one of the most active nights I've ever spent!"

Episode 131: "The Education of Ernest T. Bass" (10/12/64)   •••

DIRECTOR: Alan Rafkin; **WRITERS:** Jim Fritzell and Everett Greenbaum **CAST:** Andy Griffith, Don Knotts, Ron Howard, Howard Morris, Aneta Corsaut, Ronda Jeter

Opie likes overnight guests, so he can sleep on an
ironing board between two chairs!

Andy and Don (in the traditional Fife "salt 'n' pepper") with Juliet Prowse in a 1967 Don Knotts variety special.

Daphne prepares to lay one on a nervous "Bernie."

Episode 132: "Aunt Bee's Romance" (10/19/64)   ●●●1/2
DIRECTOR: Howard Morris; **WRITER:** Harvey Bullock **CAST:** Andy Griffith, Ron Howard, Frances Bavier, Wallace Ford, Howard McNear

Episode 133: "Barney's Bloodhound" (10/26/64)   ●●●
DIRECTOR: Howard Morris; **WRITERS:** Bill Idelson and Sam Bobrick **CAST:** Andy Griffith, Don Knotts, Howard McNear, Arthur Batanides, James Seay, Brad Trumbull

Episode 134: "Man in the Middle" (11/2/64)   ●●●
DIRECTOR: Alan Rafkin **WRITERS:** Gus Adrian and David Evans **CAST:** Andy Griffith, Don Knotts, Aneta Corsaut, Betty Lynn

Episode 135: "Barney's Uniform" (11/9/64)   ●●●
DIRECTOR: Coby Ruskin; **WRITERS:** Bill Idelson and Sam Bobrick **CAST:** Andy Griffith, Don Knotts, Allan Melvin, Yoki Shimoda, William Keene

Episode 136: "Opie's Fortune" (11/16/64)   ●●●●
DIRECTOR: Coby Ruskin; **WRITERS:** Art Baer and Ben Joelson **CAST:** Andy Griffith, Don Knotts, Ron Howard, Frances Bavier, Jon Lormer, Mary Jackson, Bill McLean **SYNOPSIS:** Opie finds a wallet containing $50, and when no one claims it, Andy allows him to keep it. Opie immediately buys a fishing pole, but later meets a farmer who reports the wallet as missing. Learning that Opie did not confess to that farmer that he had found the lost wallet, Andy angrily drags his son out of the fishing-supply store, where he is presumably on a spending spree. Later, however, he discovers that Opie was turning in his fishing rod so he could give back the money in full to the farmer. Guilt-ridden over his lack of faith in his son, Andy buys the rod back as a reward for Opie's honesty. **CRITIQUE:** Though it is initially amusing, as Opie literally counts the seconds until he becomes entitled to keep the $50, the latter part of this story is as dramatic as the series got. Despite Andy's claim early on of having full confidence in his son, he fails to give Opie the benefit of the doubt as events unfold. When Andy is forced to eat crow at the end, we share his sense of shame for having misjudged someone as good as Opie. A wonderful episode that ranks with the best of the series. **FAVORITE DIALOGUE:** Barney, reading the latest gossip to Andy: "Therrill Pike bought his boy a brand new car for his birthday." Andy: "That's nice. How old is his boy now?" Barney: "He's fifty-seven, isn't he?"

Episode 137: "Good-bye, Sheriff Taylor" (11/23/64)   ●●●1/2
DIRECTOR: Gene Nelson; **WRITERS:** Fred Freeman and Lawrence J. Cohen **CAST:** Andy Griffith, Don Knotts, Frances Bavier, George Lindsey, Howard McNear, Hal Smith, Burt Mustin, Andrew Duncan, Janet Stewart **SYNOPSIS:** Andy startles Barney when he goes on an interview for a detective's position in Raleigh. However, Barney is comforted by the possibility of being named the new sheriff. He takes on the role for a day while Andy is away, and swears in Otis, Goober, and Judd as deputies. The results are predictable: the entire town is turned into chaos. Fortunately, Andy decides to stay on as sheriff, a decision which makes Barney—and all of Mayberry—breathe a sigh of relief. **CRITIQUE:** To accept the premise of this episode, one must accept that Andy would actually entertain leaving Mayberry. There's a greater chance

Andy samples the wares of the "Merchant of Mayberry" Bert Miller (Sterling Holloway). (episode 54)

of Gomer becoming a brain surgeon than there is of this happening, but it still seems rather startling to hear Andy lay out the reasons for considering moving on. (Of course, he did so eventually at the end of the series.) There are some outstanding scenes—the topper is Barney's swearing-in of his motley "force"—each of whom has been "shanghaied" into service. **FAVORITE DIALOGUE:** Barney to his deputies: "There's only two kinds of cop—the quick and the dead!"

Episode 138: "The Pageant" (11/30/64)   •••1/2
DIRECTOR: Gene Nelson; **WRITER:** Harvey Bullock **CAST:** Andy Griffith, Don Knotts, Ron Howard, Frances Bavier, Hope Summers, Olan Soulé, Barbara Perry, James Brower **SYNOPSIS:** Aunt Bee succeeds in winning the role of Lady Mayberry in the pageant which celebrates the town's centennial. However, her enthusiasm is not matched by her talent, and it becomes clear to all that her performance will be disastrous. Andy devises a way to get her out of the pageant without hurting her feelings by inviting Clara to become a temporary cook and housekeeper while Bee is preoccupied with the play rehearsal. As planned, Bee is so reluctant to give up her kitchen to someone else, she gives the part of Lady Mayberry to Clara, who enacts it with a professional flair. **CRITIQUE:** Anytime a script allows for the residents of Mayberry to showcase their talents in the arts, you know you're in for a lot of laughs. Frances Bavier has a wonderful scene in which she proves to be hopeless during a rehearsal as Lady Mayberry. However, Don Knotts steals the most laughs with his attempt to upstage Opie with tongue-twisters. Special kudos to the largely unheralded Olan Soulé, whose portrayal of worrywart John Masters is always a joy. **FAVORITE DIALOGUE:** Andy to Barney, regarding the latter's role as an Indian chief: "Hey, Barn, I know how you can learn your part real good." Barney: "How?" Andy: "See?"

Episode 139: "The Darling Baby" (12/7/64)   •••1/2
DIRECTOR: Howard Morris; **WRITERS:** Jim Fritzell and Everett Greenbaum **CAST:** Andy Griffith, Don Knotts, Ron Howard, Frances Bavier, Denver Pyle, Maggie Peterson, The Dillards **SYNOPSIS:** Charlene Darling and her clan arrive back in Mayberry in hopes of finding a husband for her daughter—who is in danger of being an old maid at the age of three months! A crisis looms when the stubborn Darlings insist that Andy sign an agreement legally making Opie the baby's future husband! As usual, the Darlings cannot be reasoned with, so Andy signs the agreement—using Opie's trick vanishing ink. When the Darlings witness the signatures disappearing, they are convinced it is a bad omen and call off the agreement. **CRITIQUE:** You know you're in for a nutty time when Howard (Ernest T. Bass) Morris directs an episode dealing with the dizzy Darlings. Although there are an abundance of enjoyable musical interludes, there is no stinting on laughs. Denver Pyle, Maggie Peterson, and the Dillards are as watchable as ever, and Don Knotts has a howlingly funny scene in which Barney relates an ill-fated love affair with the ugly daughter of the owner of a prune-pitting operation. This one is up to the high standards of the other Darling episodes. **FAVORITE DIALOGUE:** Briscoe Darling informs Andy of the tragic demise of his wife's first husband: "He was run over by a team of hogs!"

Episode 140: "Andy and Helen Have Their Day" (12/14/64)   •••1/2
DIRECTOR: Howard Morris; **WRITERS:** Bill Idelson and Sam Bobrick **CAST:** Andy Griffith, Don Knotts, Ron Howard, Aneta Corsaut, George Lindsey, Howard Morris **SYNOPSIS:** Barney convinces Andy and Helen to spend some much needed time together by taking a picnic at Myer's

Deputy Fife finds his canine crimefighter's bark is worse than his bite in "Barney's Bloodhound." (episode 133)

Lake. Barney promises to do all of their chores for the day and to leave them in peace. No sooner do Andy and Helen arrive at the lake, however, than they are being interrupted by Barney, who seems incapable of handling the slightest problem without seeking Andy's advice. When the couple is arrested for fishing without a license, Barney causes chaos by spreading the word they are in the Justice of the Peace's office to get married. **CRITIQUE:** A predictable, but delightful tale with Barney utilizing every annoying habit he has to ensure—unintentionally—that Andy and Helen's dream date turns out to be a nightmare. We also see Barney sheepishly admit to Andy he has cheated on Thelma Lou in order to take Juanita out for a big night. ("I don't think my head hit the pillow till quarter till eleven!") George Lindsey also pops up and favors everyone with his Cary Grant imitations, and director Howard Morris does a cameo not as Ernest T. Bass but as a TV repairman. Although on-screen for only a minute, he manages to elicit some laughs. **FAVORITE DIALOGUE:** Goober, crushed upon hearing that he can't do his imitation of Cary Grant in *Picnic*, because the film actually starred William Holden: "I can't do William Holden—he talks like everybody else!"

Episode 141: "Three Wishes for Opie" (12/21/64) ●●●1/2
DIRECTOR: Howard Morris; **WRITER:** Richard M. Powell **CAST:** Andy Griffith, Don Knotts, Ron Howard, Aneta Corsaut, George Lindsey, Howard McNear, Burt Mustin

Episode 142: "Otis Sues the County" (12/28/64) ●●●1/2
DIRECTOR: Howard Morris; **WRITER:** Bob Ross **CAST:** Andy Griffith, Don Knotts, Hal Smith, Howard McNear, Jay Novello, Bartlett Robinson

Episode 143: "Barney Fife, Realtor" (1/4/65) ●●●1/2
DIRECTOR: Peter Baldwin; **WRITERS:** Bill Idelson and Sam Bobrick **CAST:** Andy Griffith, Don Knotts, Ron Howard, Frances Bavier, Amzie Strickland, Dennis Rush, Harlan Warde **SYNOPSIS:** Barney enters the real estate business as a side job and lines up a series of potential clients who are willing to sell their homes, but the plan necessitates Andy moving up to a larger house. However, when prospective buyers come to see the place, Opie shames his dad into confessing all the areas in which the house needs work. Amazingly, the couple still wants to buy it, but when Andy and Bee visit their "dream house," the owner's son informs them of a severe flooding problem. Much to Barney's chagrin, Andy decides to keep his house, thus foiling his deputy's chances of making a tidy profit. **CRITIQUE:** For once Barney has put together a logical and sensible way to make money, only to have honesty—that root of all evil!—stand between him and his pot of gold. Particularly funny are Barney's frantic efforts to minimize the effects of Opie's confessions to the would-be buyers about the number of repairs the house needs. This is preceded by a very amusing sequence in which Andy tries to justify a double standard of honesty to Opie—with predictably poor results. **FAVORITE DIALOGUE:** Barney assures Andy that his realty business will not interfere with his duties as deputy. He then answers the courthouse phone with a Freudian slip: "Fife Realty!"

Episode 144: "Goober Takes a Car Apart" (1/11/65) ●●●1/2
DIRECTOR: Peter Baldwin; **WRITERS;** Bill Idelson and Sam Bobrick **CAST:** Andy Griffith, Ron Howard, Frances Bavier, George Lindsey, Howard McNear, Wally Englehardt, Buck Young, Larry Hovis, Stanley Farrar, Johnny Coons, Tom Jacobs **SYNOPSIS:** With Barney on vacation,

Little Leon (Clint Howard), the strong, silent type, helps keep Mayberry crime free.

Andy reluctantly allows Goober to mind the courthouse for a day while he is out of town for a conference. However, Goober is constantly distracted by his work at the garage. Heeding Andy's warning not to leave the courthouse, Goober finds a way to fix an irate customer's car: he takes it apart and reassembles it inside the Sheriff's office. On his return, Andy is outraged, particularly when he learns some fellow sheriffs are dropping by from out of town. Ironically, the officers think the car is part of an innovative program to reduce speeding and indicate they will adopt a similar program. **CRITIQUE:** Barney may be away, but Goober creates more than a fair share of headaches for Andy. The funniest segment features Floyd—oblivious to the absurdity of the situation—sitting all day watching Goober's shenanigans and continuously referring to the repair job as "a beautiful piece of work!" Andy doesn't quite see it that way, and although he escapes the episode unscathed, he calmly holds a rifle on Goober in the epilogue and informs him that unless the car is removed immediately he will start shooting. **FAVORITE DIALOGUE:** Andy, reading a letter from the vacationing Barney to Goober: "'Really havin' a ball. My head hasn't hit the pillow before eleven o'clock since I got here!'" Goober: "That Barney's really got a wild streak in him!"

Episode 145: "The Rehabilitation of Otis" (1/18/65) •••1/2
DIRECTOR: Peter Baldwin; **WRITERS:** Fred Freeman and Lawrence J. Cohen **CAST:** Andy Griffith, Don Knotts, Hal Smith, Howard McNear, Frank Cady

Episode 146: "The Lucky Letter" (1/25/65) •••1/2
DIRECTOR: Theodore J. Flicker; **WRITER:** Richard M. Powell **CAST:** Andy Griffith, Don Knotts, Ron Howard, George Linsey, Howard McNear, Betty Lynn

Episode 147: "Goober and the Art of Love" (2/1/65) •••1/2
DIRECTOR: Alan Rafkin; **WRITERS;** Fred Freeman and Lawrence J. Cohen **CAST:** Andy Griffith, Don Knotts, George Lindsey, Aneta Corsaut, Betty Lynn, Josie Lloyd **SYNOPSIS:** Andy and Barney are becoming increasingly frustrated with Goober, who has been tagging along on their dates with Helen and Thelma Lou almost every night. The boys decide that Goober is lonely and encourage him to date a local wallflower named Lydia, who happens to be Thelma Lou's cousin. However, now Goober *and* Lydia accompany Andy and Barney on their dates. Lydia is a "drip" in the truest sense, and has an aversion to doing anything fun. By episode's end the problem is unresolved, and made only worse for Andy by the presence of Barney, who is now becoming as intrusive as Goober. **CRITIQUE:** There's an abundance of laughs in this well-written and directed episode. George Lindsey is as amusing as always (no surprise), but the scene-stealer proves to by Josie Lloyd, who appeared previously as Thelma Lou's *friend* Lydia, as well as in the role of Mayor Pike's daughter; and is hilarious as the dullest resident of Mayberry. The best scene has Barney and Goober spying on Andy and Helen to observe romantic techniques. **FAVORITE DIALOGUE:** Barney, encouraging Goober to start dating: "Isn't there someone you like and admire?" Goober: "Yeah, Maureen O'Sullivan—that girl who plays Jane in *Tarzan*. She sure can swim!"

Episode 148: "Barney Runs for Sheriff" (2/8/65) •••1/2

Andy and Barney almost get a bang—literally—out of "The Loaded Goat." (episode 81)

Just another day in Mayberry—Barney irate, Andy amused, and Gomer oblivious to it all!

"The Ball Game" was the classic episode inspired by Rance Howard's umpiring of son Ron's ill-fated birthday baseball game.

DIRECTOR: Alan Rafkin; **WRITER:** Richard M. Powell **CAST:** Andy Griffith, Don Knotts, Ron Howard, Frances Bavier, Howard McNear, George Lindsey, Aneta Corsaut, Betty Lynn **SYNOPSIS:** When a job offer from a large corporation falls through, Andy misses the deadline to file as a candidate for sheriff, leaving Barney as the only one running. Barney selflessly orchestrates a write-in campaign for Andy, convinced the election will be a tight one. However, he becomes jealous when he learns he has no voter support and embarks on a vigorous campaign against Andy. During a debate, Barney realizes how petty he is acting and ends up endorsing his old friend for reelection. **CRITIQUE:** Both the best and worst sides of Barney are shown in this emotional episode. When the deputy rallies support to reelect Andy, he stands tall. However, that sizable Fife ego gets in the way and when he decides to embarrass Andy by reading a list of various "malfeasances" against his boss ("Jaywalking is rampant!"), it's discomforting to watch, especially when viewing the look of pain on Andy's face. But as Andy Griffith has always maintained, the relationship between the two lawmen is anything but one dimensional, and this very good story illustrates that point amply. **FAVORITE DIALOGUE:** Floyd reacting to Andy's uninspired campaign slogan: "'Win with Taylor!' Oooo . . . That's good! . . . Kind of catchy!"

Episode 149: "If I Had a Quarter Million" (2/15/65)   ••••

DIRECTOR: Alan Rafkin; **WRITER:** Bob Ross **CAST:** Andy Griffith, Don Knotts, Howard McNear, George Lindsey, Robert Brubaker, Al Checco, Byron Foulger, Hank Patterson, Alfred Hopson

Episode 150: "TV or Not TV" (3/1/65)   ••••

DIRECTOR: Coby Ruskin; **WRITERS:** Art Baer and Ben Joelson **CAST:** Andy Griffith, Don Knotts, Ron Howard, Frances Bavier, Howard McNear, George Lindsey, Gavin McLeod, George Ives, Barbara Stuart, Charles Thompson, Warren Parker **SYNOPSIS:** When Andy is featured in a magazine story as the "Sheriff Without a Gun," two con men and their female accomplice arrive in Mayberry posing as Hollywood producers intent on filming his story. They charm everyone in town and the rue works to such an extent that they get a tour of the bank from the owner himself. Later, Barney stumbles upon them robbing the vault, but the three convince him they are rehearsing the film. However, Andy arrives in the nick of time with a posse consisting of Floyd and Goober to save the day. **CRITIQUE:** A very strong script and an excellent cast make this a memorable entry in the series. The exposure of the "producers" as crooks—splendidly enacted by Gavin McLeod, Barbara Stuart, and George Ives—comes as a surprise as this is one occasion where outsiders to Mayberry seem something other than the personifications of evil. Even Andy is slow to see through their charms, but of course he eventually does. It's also nice to see Floyd and Goober being used in a competent capacity. **FAVORITE DIALOGUE:** Barney to Mr. Harvey, the phony producer: "I wouldn't go anywhere without the old Roscoe. The Little Persuader. Blue Steel Baby. What do you fellas usually call it in your scripts?" Mr. Harvey: "We usually call it a gun."

Episode 151: "Guest in the House" (3/8/65)   •••1/2

DIRECTOR: Coby Ruskin; **WRITERS:** Fred Freeman and Lawrence J. Cohen **CAST:** Andy Griffith, Ron Howard, Frances Bavier, George Lindsey, Aneta Corsaut, Howard McNear, Jan Shutan, George Spence

Episode 152: "The Case of the Punch in the Nose" (3/15/65)   •••1/2

Opposite: Andy and Barney find
themselves with time on their hands!

201

DIRECTOR: Coby Ruskin; **WRITERS:** Bill Idelson and Sam Bobrick **CAST:** Andy Griffith, Don Knotts, Ron Howard, Frances Bavier, Howard McNear, George Lindsey, Frank Ferguson, Larry Hovis **SYNOPSIS:** While going through old files, Barney discovers an unresolved case involving a fight between Floyd Lawson and merchant Charley Foley. Despite Andy's warning to let sleeping dogs lie, Barney pursues the forgotten incident with chaotic results. The reopening of the case causes a new feud between Floyd and Charley, with the town divided in half as to who was right and everyone fighting over the issue. Ultimately, Andy gets Floyd and Charley to reason with each other and shake hands—the exact process which occurred nineteen years earlier under the previous sheriff. **CRITIQUE:** Barney's obsession with snooping into other people's affairs almost ignites a mini-revolution in this witty episode. Tensions get so high around town that even Floyd is driven to violence, like a Mayberry version of Sweeney Todd! Despite its normally serene environment, we find that Mayberry is turned into a "Naked City." Plenty of laughs from start to finish. **FAVORITE DIALOGUE:** Aunt Bee on the growing violence in Mayberry: "For heaven's sake, what's happening to this town anyway?" Andy: "Barney!"

Episode 153: "Opie's Newspaper" (3/22/65) ••••

DIRECTOR: Coby Ruskin; **WRITER:** Harvey Bullock **CAST:** Andy Griffith, Don Knotts, Ron Howard, Frances Bavier, Kelly Thordsen, Vic Raaf, Irene Tedrow, Dennis Rush, William Keene, Burt Mustin **SYNOPSIS:** Opie and a friend start a little newspaper, but when sales lag, they decide to pep it up by reporting on local gossip. The paper becomes filled with details of private conversations, many of them of an embarrassing nature. In a panic, Andy, Barney, and Aunt Bee run all over town to snatch up every copy of the paper before it can be read. They succeed in heading off a disaster, and everyone involved learns a valuable lesson about the danger of gossip. **CRITIQUE:** Although the townspeople love the local paper's gossip column, they are scared to death when Opie begins naming names in his own paper. In Mayberry, the "devastating" tidbits don't amount to much more than Andy's opinion that the preacher's sermons are often as dry as dust. Yet, in this town, that's cause for lynch mobs to be formed. The funniest bit has Andy, Barney, and Aunt Bee searching feverishly through the dump for discarded copies of Opie's paper—not so much to ensure they are destroyed, as to get a peek at the revealing column. Lots of fun throughout. **FAVORITE DIA-LOGUE:** Barney, complaining about Floyd's slow pace: "You know how Floyd is. It's impossible for him to move his scissors and jawbone at the same time!"

Episode 154: "Aunt Bee's Invisible Beau" (3/29/65) ••••

DIRECTOR: Theodore J. Flicker, **WRITERS:** Art Baer and Ben Joelson **CAST:** Andy Griffith, Don Knotts, Ron Howard, Frances Bavier, Aneta Corsaut, Hope Summers, Woodrow Chambers, Bobby Diamond, Lyle Latell, Orville Hendricks **SYNOPSIS:** Convinced by Clara that she is standing in the way of Andy's relationship with Helen, Aunt Bee decides to give him more freedom by pretending she is dating the butter-and-egg man from Mt. Pilot. The plan backfires when Barney discovers Bee's beau is married. Andy has a confrontation with the man, who obviously takes offense at the accusations. Later, Andy learns the truth and assures Aunt Bee that she is not intruding and that he welcomes her presence in his life at all times. **CRITIQUE:** There are some highly dramatic moments in this episode, despite a good deal of levity. Aunt Bee is

Warren tries to explain
his way out of his latest
disaster.

EVERY DAY THIS MAN COMMITS A CRIME.

HE ALWAYS STEALS THE SHOW.

the Andy Griffith Show

WAAA-TV 00, 10:00 p.m. M–F

Promo ad for use by syndication networks.

haunted by the possibility that she has become a liability to Andy, and her attempts to pretend she has a beau to keep her busy are quite affecting. Andy's meeting with the innocent merchant begins on a humorous vote when the man thinks Andy is there to complain about some broken eggs. When Andy gets around to accusing the innocent man of trifling with Bee, it is quite dramatic. Aunt Bee learns her lesson by episode's end with a poignant scene in which Andy reaffirms his devotion to her. (Note: the epilogue introduces a new butter-and-egg man. Why doesn't Bee apologize to her former delivery man rather than leave their relationship disrupted by her fib?) **FAVORITE DIALOGUE:** Andy to Aunt Bee at the episode's finale: "You and Opie and myself are a family. Now, maybe someday Helen will join us, and I want you to know that if Helen and I do decide to get married, things are going to go on just the way they are. You're going to go right on living with us, because I wouldn't have it any other way."

Episode 155: "The Arrest of the Fun Girls" (4/5/65) ••••
DIRECTOR: Theodore J. Flicker; **WRITER:** Richard M. Powell **CAST:** Andy Griffith, Don Knotts, Frances Bavier, Jean Carson, Joyce Jameson, Aneta Corsaut, Betty Lynn, Hal Smith **SYNOPSIS:** It's disaster time again for Andy and Barney when Skippy and Daphne, "the Fun Girls" from Mt. Pilot, descend again on Mayberry eager to do some partying with their favorite lawmen. As usual, Andy and Barney try to keep the women's presence a secret from Thelma Lou and Helen, and as usual, they fail. After being "invited" out of town, "the Fun Girls" return in the evening and cause even more headaches when Thelma Lou and Helen encounter them in the jail with Andy and Barney. The boys have to use all their resources to maintain their relationships with their girlfriends, while trying to escape the clutches of "the Fun Girls." **CRITIQUE:** The final appearance of Daphne and Skippy is every bit up to the standards set by their earlier guest shots. As played by Jean Carson (in a new hairdo) and Joyce Jameson, these characters are among the best loved of the series. Like Ernest T. Bass, however, there was a need to use them very sparingly, thus ensuring their presence was somewhat of an event. With Don Knotts leaving the series in the next season, it was decided not to have "the Fun Girls" reappear, lest the magic be lost without the character of Barney to play off. Nevertheless, it was one heck of a ride with the gals from Mt. Pilot. **FAVORITE DIALOGUE:** Andy, exasperated at the troubles caused by "the Fun Girls," snaps when criticized by Barney: "Oh, shut up, Bernie, just shut up!"

Episode 156: "The Luck of Newton Monroe" (4/12/65) •••
DIRECTOR: Coby Ruskin; **WRITERS:** Bill Idelson and Sam Bobrick **CAST:** Andy Griffith, Don Knotts, George Lindsey, Howard McNear, Don Rickles

Episode 157: "Opie Flunks Arithmetic" (4/19/65) •••1/2
DIRECTOR: Coby Ruskin; **WRITER:** Harvey Bullock **CAST:** Andy Griffith, Don Knotts, Ron Howard, Frances Bavier, Aneta Corsaut

Episode 158: "Opie and the Carnival" (4/26/65) •••1/2
DIRECTOR: Coby Ruskin; **WRITERS:** Fred Freeman and Lawrence J. Cohen **CAST:** Andy Griffith, Ron Howard, Frances Bavier, George Lindsey, Richard Keith, Lewis Charles, Billy Halop

Barney must be set for a hot night on the town, as he's decked out in the old "salt 'n' pepper." ("It's good for the dips!")

Episode 159: "Banjo-Playing Deputy" (5/3/65) ••1/2
DIRECTOR: Coby Ruskin; **WRITER:** Bob Ross **CAST:** Andy Griffith, Ron Howard, Frances Bavier, Howard McNear, Jerry Van Dyke, Herbie Faye, Sylvia Lewis, Hope Summers, Mary Lansing, Jean Inness, Robert Carricart, Lee Van Cleef, Tom Steele, Bill Catching

Episode 160: "Opie's Job" (9/13/65) ••••
DIRECTOR: Larry Dobkin; **WRITERS:** Art Baer and Ben Joelson **CAST:** Andy Griffith, Ron Howard, Frances Bavier, Howard McNear, George Lindsey, Norris Goff, Ronda Jeter, John Bangert **SYNOPSIS:** Opie and another boy compete for a delivery job at the local grocery store, and the owner, Mr. Doakes, hires them both for a week with the understanding that the more efficient one will get the job permanently. Both boys run themselves ragged, but Opie emerges the winner. However, no sooner does Andy brag to his friends about Opie's work ethic, than he learns his son has been fired for requesting time off to play baseball. Andy chastises him, but feels guilty when Opie tells him he intentionally got fired so the other boy could get the job and use the money to help pay his ailing father's bills. **CRITIQUE:** Throughout the run of the series, the producers learned that stories centering on Opie were consistently among the most popular. This is largely due the acting skills of Andy Griffith and Ronny Howard. Outstanding writing was also a factor, as this episode demonstrates. Opie's selflessness in allowing his competitor to get the job is done in such a way that it does not appear to be an act of charity. The scene in which Andy once again discovers he should give his son the benefit of a doubt makes this episode one of the most touching of the series. **FAVORITE DIALOGUE:** Andy to Opie, upon learning why his son has lost his job: "You know, when I was bragging on you to Floyd and Goober, I told them how proud I was to have a boy like you. But that wasn't quite true—you're a man."

Episode 161: "Andy's Rival" (9/20/65) •••1/2
DIRECTOR: Peter Baldwin; **WRITER:** Laurence Marks **CAST:** Andy Griffith, Ron Howard, Frances Bavier, Aneta Corsaut, George Lindsey, Charles Aidman

Episode 162: "Malcolm at the Crossroads" (9/27/65) •••
DIRECTOR: Gary Nelson; **WRITER:** Harvey Bullock **CAST:** Andy Griffith, Howard McNear, George Lindsey, Bernard Fox, Howard Morris, Dennis Bradshaw, Kenneth Butts **SYNOPSIS:** When Malcolm Merriweather visits Mayberry, Andy gives him the job of school crossing guard, replacing Ernest T. Bass, whose violent temper has caused him to be fired. Jealous of the dignified Malcolm, whose militaristic methods of handling traffic have won him acclaim, Ernest T. challenges him to a fight. Malcolm accepts, although even an intense course in fist-fighting from Goober can't change the fact he will suffer a terrible beating. When the moment of the showdown comes, Andy convinces Ernest T. that Malcolm is actually from Ireland. Unwilling to battle a person of similar ancestry, Ernest T. calls off the fight and proclaims Malcolm his friend for life. **CRITIQUE:** The welcome return of dependable Bernard Fox as Malcolm Merriweather, coupled with the antics of Howard Morris's Ernest T. proves an unbeatable combination in this wild episode. It's the ultimate culture clash, and one that brings predictable, but nonetheless amusing, situations at every turn. (Although it should be stated that Ernest T. looks somewhat less menacing in color than he did in black

The sheriff of Mayberry knows no rest, and trouble can come calling any time of the day or night.

and white, Howard Morris seems to turn up the volume to compensate for this potentially civilizing effect on his character!) This episode marks the last appearances of Ernest T. Bass and Malcolm Merriweather. **FAVORITE DIALOGUE:** Ernest T. on his wedding plans: "I need twelve dollars for the honeymoon—tents cost something' fierce!"

Episode 163: "Aunt Bee, The Swinger" (10/4/65) •••

DIRECTOR: Larry Dobkin; **WRITER:** Jack Elinson **CAST:** Andy Griffith, Ron Howard, Frances Bavier, Aneta Corsaut, Howard McNear, Charlie Ruggles

Episode 164: "The Bazaar" (10/11/65) ••

DIRECTOR: Sheldon Leonard; **WRITERS:** Art Baer and Ben Joelson **CAST:** Andy Griffith, Ron Howard, Frances Bavier, George Lindsey, Jack Burns, Hope Summers, Amzie Strickland, Mary Lansing, Janet Stewart, Claudia Bryar, Joe Di Reda, Pam Ferdin, Sam Edwards **SYNOPSIS:** Andy's new deputy, Warren Lawson (Floyd's nephew), is a "by-the-book" police officer who brings law enforcement to ridiculous extremes. Finding the Ladies Auxiliary in violation of gambling laws when they hold a bingo game for charity, he arrests the entire group—including Aunt Bee. Andy suspends their sentences, but the women insist on a jury trial. With the jail overcrowded and Warren unwilling to drop the charges, Andy tricks him into making a harmless bet and then arrests *him* for gambling. The ploy works and Warren concedes defeat, dropping the charges against the ladies. **CRITIQUE:** This first appearance of Jack Burns as Warren represents one of the series' rare missteps. Although Burns was supposed to be allowed to embellish Warren with a unique personality, the ghost of Barney Fife following Don Knotts's departure was in everyone's minds. From his first appearance, Burns was hampered with material that would have worked well for Knotts but failed to soar with another actor delivering the lines. Andy's good-natured tolerance of Barney's absurd actions is not to be found here, and when he refers to Warren as "my idiot deputy," it sounds all too cruel because it appears Andy means it. None of this is Jack Burns's fault, as Andy pointed out years later. Burns gamely does his best though it was obvious from minute one the Warren character was not working well. It should be pointed out that Burns did contribute a good number of laughs in several of the dozen episodes he appeared in. No one could have filled the shoes of Don Knotts, but Jack Burns had the guts to try. **FAVORITE DIALOGUE:** Andy to Opie, as he reacts to another of Warren's mishaps: "You'd better stay here. I'm not sure even I'm old enough to hear what I'm gonna say!"

Episode 165: "A Warning From Warren" (10/18/65) •••

DIRECTOR: Alan Rafkin; **WRITERS:** Fred Freeman and Lawrence J. Cohen **CAST:** Andy Griffith, Jack Burns, George Lindsey, Howard McNear, Aneta Corsaut, Charles Smith

Episode 166: "Off to Hollywood" (10/25/65) ••••

DIRECTOR: Alan Rafkin; **WRITERS:** Bill Idelson and Sam Bobrick **CAST:** Andy Griffith, Jack Burns, Ron Howard, Frances Bavier, Aneta Corsaut, George Lindsey, Howard McNear, Owen Bush, Maudie Prickett **SYNOPSIS:** A Hollywood film studio reads about Andy in a magazine article entitled "Sheriff Without a Gun" and sends him $1,000 for the film rights to his life story. While conservative Andy wants to bank the money, Helen and Aunt Bee convince him to take the family on a trip to Hollywood, and he reluctantly agrees. Andy is soon besieged with requests from all the locals, for everything from obtaining autographed photos of Tony Curtis to ensuring he uses his "influence" in Hollywood to make stars out of relatives. Finally, on the plane, Andy has a last-minute crisis when he recalls he left the gas on in the house. **CRITIQUE:** The Taylors' road trip to Hollywood begins with this superb episode, one of the most memorable of the post-Barney years. Everyone's at his peak, including Andy, whose idea of "living it up" with his newfound money consists of having shrimp cocktail and ice cream for dinner. Jack Burns, George Lindsey, and Howard McNear are particularly funny here. Excellent writing, direction, and acting throughout. **FAVORITE DIALOGUE:** Floyd extolling the virtues of land he wants to sell Andy: "It's a beautiful spot. Fill in that swamp and you'll have a paradise. One of these days put on your wading boots and go over and take a look at it."

Episode 167: "The Taylors in Hollywood" (11/1/65) ●●●●

DIRECTOR: Alan Rafkin; **WRITERS:** Bill Idelson and Sam Bobrick **CAST:** Andy Griffith, Ron Howard, Frances Bavier, Gavin MacLeod, Hayden Rorke, Eddie Quillan, Ross Elliott, Robert Nichols, Herb Vigran, Yvonne Lime **SYNOPSIS:** The Taylors arrive in Hollywood and are immediately mesmerized by the excitement. However, when Andy is invited to visit the set of "Sheriff Without a Gun" he is shocked to find the script has depicted Mayberry as a cesspool of violence, and his character as a hard-bitten, no-nonsense man of action. Outraged, Aunt Bee insists that Andy protest. However, the next day she sings a different tune when she observes the role of Aunt Bee is being played by a vivacious actress who saves the Andy Taylor character through her proficiency with guns. **CRITIQUE:** "Opening up" the show by bringing the Taylors to Tinseltown proves to be an invigorating change of pace. There are the expected jokes, with Andy, Opie, and Aunt Bee staring open-mouthed at movie star homes (why they would choose Cesar Romero's house will forever remain a mystery!), their plush hotel suite, and the outdoor pool. However, the funniest moments involve the Taylors watching in horror as Gavin MacLeod (hilariously overacting in an absurd toupeé) attempts to elevate the character of Andy Taylor to legendary status by disposing of villains left and right. Equally amusing is the portrayal of Aunt Bee as a virtual gun moll. (Talk about a "Bee" movie!) **FAVORITE DIALOGUE:** The tour bus driver describes the Whiskey a-Go-Go nightclub to the Taylors: "That's one of those go-go places where the people twist and swim and jerk." Aunt Bee: "Oh, the poor folks!"

Episode 168: "The Hollywood Party" (11/8/65) ●●●1/2

DIRECTOR: Alan Rafkin; **WRITERS:** Fred Freeman and Lawrence J. Cohen **CAST:** Andy Griffith, Ron Howard, Frances Bavier, Aneta Corsaut, Ruta Lee, Sid Melton, Herb Vigran **SYNOPSIS:** Andy is asked to pose for publicity photos with actress Darlene Mason (Ruta Lee). When the shots hit the papers in Mayberry, Helen Crump tells Andy over the phone she is breaking up with him. Annoyed, Andy makes a dinner date with Darlene, but has guilty feelings. He explains his dilemma to her and she calls Helen and patches everything up. **CRITIQUE:** Andy Taylor acts a bit out of character here, and bows to some human temptations by enjoying the company of a famous actress. When Helen acts jealous, Andy becomes even more aggressive, and darn it if it doesn't appear something of a rather intimate nature isn't in the making when he arrives at Darlene's apartment. However, this isn't "Last Tango in Mayberry," so the sexual element is quickly doused. It's fun to see Andy Griffith play

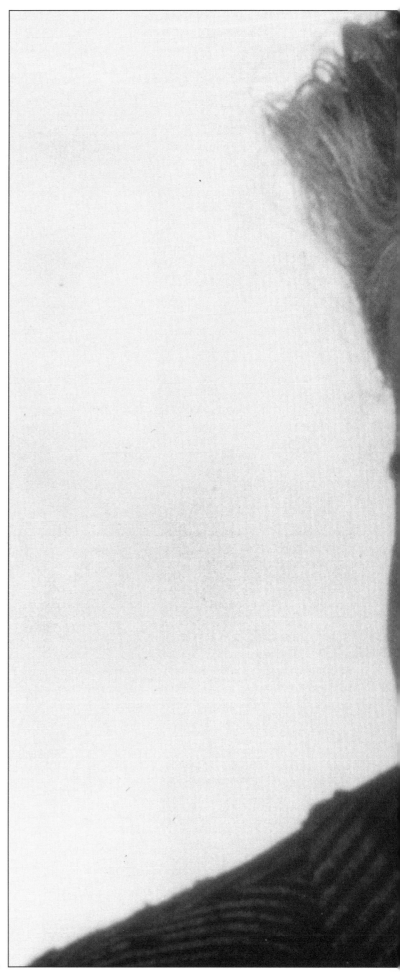

Frances Bavier as everyone's favorite aunt—Bee Taylor.

A TVQ survey in 1966 showed Andy Griffith to be the fourth most popular television comedian, standing above such stalwarts as Lucille Ball, Danny Thomas, Danny Kaye, Carol Burnett and Jackie Gleason.*

But it takes more than a star to make a strong show.

For one, it takes a strong cast of characters. Like Sheriff Andy and bumbling Barney Fife...wide-eyed Opie and good-as-gold Aunt Bee in her kitchen...Gomer and Goober, sometimes at the service station but always in the midst of any mischief...Floyd, the barber and town gossip...tippling Otis Campbell, more often in jail than out...and Andy's girl, Helen, always just a ring away from becoming Mrs. Sheriff of Mayberry.

For another thing, it takes professionalism in every phase of production to achieve the easy interplay among these familiar characters and consistently come up with warmhearted, relaxing half hours of pure entertainment.

"The Andy Griffith Show" has it all. Which is why...

This promotional brochure for *The Andy Griffith Show* summarizes the reasons for the show's success.

nervous à la Don Knotts, and his predicament allows him to explore new comedic avenues. There's also a fun bit with a studio publicity hack played by Sid Melton, involving his plans to build Andy Taylor into a character of mythical proportions. **FAVORITE DIALOGUE:** Publicity man to Andy: "How many girls you got back there in Blueberry?" Andy: "Mayberry!!"

Episode 169: "Aunt Bee on TV" (11/15/65)   •••

DIRECTOR: Alan Rafkin; **WRITERS:** Fred Freeman and Lawrence J. Cohen **CAST:** Andy Griffith, Ron Howard, Frances Bavier, Aneta Corsaut, George Lindsey, Howard McNear, Hope Summers, William Christopher, Amzie Strickland

Episode 170: "The Cannon" (11/22/65)   •••

DIRECTOR: Alan Rafkin; **WRITER:** Jack Elinson **CAST:** Andy Griffith, Frances Bavier, Jack Burns, George Lindsey, Howard McNear, Justin Smith, Byron Foulger, Vaughn Taylor, J. Edward McKinley, Sally Mansfield, Robert Carnes, Douglas McCairn

Episode 171: "A Man's Best Friend" (11/29/65)   ••••

DIRECTOR: Alan Rafkin; **WRITERS:** Art Baer and Ben Joelson **CAST:** Andy Griffith, Ron Howard, Frances Bavier, George Lindsey, Howard McNear **SYNOPSIS:** Opie is convinced by a new playmate to help him play a cruel joke on Goober. They place a tiny walkie-talkie under the collar of Goober's dog, thus convincing Goober the mutt can talk. Goober foolishly announces to everyone that he has a talking dog and he will make a fortune, and humiliates himself by doing tricks for the canine in preparation of their comedy act. Andy discovers the ruse and informs an obviously hurt Goober. To teach the boys a lesson, Andy and Goober devise their own brand of practical joke. **CRITIQUE:** This episode is both hilarious and poignant, as we watch Goober pathetically play into the hands of his tormentors by insisting his dog can talk. It speaks well for his character, however, that when he is confronted with the deception, his first reaction is to remain cheerful so as not to make the boys feel bad. Such scenes illustrate that the Goober character was far more in-depth than many viewers recall, and in his naive way, he often showed more class and wisdom than the "normal" people around. Special praise for George Lindsey, who gives what might be his finest performance as Goober. **FAVORITE DIALOGUE:** Goober on how he named his new dog: "He hasn't got any spots on him, so I named him Spot!"

Episode 172: "Aunt Bee Takes a Job" (12/6/65)   •••1/2

DIRECTOR: Alan Rafkin; **WRITERS:** Bill Idelson and Sam Bobrick **CAST:** Andy Griffith, Frances Bavier, Jack Burns, James Milhollin, Milton Frome, Herbie Faye, Maggie Magennis, Jason Johnson, Don Gazzaniga

Episode 173: "The Church Organ" (12/13/65)   •••

DIRECTOR: Lee Philips; **WRITER:** Paul Wayne **CAST:** Andy Griffith, Ron Howard, Frances Bavier, Jack Burns, George Lindsey, Howard McNear, Aneta Corsaut, Hope Summers, William Keene, Woodrow Chambliss, Pitt Herbert, Robert B. Williams

Episode 174: "Girl-Shy" (12/20/65)   ••

DIRECTOR: Lee Philips; **WRITERS:** Bill Idelson and Sam Bobrick **CAST:** Andy Griffith, Frances Bavier, Jack Burns, Aneta Corsaut, George Lindsey

To allow Barney to foil the Darlings' plan for his shotgun wedding to Charlene, Andy stalls for time in "Divorce, Mountain Style."

Episode 175: "Otis, the Artist" (1/3/66) ●●●1/2
DIRECTOR: Alan Rafkin; **WRITERS:** Fred Freeman and Lawrence J. Cohen **CAST:** Andy Griffith, Ron Howard, Frances Bavier, George Lindsey, Jack Burns, Hal Smith

Episode 176: "The Return of Barney Fife" (1/10/66) ●●●1/2
DIRECTOR: Alan Rafkin; **WRITERS:** Bill Idelson and Sam Bobrick **CAST:** Andy Griffith, Don Knotts, Ron Howard, Frances Bavier, Aneta Corsaut, Betty Lynn, Barbara Perry, Virginia Sale, Burt Mustin, Alberta Nelson, Ted Jordan **SYNOPSIS:** Barney Fife returns from Raleigh to attend his high school reunion in Mayberry, hoping to perhaps rekindle his romance with Thelma Lou. When they do reunite, the old sparks seem to still be there—until she introduces him to her husband. Barney is devastated until a former classmate approaches and eases his pain by confessing she was always secretly in love with him. This appeals to Barney's oversize ego, and he is able to enjoy the remainder of the reunion. **CRITIQUE:** This was the first of Don Knotts's return visits to *The Andy Griffith Show*, each of which proved to be a ratings block-buster. This is a flashier Barney: he has a used car, wears monogrammed dress shirts, owns those fancy "Eye-talian" suits, and brags about having a credit card. Yet, he breaks out the old salt "n" pepper suit and the chemistry with the friendly folk of Mayberry is resumed in amusing fashion. Still, this is a bittersweet story that explores the inner psyche of Barney, revealing him as a lonely, tragic figure. This show is also somewhat downbeat because this proved to be Betty Lynn's final appearance in the series (ironically the only time she appeared in a color episode). Her contributions to the show cannot be overstated. In all, an intriguing episode that runs the gamut from humor to pathos, with Knotts in top form. **FAVORITE DIALOGUE:** Opie, upon seeing Barney in his old salt 'n' pepper suit: "Gee, that suit looks better than ever, Barney!"

Episode 177: "The Legend of Barney Fife" (1/17/66) ●●●●
DIRECTOR: Aaron Ruben; **WRITER:** Harvey Bullock **CAST:** Andy Griffith, Don Knotts, Frances Bavier, Jack Burns, George Lindsey, Howard McNear, Frank Cady, Harry Holcomb, Ted White **SYNOPSIS:** Barney becomes tired of hearing people praise his replacement, Warren, but takes a liking to Warren when he discovers the deputy idolizes him. When a vicious criminal escapes from jail and heads toward Mayberry to avenge his arrest by Barney years before, Fife attempts to flee, but is stuck in town due to car problems. Warren begins to suspect Barney's cowardice when the latter makes every effort to avoid the manhunt for the crook. Barney eventually summons his courage and stumbles upon the villain. Due to some strategy by Andy, Barney is made to believe that he knocked the man unconscious and is made a local hero, absolving himself in the eyes of Warren. **CRITIQUE:** Part two of Barney's return to Mayberry is far more lighthearted than the previous episode, although it provides still another monumental psychological barrier for the timid lawman to overcome: his cowardice. Fellow bumbler Warren, however, fares well in this episode and is shown to be both courageous and competent. Jack Burns is given a decidedly lesser role and does not try to upstage Don Knotts. There's a priceless scene in which Barney drives Goober crazy with contradictory instructions about repairing his car. Also, pay attention to Andy's subtle but perfect comic timing. **FAVORITE DIALOGUE:** Barney, reflecting on being the object of Warren's hero worship: "Lots of fellas have idols. I had one when I was a kid—Skeets Gallagher, sidekick to Tailspin Tommy!"

Fan Bob Scheib's meticulous reconstruction of Wally's Garage which adjoins his home in Ohio. (courtesy Bob Scheib)

Even a professional lawman like Sheriff Taylor can (almost) succumb to the charms of a pretty temptress.

Episode 178: "Lost and Found" (1/24/66) ●●●
DIRECTOR: Alan Rafkin; **WRITERS:** John L. Green and Paul David **CAST:** Andy Griffith, Ron Howard, Frances Bavier, Jack Burns, George Lindsey, Hope Summers, Jack Dodson, Arthur Mallet **SYNOPSIS:** Aunt Bee loses a precious pin that is a family heirloom, and receives compensation from the insurance company. She uses the money to have a garbage disposal installed, but panics when she later finds the pin, distraught as to how she will repay the insurance company. The situation is inadvertently solved for her when Goober and Warren accidentally drop the pin down the new disposal unit. **CRITIQUE:** The prospect that someone would actually repay an insurance company for an item reported lost and later found will strain credibility in most sitcoms, but on *The Andy Griffith Show* it would be inconceivable for the characters to react any differently. There is also a very funny bit in which Warren and Goober present Andy with the "thief" who stole the pin, only to find he is a loafer willing to do "time" in return for a few meals. Jack Dodson makes his first appearance on the series here, playing insurance adjuster Ed Jenkins. He so impressed Andy that he was soon offered the role of Howard Sprague. **FAVORITE DIALOGUE:** Aunt Bee reacting to Clara's suggestion that the pin may have been stolen: "Of course not! Andy doesn't allow thieves in Mayberry!"

Episode 179: "Wyatt Earp" (1/31/66) ●●●1/2
DIRECTOR: Alan Rafkin; **WRITER:** Jack Elinson **CAST:** Andy Griffith, Ron Howard, George Lindsey, Jack Burns, Howard McNear, Pat Hingle, Richard Jury, Richard Keith

Episode 180: "Aunt Bee Learns to Drive" (2/7/66) ●●●1/2
DIRECTOR: Lee Philips; **WRITER:** Jack Elinson **CAST:** Andy Griffith, Ron Howard, Frances Bavier, George Lindsey, Aneta Corsaut, Raymond Kark

Episode 181: "Look, Paw, I'm Dancing" (2/14/66) ●●●1/2
DIRECTOR: Lee Philips; **WRITER:** Ben Starr **CAST:** Andy Griffith, Ron Howard, Frances Bavier, Aneta Corsaut, George Lindsey, Howard McNear, Ronda Jeter, Richard Keith

Episode 182: "The Gypsies" (2/21/66) ●●
DIRECTOR: Alan Rafkin; **WRITER:** Ronald MacLane **CAST:** Andy Griffith, Ron Howard, Frances Bavier, Aneta Corsaut, George Lindsey, Vito Scotti, Jamie Farr, Hope Summers, Francesca Bellini, Jason Johnson, Argentina Brunetti

Episode 183: "Eat Your Heart Out" (2/28/66) ●●●
DIRECTOR: Alan Rafkin; **WRITER:** Art Baer and Ben Joelson **CAST:** Andy Griffith, George Lindsey, Howard McNear, Aneta Corsaut, Alberta Nelson

Episode 184: "A Baby in the House" (3/7/66) ●●
DIRECTOR: Alan Rafkin; **WRITERS:** Bill Idelson and Sam Bobrick **CAST:** Andy Griffith, Ron Howard, Frances Bavier, George Lindsey, Aneta Corsaut, Jim Connell, Candace Howard, Ronny Dapo, Alvy Moore

Episode 185: "The County Clerk" (3/14/66) ••••
DIRECTOR: Alan Rafkin; **WRITERS:** Bill Idelson and Sam Bobrick **CAST:** Andy Griffith, Ron Howard, Aneta Corsaut, Jack Dodson, Nina Shipman, Mabel Albertson, Jim Begg, Coleen O'Sullivan **SYNOPSIS:** County clerk Howard Sprague, a shy mother's boy, finds himself smitten by Irene Fairchild, a gorgeous municipal health official, and at Helen's urging, Andy sets up a double date with Howard and Irene. However, Howard's domineering mother tries to dissuade her son from going by feigning illness. Although Irene and Howard get along well, Andy can see that a solution must be found to keep Mrs. Sprague from ruining her middle-age son's social life. The answer: Mother Sprague now comes along on the double dates, and it is left to Andy to dance with her and keep her occupied! **CRITIQUE:** This is an important episode in *The Andy Griffith Show* canon, as it introduced Jack Dodson in the pivotal role of Howard Sprague. Dodson immediately proved to be a winner by embellishing Howard with enough fascinating traits to make him both lovable and exasperatingly naive. In the dictionary, under the word "dull" you'll probably find a picture of Howard Sprague. It may defy logic that a lively go-getter like Irene Fairchild would want to date this mother's boy, but after all, he is a nice guy. Mabel Albertson is excellent as Mayberry's Ma Barker, and there are nonstop laughs throughout the episode. The Howard Sprague character would play an important contribution to the success of later episodes, and Dodson's superb portrayal makes it impossible to envision anyone else in the role. **FAVORITE DIALOGUE:** Mrs. Sprague to Andy: "You know, Andrew, Howard's work is quite different from yours. Howard has to work with his mind!"

Episode 186: "The Foster Lady" (3/21/66) •••
DIRECTOR: Alan Rafkin; **WRITERS:** Jack Elinson and Iz Elinson **CAST:** Andy Griffith, Ron Howard, Frances Bavier, George Lindsey, Howard McNear, Robert Emhardt, Ronnie Schell, Marc London, Burt Taylor

Episode 187: "Goober's Replacement" (3/28/66) •••1/2
DIRECTOR: Alan Rafkin; **WRITERS:** Howard Merrill and Stain Dreben **CAST:** Andy Griffith, Ron Howard, George Lindsey, Howard McNear, Alberta Nelson, Cliff Norton, Jason Johnson, Charles Smith, Maudie Prickett, Burt Mustin, David Azar

Episode 188: "The Battle of Mayberry" (4/4/66) •••1/2
DIRECTOR: Alan Rafkin; **WRITERS:** John L. Green and Paul David **CAST:** Andy Griffith, Ron Howard, Frances Bavier, Aneta Corsaut, Howard McNear, George Lindsey, Hope Summers, Norman Alden, Clinton Sundberg, Arthur Malet **SYNOPSIS:** In researching the famous Battle Of Mayberry for an essay contest, Opie finds that virtually every town resident claims his or her ancestor was a hero in the clash between pioneers and Indians. The project causes hard feelings among Mayberrians, who debate their ancestor's contribution to the "bloody battle." However, Opie discovers the "battle" consisted of a minor argument that ended with settlers and Indians getting drunk and creating the myth about the fierce confrontation. When his story is published, the townsfolk are resentful at having their legend destroyed. Opie is redeemed, though, when the essay is complimented for its honesty on a radio broadcast by the governor. **CRITIQUE:** It's a battle royale of egos—Mayberry style—when everyone in town gets to argue the merits of their ancestors' contribution to a battle whose only casualties were a cow and a mule. Hearing the

"The Return of Barney Fife" episode earned Don Knotts another Emmy.

Opie and Andy release the baby birds in "Opie the Birdman." (episode 96)

Opposite: Denver Pyle uses his head to find a way to cool an overheated radiator in "The Darlings Are Coming," the bizarre backwoods clan's first appearance on the series.

endless arguments about the myth of the battle makes for some very amusing moments. **FAVORITE DIALOGUE:** Andy debunks the Battle of Mayberry myth: "There's not too much pride in fifty Indians and fifty settlers sitting around getting gassed!"

Episode 189: "A Singer in Town" (4/11/66) •••
DIRECTOR: Alan Rafkin; **WRITERS:** Howard Merrill and Stan Dreben **CAST:** Andy Griffith, Ron Howard, Frances Bavier, George Lindsey, Howard McNear, Hope Summers, Jesse Pearson, Byron Folger, Edgar Hess, Tom D'Andea, Joel Redlin

Episode 190: "Opie's Girlfriend" (9/12/66) ••
DIRECTOR: Lee Philips; **WRITER:** Budd Grossman **CAST:** Andy Griffith, Ron Howard, Frances Bavier, George Lindsey, Aneta Corsaut, Howard McNear, Mary Ann Durkin

Episode 191: "The Lodge" (9/19/66) ••••
DIRECTOR: Lee Philips; **WRITERS:** Jim Parker and Arnold Margolin **CAST:** Andy Griffith, Ron Howard, Frances Bavier, Jack Dodson, George Lindsey, Howard McNear, Mabel Albertson, George Cisar, Burt Mustin, Sam Edwards, Ralph Rose **SYNOPSIS:** When Howard Sprague announces he is applying for membership in the social club known as "the Regal Order of the Golden Door to Good Fellowship," his overpossessive mother pulls out all the stops to ensure he does not get accepted. She convinces Goober that Howard's father was ruined through his compulsive gambling and that Howard will share the same fate if he is subjected to the card games at the lodge. Goober casts the only dissenting vote, thereby excluding Howard from the group. Later, Andy uncovers the story and Howard assures Goober that his mother has deceived him. Howard is then voted into the lodge as a member in good standing. **CRITIQUE:** This very amusing episode was one of the first to prominently feature Jack Dodson's wonderful interpretation of Howard Sprague. Howard is the very personification of the dullard and his attempt to be "one of the guys" at lounge is a joy, trying to impress everyone by citing census statistics. Mabel Albertson is such a "mother from hell" that at times her claustrophobic relationship with Howard looks like a Mayberry version of the Bateses from *Psycho*. Curiously, she is one of the few characters who is not given any redeeming qualities. The biggest laugh comes in a scene where the lodge members cast their secret ballots, while following some ludicrous formalities. The scene is also of interest to fans because it's the first—and probably last—time we'll get to see Andy Griffith in a fez! (Sorry, Andy, but you didn't start a stampede to local hat stores!) **FAVORITE DIALOGUE:** Howard trying to lure Andy for a night on the town: "I see they got a wild one over at the show—something about blondes!"

Episode 192: "The Barbershop Quartet" (9/26/66) ••1/2
DIRECTOR: Lee Philips; **WRITER:** Fred S. Fox **CAST:** Andy Griffith, Ron Howard, Frances Bavier, Jack Dodson, Howard McNear, Hamilton Camp, Burt Mustin, Blackie Hunt, Ken Mayer, Vernon Rich, Harry Arnie

Episode 193: "The Ball Game" (10/3/66) ••••
DIRECTOR: Lee Philips; **WRITER:** Sid Morse (based on an idea by Rance Howard) **CAST:** Andy Griffith, Ron Howard, Frances Bavier, George Lindsey, Aneta Corsaut, Howard McNear, Jack Dodson, John Reilly **SYNOPSIS:** Andy reluctantly agrees to umpire a pivotal ball game between

the Mayberry and Mt. Pilot Little League teams. The Mayberry team finds itself trailing until the ninth inning, when Opie smacks a hit which could tie it up. But Andy calls him out in a close play at the plate. Despite Andy's pleas that he had to remain unbiased and honest, the towns-people accuse him of selling out Opie and Mayberry. Disgusted with their attitude, Howard Sprague writes a moving newspaper column extolling Andy's honesty and willingness to make a tough decision. Guilt-ridden, Andy's friends and family apologize. Later, Helen Crump confides in Aunt Bee that she has a photo which shows Opie was indeed safe, but refuses to show it out of respect for Andy's attempt to do the best he could as umpire. **CRITIQUE:** This popular episode—one of Ron Howard's favorites—was suggested by a real-life incident wherein his dad Rance called him out in a crucial play at homeplate. Here, Andy's integrity forces him to do the right thing, even at the cost of his reputation. The script takes some knocks at people whose fanaticism about sports allows them to advocate cheating. Andy's outburst at Floyd and Goober is a dramatic highlight, matched by their reconciliation with him later. An outstanding episode in every respect. **FAVORITE DIALOGUE:** "Coach" Goober to his team: "Go out there and hit one for the old Goob."

Episode 194: "Aunt Bee's Crowning Glory" (10/10/66)   ●●●1/2
DIRECTOR: Lee Philips; **WRITER:** Ronald Axe **CAST:** Andy Griffith, Ron Howard, Frances Bavier, Howard McNear, Aneta Corsaut, Hope Summers, Ian Wolfe, Carol Veazie, Ruth Thom, Janet Stewart **SYNOPSIS:** Tired of her hair problems, Aunt Bee shocks everyone by buying a blond wig. The decision is the talk of all Mayberry, with friends and family snickering at her behind her back. The wig also causes problems when the new preacher gives a lecture on the shame of vanity, causing Bee to become obsessed with keeping her secret from him. Eventually, she confesses and is relieved to find he is not critical. Seeing his favorable reaction to the wig, Clara then attempts to "snare" the preacher—by purchasing a blond wig of her own! **CRITIQUE:** Although Aunt Bee looks rather good in her store-bought locks, Mayberrians dislike change, and Bee's fashion statement almost approaches the level of a scandal. Andy acts like a chauvinist, and Floyd is completely obsessed with finding out if the wig consists of Chinese hair. A witty tale with Frances Bavier in top form, bearing a remarkable resemblance here to Kathy Bates in *Fried Green Tomatos*!) **FAVORITE DIALOGUE:** Opie to Clara: "Do you have to go to the beauty shop, too?" Clara: "I was there this morning!"

Episode 195: "The Darling Fortune" (10/17/66)   ●●●1/2
DIRECTOR: Lee Philips; **WRITERS:** Jim Parker and Arnold Margolin **CAST:** Andy Griffith, Frances Bavier, George Lindsey, Aneta Corsaut, Denver Pyle, Maggie Peterson, The Dillards **SYNOPSIS:** Having sold a piece of land for "a fortune" ($300), Briscoe Darling brings his boys to town in search of wives. They are encouraged by the sighting of an owl, which superstition tells them they will be successful. Unfortunately, the first "bride" Briscoe settles on is Helen Crump, whom they drive into a panic with their overbearing attempts to "woo" her. Faced with obstinate foes, Andy learns he can outfox them using his own brand of superstition. He and Goober arrange for the Darlings to see another owl, thus negating the idea that a marriage is imminent. **CRITIQUE:** The Darlings are always a welcome sight and a hoot-and-a-half in Mayberry. That's literally the case here, when Goober sits in a tree using a dead owl as a puppet to convince the Darlings to leave town. Poor Helen Crump is the recipient of the Darlings' unwanted attentions, which gives Aneta Corsaut the opportunity to shriek with more horror than she demonstrated

when confronted with *The Blob*! **FAVORITE DIALOGUE:** Briscoe reacts favorably to Aunt Bee's steak dinner: "Gotta learn what kinda animal you chopped that off of!"

Episode 196: "Mind Over Matter" (10/31/66) •••1/2

DIRECTOR: Lee Philips; **WRITERS:** Ron Friedman and Pat McCormick **CAST:** Andy Griffith, Ron Howard, Frances Bavier, George Lindsey, Howard McNear **SYNOPSIS:** When Goober is involved in a minor accident, Floyd and Aunt Bee convince him he has severe whiplash. Bee takes him into the Taylor household, where Goober's psychosomatic problems are tended to by the family. Goober proves an obnoxious guest who revels in the attention, much to the chagrin of Andy, who is run ragged caring for him. Finally, Andy tricks Goober into raising his arms above his head—a sign that his whiplash is nonexistent. In joy, Goober throws a football to Andy, causing Andy to fall and develop a legitimate back injury. **CRITIQUE:** This is *The Man Who Came to Dinner*—with Goober in the Monty Woolley role, and every bit as demanding. Poor Andy must cope with shaving his "guest," as well as giving him continuous massages. Howard McNear is in top form, providing Goober with tall tales of locals who have died from similar symptoms. Andy's slow burn is more evident than ever, and the last scene, in which he develops a back problem is great. **FAVORITE DIALOGUE:** Floyd to Goober, describing a local man who supposedly died from whiplash while trying to raise his arms above his head: "They had to bury him in an extra-wide coffin, because they couldn't get his arms down!"

Episode 197: "Politics Begin at Home" (11/7/66) •••

DIRECTOR: Lee Philips; **WRITER:** Fred S. Fox **CAST:** Andy Griffith, Ron Howard, Frances Bavier, George Lindsey, Jack Dodson, Howard McNear, Hope Summers, Ruth Thom, Maxine Semon

Episode 198: "The Senior Play" (11/14/66) •••

DIRECTOR: Lee Philips; **WRITER:** Sid Morse **CAST:** Andy Griffith, Aneta Corsaut, George Lindsey, Howard McNear, Jack Dodson, Leon Ames, Chuck Brummit, Cynthia Hull, Mary Jackson

Episode 199: "Opie Finds A Baby" (11/21/66) •••

DIRECTOR: Lee Philips; **WRITERS:** Stan Dreben and Sid Mandel **CAST:** Andy Griffith, Ron Howard, Frances Bavier, George Lindsey, Sheldon Collins, Jack Nicholson, Jamie Kelly, James McCallion

Episode 200: "Big Fish in a Small Town" (11/28/66) •••1/2

DIRECTOR: Lee Philips; **WRITERS:** Bill Idelson and Sam Bobrick **CAST:** Andy Griffith, Ron Howard, George Lindsey, Howard McNear, Sam Reese **SYNOPSIS:** When Howard Sprague announces he wants to participate in the annual fishing tournament, the townspeople's worst nightmare is realized when an overequipped Howard wreaks havoc on the lake. Ironically, he succeeds in catching Old Sam, a legendary trout which residents of Mayberry have been competing to land for many years. Howard becomes a local celebrity and donates the fish to an aquarium. However, he finds the townsfolk are saddened at the loss of a fish that had become part of Mayberry's heritage. Howard orders the fish returned to Myer's Lake so the locals can resume their quest to catch it. **CRITIQUE:** This episode has an abundance of laughs and sentimental-

A rare production shot of Andy and Ron enacting a scene.

ity, and is highlighted by Jack Dodson's delightful comic performance. Here, the character of Howard Sprague goes through an emotional roller coaster, first shunned as a novice fisherman, then scorned by all when he manages to capitalize on some amazing beginner's luck. Talk about a guy who can't win! The outcome of the story is telegraphed from the start, but this is a fine episode that remains one of Dodson's personal favorites. **FAVORITE DIALOGUE:** Andy to Howard, upon seeing the latter's cumbersome fishing gear: "Are you going to the moon??"

Episode 201: "Only a Rose" (12/5/66)   ●●●1/2
DIRECTOR: Lee Philips; **WRITERS:** Jim Parker and Arnold Margolin **CAST:** Andy Griffith, Ron Howard, Frances Bavier, Howard McNear, Hope Summers, Maxine Semon, John Reilly, Ruth Thom

Episode 202: "Otis, the Deputy" (2/12/66)   ●●●1/2
DIRECTOR: Lee Philips; **WRITERS:** Jim Parker and Arnold Margolin **CAST:** Andy Griffith, Hal Smith, Jack Dodson, Charles Dierkop, Joe Turkell **SYNOPSIS:** When Andy is captured by bank robbers and held captive in a remote cabin, Howard teams up with Otis to rescue him. However, Otis gets drunk, as usual, and Howard must save Andy by himself. Through a mishap, he too gets captured, leaving the ossified Otis to save the day. Amazingly, he does, by knocking out one of the crooks and allowing Andy and Howard to nab the other one. **CRITIQUE:** A very funny episode remindful of "Convicts at Large." With his life in danger, Andy must also worry about the well-intentioned, but ill-planned actions of Howard and Otis. The most amusing bit finds Andy and Howard trying to toss cups of water through the window onto a drunken Otis to wake him up, without the crooks seeing. Predictably, Howard only succeeds in drenching Andy—an old gag, but when done by pros, it's hilarious. **FAVORITE DIALOGUE:** Howard to Otis: "We'll just have to sweat it out. That's police terminology!"

Episode 203: "Goober Makes History" (12/19/66)   ●●●1/2
DIRECTOR: Lee Philips; **WRITERS:** John L. Green and Paul David **CAST:** Andy Griffith, Frances Bavier, George Lindsey, Howard McNear, Jack Dodson, Aneta Corsaut, Richard Bull, Vivian Rhodes, Christine Burke **SYNOPSIS:** Goober drops out of an adult-education history class, embarrassed by his inability to contribute to the discussions. When he returns from a hunting trip sporting a beard, many of his friends tell him it makes him look like an intellectual. Now overly confident, Goober rejoins the class and becomes a conceited bore who feels he has all the answers to life's questions. His behavior finally alienates so many of the townsfolk that Andy must tell him the truth. Initially hurt, Goober recovers and resumes classes with a better attitude and a determination to learn rather than show off. **CRITIQUE:** George Lindsey gets to play against type when Goober becomes a pseudo-intellectual snob. The transformation is as amusing at it sounds, as Goober becomes adept at talking a great deal without making any sense. The funniest scenes feature Floyd first convincing Goober he is a great thinker, then scheming to tell him the opposite is true. Sharply written, with Lindsey doing yeoman work. **FAVORITE DIALOGUE:** Goober on how his beard has increased his intellectualism: "I've had this beard inside me a long time and I've been holding it back." Floyd: "Oooo . . . Another deep one!"

Episode 204: "A New Doctor in Town" (12/26/66)   ●●●
DIRECTOR: Lee Philips; **WRITERS:** Ray Brenner and Barry E. Blitzer **CAST:** Andy Griffith, Ron Howard, Frances Bavier, Howard McNear,

Rap, it ain't, but good music it is. The ultra-rare original soundtrack to *The Andy Griffith Show*. (courtesy Jim Clark Collection)

Sheriff Andy Taylor prepares to leave Mayberry in the capable hands of Ken Berry's Sam Jones in the last episode of *The Andy Griffith Show*, "Mayberry R.F.D." (episode 249)

Aneta Corsaut, William Christopher, Hope Summers, Sari Price

Episode 205: "Don't Miss a Good Bet" (1/2/67) •••1/2
DIRECTOR: Lee Philips; **WRITER:** Fred S. Fox **CAST:** Andy Griffith, Ron Howard, Frances Bavier, George Lindsey, Howard McNear, Aneta Corsaut, Roger Perry, Dick Ryan

Episode 206: "Dinner at Eight" (1/9/67) ••••
DIRECTOR: Lee Philips; **WRITER:** Budd Grossman **CAST:** Andy Griffith, Ron Howard, Frances Bavier, George Lindsey, Jack Dodson, Aneta Corsaut, Mabel Albertson, Emory Parnell **SYNOPSIS:** With Aunt Bee visiting her sister and Opie away on a scouting trip, Andy looks forward to a relaxing weekend by himself. Unfortunately, Goober not only moves in to keep him company and cook meals, but also takes two messages: Helen is expected Andy for dinner and Howard called about rescheduling a meeting. Following a spaghetti dinner, Goober remembers the messages but transposes them, thus making Andy—already stuffed from dinner—arrive at Howard's house to eat another meal. The Spragues are mystified by his presence, but eat again to please Andy. The main course? Spaghetti. Andy then learns the message was mixed up, forcing him to eat a third spaghetti dinner at Helen's! **CRITIQUE:** One of the best of the post-Barney episodes. This is a laugh riot from start to finish, filled with memorable dialogue. The funniest sequence finds Andy literally stuffing himself at a dinner Helen is holding for a visiting uncle. Superbly written, acted, and directed throughout and a highlight of the series later episodes. **FAVORITE DIALOGUE:** Howard Sprague to Andy: "Mother likes me to get plenty of vitamin C during the flu season!"

Episode 207: "A Visit to Barney Fife" (1/16/67) ••••
DIRECTOR: Lee Philips; **WRITERS:** Bill Idelson and Sam Bobrick **CAST:** Andy Griffith, Don Knotts, Betty Kean, Richard X. Slattery, Margaret Teele, Richard Chambers, Gene Rutherford, Robert Ball, Luana Anders, Peter Madsen, Charles Horvath **SYNOPSIS:** While in Raleigh on business, Andy pays a visit to Barney who is now a detective. Once in police headquarters, however, he sees that Barney is treated as a gofer and learns from the captain that Fife's job is in jeopardy. Meanwhile, the department is frustrated by a series of supermarket robberies which seem to indicate there is a leak of inside information. Andy drops in on Barney at a boardinghouse and is introduced to Fife's "second family"—the Parkers, a beer-guzzling group of suspicious individuals who constantly prod the gullible Barney into revealing strategies the police will use to capture the robbery gang. Andy suspects the Parkers are the criminals, but does not tell Barney his theory. He gives misinformation to the gang, then sets a trap. When the robbers are captured, he arranges for Barney to take credit and his friend becomes a hero in the department.
CRITIQUE: This is the most amusing of Don Knotts's return visits to *The Andy Griffith Show*. The hilarity begins with Andy and Barney sitting at the latter's "desk" in police headquarters—a useless board extending from the wall at an absurd height. Later Barney gives Andy a tour of his tiny room, and proves his interior decorating is a marvel to behold. Prints of "Blue Boy" and "The Laughing Cavalier" are taped to one wall, while a Mayberry High pennant graces the opposite wall. (Barney attributes his newfound love of art to having fallen under the spell of a big city "culture kick" and that "arty crowd" he hangs around with.) Equally funny is the Parkers' obvious manipulation of Barney, enforced by a

sexpot daughter who continuously flirts with him. Still, the greatest pleasure is seeing Knotts and Griffith together, and this is often demonstrated not in the laugh-packed scenes, but in those quiet ones that convey their mutual admiration. **FAVORITE DIALOGUE:** Barney, glancing at the streets of Raleigh: "It's a jungle out there, Ang."

Episode 208: "Barney Comes to Mayberry" (1/23/67) ●●●●

DIRECTOR: Lee Philips; **WRITER:** Sid Morse **CAST:** Andy Griffith, Don Knotts, Ron Howard, Frances Bavier, George Lindsey, Aneta Corsaut, Diahn Williams, Chet Stratton, May Lou Taylor, Ollie O'Toole, Christine Burke, Steve Dunn, Luana Anders, Patty Regan **SYNOPSIS:** Barney returns to Mayberry where he is reunited with former high-school flame Teena Andrews, now a famous movie star who has also returned to hold the premiere of her latest film in town. When Teena has Barney escort her to the premiere, Barney mistakenly assumes the old romance is back, and begins to talk marriage. He soon learns Teena has left town to meet with her fianceé. Depressed, Barney returns to Raleigh. Here, his spirits are raised when he becomes a "catch" among the girls in the office, who are impressed that he took Teena to the premiere. **CRITIQUE:** As with most of Barney's return visits to Mayberry, this one proves to be a bittersweet affair. We get to see him putting "the moves" on a slightly drunken Teena. For once Barney has reason to believe his attentions are desired, as Teena gives him every indication the romance is back. The inevitable heartbreak Barney suffers is painful to watch, and only slightly compensated by an obligatory "feel good" ending. Like most great comic actors, Don Knotts excels not only with laughs, but with pathos as well. His occasional visits to Mayberry are classic episodes. **FAVORITE DIALOGUE:** A dejected Barney tells Andy why his revolver is his only true love: "This right here is the only love a lawman ought to have—you can depend on her."

Episode 209: "Andy's Old Girlfriend" (1/30/67) ●●●●

DIRECTOR: Lee Philips; **WRITER:** Sid Morse **CAST:** Andy Griffith, Ron Howard, Jack Dodson, Aneta Corsaut, Joanna McNeil **SYNOPSIS:** Trouble brews between Andy and Helen when his former girlfriend Alice moves back to Mayberry, and temporarily stays at the Taylor home. Initially jealous, Helen warms to Alice when Andy sets the latter up on dates with Howard Sprague. However, when the four spend a weekend at Alice's cabin in the woods, disaster looms. Andy and Alice can't sleep and innocently bump into each other in the woods at night. They later get lost, and their absence is discovered by Helen and Howard. To make matters worse, they try to cover up the situation only to be confronted with angry reactions from their respective dates. The situation is resolved when Helen runs into the woods, she, too gets lost. Seeing Andy's story is plausible, she patches up her differences with him. **CRITIQUE:** An extremely enjoyable episode filled with wonderful performances. Andy Griffith plays against type, with a frantic, nervous behavior that demonstrates his talents go far beyond being a straight man. His constant attempts to placate Helen by reminding her his relationship with Alice is strictly platonic are often hilarious. Jack Dodson and Aneta Corsaut are particularly delightful, and Joanna McNeil is perfect as the sensuous Alice. **FAVORITE DIALOGUE:** Howard, defending his habit of brushing his teeth for fifteen minutes: "I know there's lots of toothpaste that prevent cavities, but I like to wage my own battle!"

Episode 210: "Aunt Bee's Restaurant" (2/6/67) ●●●

Opposite: Andy and Helen feeling rather romantic. Must be near Myer's Lake.

DIRECTOR: Lee Philips; **WRITERS:** Ronald Axe and Lee Roberts **CAST:** Andy Griffith, Frances Bavier, Jack Dodson, Aneta Corsaut, George Lindsey, Keye Luke, Lloyd Kino, Ruth Thom, Jason Johnson

Episode 211: "Floyd's Barber Shop" (2/13/67)   •••1/2

DIRECTOR: Lee Philips; **WRITERS:** Jim Parker and Arnold Margolin **CAST:** Andy Griffith, Ron Howard, Frances Bavier, Howard McNear, Jack Dodson, George Lindsey, Dave Ketchum, George Cisar, James O'Rear, William Chalee **SYNOPSIS:** When Howard Sprague buys the building housing Floyd's Barber Shop as an investment, he raises the rent slightly. Outraged, Floyd closes the place and threatens to move to Mt. Pilot. Meanwhile, Andy is continuously distracted from his work when all the loafers from Floyd's move into the courthouse. Andy arranges a meeting between Howard and Floyd, and cleverly mocks the relevance of the barbershop to Mayberry. As hoped, both Howard and Floyd team up to defend the shop. Now united, they come to terms on a compromise that convinces Floyd to stay in Mayberry. **CRITIQUE:** A wonderful episode with Mayberry's two most mild-mannered citizens locked in a battle of egos and wills. Howard's proposal of a modest rent increase (to $65 a month!) causes Floyd to accuse him of "taking the food right out of my mouth!" The significance of the unique "culture" that Floyd's shop brings to Mayberry is dramatized in a scene in which the owner of a chain of barbershops makes a bid on Floyd's place, with the promise of modernizing it and depersonalizing it as well. This makes everyone realize that the barber shop—at least under Floyd's management—is the cultural heart of the town. **FAVORITE DIALOGUE:** Floyd recalls to Andy the many times he cut his hair as a child: "You always wanted to eat the shaving cream! You thought it was ice cream. You were pretty stupid, you know that?"

Episode 212: "The Statue" (2/20/67)   •••

DIRECTOR: Lee Philips; **WRITER:** Fred S. Fox **CAST:** Andy Griffith, Frances Bavier, Howard McNear, Jack Dodson, George Lindsey, Hope Summers, Richard Collier, Dale McKennon, George Cisar

Episode 213: "Helen, The Authoress" (2/27/67)   ••••

DIRECTOR: Lee Philips; **WRITER:** Douglas Tibbles **CAST:** Andy Griffith, Ron Howard, Aneta Corsaut, Howard McNear, George Lindsey, Jack Dodson, Keith Andes, Elaine Joyce, Laurie Main **SYNOPSIS:** Andy is elated when Helen learns that her children's book has found a major publisher. However, when she has to spend an inordinate amount of time working on the manuscript, her social life with Andy is greatly reduced. He eventually becomes jealous of the money and fame Helen is receiving, and he comes to resent her book. He breaks up with Helen and dates an airheaded bombshell. When Helen sees them together, she is hurt and angered. Ultimately, Andy realizes he is being petty and apologizes to Helen and promises support for her work. **CRITIQUE:** Women's lib is once again at the forefront of an episode, and even in prehistoric 1967, Andy's attitude seems hopelessly outdated. It does make for a dandy show, however, as there has never been this much tension between Andy and Helen before. Andy's uncharacteristic severing of his relationship with Helen is a real shock, but nothing compared to his blatant dating of a local sexpot who makes either of "the Fun Girls" looks like Mother Teresa. Aneta Corsaut is in top form here. **FAVORITE DIALOGUE:** Helen is given an "unpretentious" pen name by her publisher: "Helene Alexia DuBois."

Episode 214: "Good-bye, Dolly" (3/6/67) •••1/2
DIRECTOR: Lee Philips; **WRITERS:** Michael L. Morris and Seamon Jacobs **CAST:** Andy Griffith, Ron Howard, Frances Bavier, George Lindsey, Jack Dodson, Tom Tully, Sheldon Golomb

Episode 215: "Opie's Piano Lesson" (3/13/67) •••1/2
DIRECTOR: Lee Phillips; **WRITERS:** Leo and Pauline Townsend **CAST:** Andy Griffith, Ron Howard, Frances Bavier, Hope Summers, Sheldon Collins, Rockne Tarrington, Richard Bull, Maudie Prickett, Chuck Campbell, Johnny Jenson, Kirk Travis

Episode 216: "Howard, the Comedian" (3/20/67) •••1/2
DIRECTOR: Lee Philips; **WRITERS:** Michael Morris and Seaman Jacobs **CAST:** Andy Griffith, Ron Howard, Frances Bavier, George Lindsey, Howard McNear, Jack Dodson, Hope Summers, Dick Haynes, Dick Curtis, Tol Avery **SYNOPSIS:** When Howard's comedy act proves a hit at the local lodge, the people of Mayberry encourage him to perform on a TV talent show. When he does, however, he "personalizes" the routines by good-naturedly kidding the local residents. The reaction among his thin-skinned friends is one of outrage, and Howard is ostracized. However, the folks begin to revel in the attention the TV show brings them and for once they feel like celebrities. When Howard formally apologizes to them, he is shocked to find they now encourage him to continue teasing them in his routines. **CRITIQUE:** The prospect of Howard Sprague "wowing" people with a comedy routine might seem more at home in a science-fiction show. It is to Jack Dodsons credit that he makes Howard's unlikely talent seem plausible. Alan King, he ain't, but the laughs he gets seem deserved. **FAVORITE DIALOGUE:** Howard on Bee's ancestors: "Aunt Bee's family came over on the *Mayflower*. Of course, in those days the immigration laws weren't as strict!"

Episode 217: "Big Brothers" (3/27/67) •••1/2
DIRECTOR: Lee Philips; **WRITER:** Fred S. Fox **CAST:** Andy Griffith, Jack Dodson, George Lindsey, Howard McNear, Scott Lane, Elizabeth Macrae, Scott Lane **SYNOPSIS:** Agreeing to tutor Tommy Parker, a troubled student, Howard is manipulated by the boy into spending most of his time with his gorgeous sister, Betty, whom Howard drives to and from her job at a dance hall while Tommy goofs off. Suspicious as to why Tommy is not improving in school, Andy learns the truth and confronts Howard, and tells him that his poor performance as a role model has so disappointed Tommy that, ironically, the boy is determined to do better so that he can be more successful than Howard. Howard admits his errors, and buckles down to correct his mistakes. **CRITIQUE:** Poor Howard Sprague! He finally has a semi-fling with a seductive woman, only to end up getting chastised and looking foolish. His preoccupation with Betty (who does appear to be pretty "loose") causes him to start wearing fedoras (with feathers, 'natch), a plaid sports jacket, black-and-white shoes, and an ascot. (Which causes him to look like a Mayberry version of Rex Reed!) The dance hall where Betty works is about as shocking as an Elks Club, but for Howard it's living on the edge. A good exploration of the Sprague psyche, made very watchable by the wonderful Jack Dodson. **FAVORITE DIALOGUE:** Howard "relating" to his teenage protégé by using terms like "groovy" and "pal."

Episode 218: "Opie's Most Unforgettable Character" (4/3/67) •••

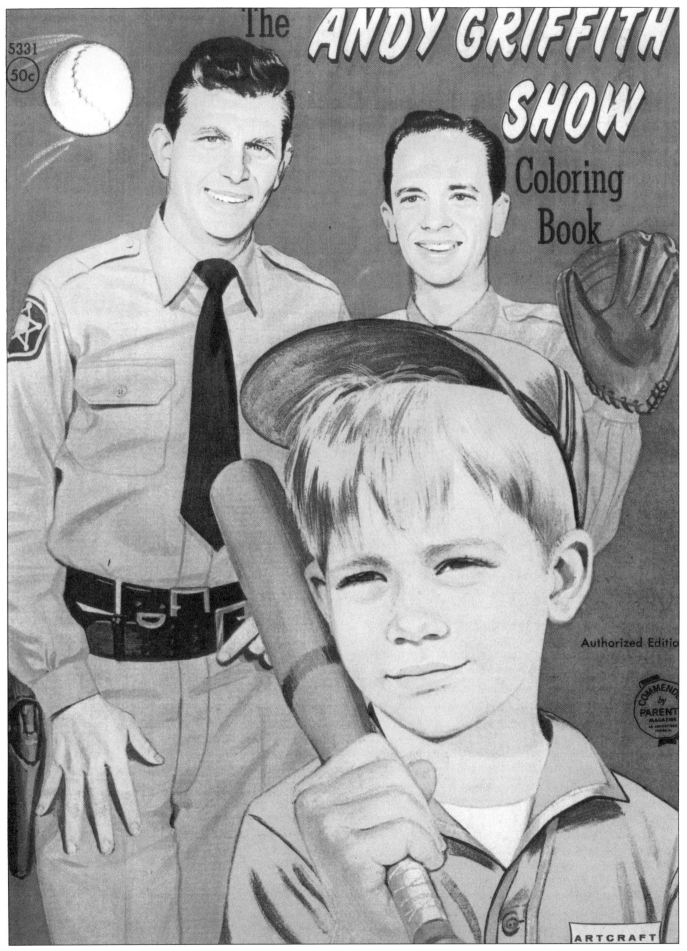

These rare fifty-cent coloring books from the early 1960s sell for over $100 each. (courtesy Dennis Hasty Collection)

5644
50c

RONNY HOWARD
of the Andy Griffith Show
PICTURES to COLOR
Authorized Edition

Andy Griffith
as
SHERIFF ANDY TAYLOR

Don Knotts
as
BARNEY FIFE

Frances Bavier
as
AUNT BEE

*Ronny Howard as OPIE
has a sundae in Mayberry's drug store*

Andy and Don reprise their Broadway roles in the screen version of *No Time for Sergeants*.

DIRECTOR: Lee Philips; **WRITERS:** Michael Morris and Seaman Jacobs **CAST:** Andy Griffith, Ron Howard, Frances Bavier, George Lindsey, Jack Dodson, Aneta Corsaut, Sheldon Collins, Joy Ellison

Episode 219: "Goober's Contest" (4/10/67)   •••1/2

DIRECTOR: Lee Philips; **WRITERS:** Ron Friedman and Pat McCormick **CAST:** Andy Griffith, Ron Howard, Frances Bavier, George Lindsey, Howard McNear, Rob Reiner, Owen Bush, Edgar Hess **SYNOPSIS:** To generate more business for the gas station, Goober initiates a contest in which $200 in prizes will be awarded in $5 increments. By mistake, a gift is awarded to Floyd in the amount of $200. Though Goober explains it was a printing error, Floyd insists upon being paid in full. Even Andy's intervention fails to soothe Floyd, so he initiates another strategy: arresting Goober for nonpayment of the prize money. As expected, when Floyd hears of Goober's dilemma, his affection for his friend causes him to drop his claim. **CRITIQUE:** This sharply written episode is a bittersweet affair as it represents Howard McNear's last performance on *The Andy Griffith Show*. Howard's health has been deteriorating, and this is painfully evident in his physical condition on-screen. To his credit, his health problems had never been apparent in other episodes, but in the end courage could not win out over the effects of his recent stroke. Like a trooper, Howard endures great physical discomfort to ensure this episode was completed, and it has many laughs (keep an eye out for the young Rob Reiner with a full head of hair). While one can only speculate on the contributions McNear could have made to the final season of the series, and perhaps *Mayberry R.F.D.*, we must be grateful for the work he did complete. Fittingly, his performances are held in greater esteem by fans today than ever before. Fate accomplishes what no script writer would have ever dared to envision—the closing of Floyd's Barber Shop. Life in Mayberry would go on, of course, but the town would always seem a bit emptier without the comforting presence of the kindly barber and his trademark promise of "Two Chairs—No Waiting!" **FAVORITE DIALOGUE:** Floyd offers Goober a free shampoo in return for winning the $200 prize: "I'll use my French soap. It'll make you smell like Morris Chevalier!"

Episode 220: "Opie's First Love" 9/11/67   ••••

DIRECTOR: Lee Philips; **WRITERS:** Ron Friedman and Pat McCormick **CAST:** Andy Griffith, Ron Howard, Frances Bavier, George Lindsey, Aneta Corsaut, Suzanne Cupito, Sheldon Collins, Joy Ellison, Owen Bush, David Alan Bailey, Kevin Tate **SYNOPSIS:** Opie is elated at the prospect of his first date—taking cute classmate Mary Alice Carter to Arnold's party. Elation turns to despair, however, when Mary Alice breaks the date to attend the party with the school heartthrob, Fred. Seeing Opie's rejection, Andy relates a story about how he overcame a similar experience in his youth. Inspired, Opie attends the party "stag," only to find Mary Alice being neglected by Fred. She apologizes to Opie and becomes his date for the evening. To Andy and Helen's surprise, Opie offers to pay for a double date at the diner. **CRITIQUE:** Another wonderful episode that draws from an experience most of us have encountered, in this case, cruel treatment by a would-be paramour. Opie's anticipation for his date is so great, his later rejection by Mary Alice is almost heartbreaking. Opie gets the last laugh, of course, and his ultimate triumph is handled with the kind of dignity one would expect of him. A sweet, enticing episode that beautifully conveys the awkward "coming of age" each teen-ager experiences. Suzanne Cupito (Mary Alice), by the way, grew up and reemerged years later as glamorous Morgan

Brittany. **FAVORITE DIALOGUE:** Goober to Opie: "Your daddy's tellin' me about your new threads—that's clothes in hipster talk!"

Episode 221: "Howard, the Bowler" (9/18/67) •••

DIRECTOR: Lee Philips; **WRITERS:** Dick Bensfield and Perry Grant **CAST:** Andy Griffith, Ron Howard, Frances Bavier, Jack Dodson, George Lindsey, Paul Hartman, Norman Alden, Bob Becker

Episode 222: "A Trip to Mexico" (9/25/67) •••

DIRECTOR: Lee Philips; **WRITERS:** Dick Bensfield and Perry Grant **CAST:** Andy Griffith, Ron Howard, Frances Bavier, Jack Dodson, George Lindsey, Paul Hartman, Aneta Corsaut, Hope Summers, Ruth Thom, Vincent Barnett, Jose Gonzalez-Gonzalez, Anthony Jochim, Manuel Martin, Eddie Carroll, Natividad Vacio

Episode 223: "Andy's Trip to Raleigh" (10/2/67) ••••

DIRECTOR: Lee Philips; **WRITER:** Joseph Bonnaduce **CAST:** Andy Griffith, Aneta Corsaut, Jack Dodson, George Lindsey, Whitney Blake, Paul Hartman **SYNOPSIS:** Andy has to cancel a date with Helen so that he can spend the weekend in Raleigh reviewing his testimony for an upcoming trial. The lawyer proves to be a stunning blonde who persuades Andy to join her in her pool. When Helen finds out the lawyer was a woman, Andy lies and tells her she was very unattractive. However, when the lawyer shows up in Mayberry unexpectedly, Helen becomes enraged. After many apologies and explanations, Andy is forgiven—but not before Helen tantalizes him by implying she met a handsome stranger when she spent the day at Myer's lake. **CRITIQUE:** A first-rate episode. Andy's comic timing is especially impressive, as in the scenes in which he tries desperately to explain his sunburn to Helen following the weekend of "work" in Raleigh. Aneta Corsaut again demonstrates she is the most liberated woman in Mayberry, and her sarcastic digs at the nervous Andy makes for great comedy. The show also benefits from guest star Whitney Blake's vivacious lawyer. (To show how times have changed, the script makes reference to only two or three female attorneys in the entire state!) **FAVORITE DIALOGUE:** Goober tries to prevent the female lawyer from "dropping in" on Andy: "He went to New York yesterday, then on to Alaska. I don't know if he'll ever be back!"

Episode 224: "Opie Steps Up in Class" (10/9/67) •••1/2

DIRECTOR: Lee Philips; **WRITER:** Joseph Bonnaduce **CAST:** Andy Griffith, Ron Howard, Frances Bavier, Jack Dodson, Paul Hartman, Joyce Van Patten, Sandy Kenyon, Don Wyndham, Ivan Bonar, Ward Ramsey, Monty Margetts, Thom Carney

Episode 225: "Howard's Main Event" (10/16/67) ••••

DIRECTOR: Lee Philips; **WRITERS:** Earl Barrett and Robert C. Dennis **CAST:** Andy Griffith, Jack Dodson, George Lindsey, Aneta Corsaut, Arlene Golonka, Allan Melvin, Wayne Heffley **SYNOPSIS:** Howard begins dating Millie, the new girl in the bakery, but finds trouble when Clyde, a jealous former boyfriend, shows up and warns him to keep away from "his" girl. Seeking protection, Howard begins sticking by Andy day and night, until the latter convinces him that the indignity of hiding hurts more than a punch in the nose. Inspired, Howard seeks out Clyde and challenges him to a fight. Surprisingly, the bully gets cold feet and runs. With renewed confidence, Howard then tells off another bully who is

Andy Griffith and Howard McNear in a
network promotional telop slide.

flirting with Millie—only to receive a punch in the stomach! **CRITIQUE:** Say this for Howard Sprague—although mild-mannered, he can be a man of "true grit." The bully this time around is played by Allan Melvin, whose numerous appearances on the show should have qualified him for semi-regular status. This episode introduced Arlene Golonka as Millie, the girl who would capture Howard's heart, at least on a periodic basis. This story did a lot to change Howard's image from hopeless Mama's boy to independent man. His preposterous excuses to stay near Andy's side are quite amusing. **FAVORITE DIALOGUE:** Howard tries to induce Andy into buying a rum cake at the bakery: "Well, actually the alcoholic content of rum cake is negligible." Andy: "If you want to take your chances with rum cake, Howard, you're on your own. I have to go to work!"

Episode 226: "Aunt Bee, the Juror" (10/3/67)   •••1/2
DIRECTOR: Lee Philips; **WRITER:** Kent Wilson **CAST:** Andy Griffith, Ron Howard, Frances Bavier, George Lindsey, Jack Nicholson, Jim Begg, Tom Palmer, Rhys Williams, Henry Beckman, Tol Avery, Richard Chambers, Arthur Hansen, Pete Madsen, Alan Dexter, Emory Parnell, Frederic Downs **SYNOPSIS:** Aunt Bee is called to jury duty and must render a verdict on a young man named Marvin Jenkins who has been accused of looting a local store. Jenkis protests his innocence, but the eleven men on the jury feel he is guilty and want to hand up immediate verdict to that effect. However, Bee insists on the man's innocence and infuriates the others when she refuses to relent. As the hung jury is about to be dismissed, Andy turns up the real thief who has been observing the trial all along, and Bee emerges a true hero. **CRITIQUE:** Bedsides a clever script and an excellent performance by Frances Bavier, this episode is notable for the second series appearance of Jack Nicholson, albeit it in a very small role. His contribution to the episode is minimal, save for the "camp" value of seeing Hollywood's later-notorious bad boy paying homage to Aunt Bee and being billed behind Tol Avery (the former "Ben Weaver"). With twelve guest stars, this is like Mayberry's version of *Ben Hur*. Yet, this is Bavier's show all the way. She causes such a stir among her fellow jurors that a better title for this episode might have been "Eleven Angry Men." **FAVORITE DIALOGUE:** Aunt Bee, explaining to the court what she does for a living: "Oh, I take care of my nephew Andy Taylor and his son Opie. They're sitting right over there. Stand up, boys!" (Cut to Andy, looking for the nearest rock to crawl under!)

Episode 227: "Tape Recorder" (10/3/67)   •••
DIRECTOR: Lee Philips; **WRITERS:** Michael L. Morris and Seamon Jacobs **CAST:** Andy Griffith, Ron Howard, Frances Bavier, George Lindsey, Herbie Faye, Sheldon Collins, Jerome Guardino, Troy Melton

Episode 228: "Opie's Group" (11/6/67)   •••
DIRECTOR: Lee Philips; **WRITER:** Douglas Tibbles **CAST:** Andy Griffith, Ron Howard, Frances Bavier, George Lindsey, Paul Hartman, Hope Summers, Sheldon Collins, Jim Kidwell, Joe Leitch, Gary Chase, Kay Ann Kemper

Episode 229: "Aunt Bee and the Lecturer" (11/13/67)   •••1/2
DIRECTOR: Lee Philips; **WRITERS:** Seaman Jacobs and Ed James **CAST:** Andy Griffith, Ron Howard, Frances Bavier, Aneta Corsaut, George Lindsey, Jack Dodson, Hope Summers, Edward Andrews

Chicago Tribune TV WEEK

Complete Program Listings, Jan. 13-19, 1962

PART 3, SECTION 2

It's His Own Fault: DON KNOTTS Cast Himself for This Role

Inside in Color: Life Can Be Beautiful on the Prairies These Days

Episode 230: "Andy's Investment" (11/20/67) •••1/2
DIRECTOR: Alan Rafkin; **WRITERS:** Michael Morris and Seamon Jacobs **CAST:** Andy Griffith, Ron Howard, Frances Bavier, Jack Dodson, Aneta Corsaut, Paul Hartman, Ken Lynch, Roy Jenson, Richard Collier, Ceil Cabot, Maudie Prickett, Jesslyn Fax

Episode 231: "Howard and Millie" (11/27/67) •••1/2
DIRECTOR: Peter Baldwin; **WRITER:** Joseph Bonnaduce **CAST:** Andy Griffith, Ron Howard, George Lindsey, Jack Dodson, Aneta Corsaut, Arlene Golonka, Elizabeth Harrower, Steve Pendleton, Robert B. Williams, Ida Mae MacKenzie, Carol Veazie, Roy Engel **SYNOPSIS:** Although only having dated her for a few months, Howard Sprague proposes to Millie, who eagerly accepts. They plan a wedding in Millie's hometown of Wheeling, West Virginia, and Andy and Helen accompany them to serve as best man and maid of honor. The overnight train trip proves to be uncomfortable, as the gloom fades between Howard and Millie when they discover how opposite they are. By the time they arrive in Wheeling, the two aren't speaking. They quickly find a solution to the problem and inform the family that they've found a way to overcome their differences: by calling off the wedding and resuming their relationship as boyfriend and girlfriend. **CRITIQUE:** Howard Sprague should know that every effort to go against type by doing something impetuous will lead to disaster. This insightful episode shows the "darker" side of Howard and Millie. There's some great dialogue when Howard relates his honeymoon plans to an unimpressed Millie (they include a King Arthur pageant and a tour of a cave!). Arlene Golonka is especially amusing when she reveals herself to be a disheveled grouch in the morning, in contrast to Howard's nauseating cheerfulness. A delightful send-up of impromptu marriages. **FAVORITE DIALOGUE:** Howard stresses the benefits of dining on fish to Andy: "You know what I like about fish? It combines a high nutritional value with flavor at a modest price." Andy: You can't ask more of a fish than that!"

Episode 232: "Aunt Bee's Cousin" (12/4/67) •••
DIRECTOR: Lee Philips; **WRITERS:** Dick Bensfield and Perry Grant **CAST:** Andy Griffith, Ron Howard, Frances Bavier, George Lindsey, Aneta Corsaut, Jack Dodson, Hope Summers, Paul Hartman, Jack Albertson, Ann Morgan Guilbert

Episode 233: "Suppose Andy Gets Sick" (12/11/67) ••••
DIRECTOR: Peter Baldwin; **WRITER:** Jack Raymond **CAST:** Andy Griffith, Ron Howard, Frances Bavier, George Lindsey, Paul Hartman, Jack Dodson, Vince Barnett, Charles Thompson, Anthony Jochim, Hollis Morrison **SYNOPSIS:** Confined to bed with the flu, Andy makes the mistake of deputizing Goober, hoping to get some much-needed rest. Unfortunately, Goober carries a safe-driving campaign to an extreme and tickets seemingly everyone in town. He also wrecks the squad car, and makes uninvited and disturbing visits to Andy's room. His behavior prompts Howard Sprague to stop by also, as does Emmett to "help" Andy by installing a light. Ultimately, Andy recognizes he would have gotten more rest by simply staying on the job. **CRITIQUE:** The author confesses to having a weakness for those shows in which Andy vows to get "peace and quiet" away from the courthouse. And this humorous tale culminates in a memorable scene in which his friends converge on his cramped bedroom uninvited in such a way as to be reminiful of the Mary Prathers's classic stateroom sequence from *A Night at the Opera*. **FAVORITE DIA-**

Best buddies on and off television, Don and Andy costarred in a CBS variety special in 1967.

LOGUE: A Frantic Andy hears Goober crash the squad car outside the Taylor home. Andy: "What about the squad car??" Emmett: "We'll be able to tell more about it once they get it back on the wheels!"

Episode 234: "Howard's New Life" (12/18/67) ••••

DIRECTOR: Lee Philips; **WRITERS:** Dick Bensfield and Perry Grant **CAST:** Andy Griffith, Ron Howard, Frances Bavier, Harry Dean Stanton, George Lindsey, Jack Dodson, Paul Hartman, Don Keefer, Sam Green, Mark Brown, Sir Lancelot (SIC) **SYNOPSIS:** Bored by his humdrum existence as county clerk, Howard Sprague becomes inspired by a documentary about the beauty of life in the Caribbean. He shocks his friends by announcing he has quit his job and has purchased a one-way ticket to a remote island where he intends to live the life of an adventurer. There's trouble in paradise, however, as Howard soon becomes restless and discovers the only other inhabitants of the island are a group of burned-out souls who sit motionless for hours in the general store. When a nightmare convinces him he will end up a similar fashion, Howard returns to Mayberry. Although his trip was a failure, Andy correctly points out that it will be an adventure Howard will never forget. **CRITIQUE:** This is arguably the most memorable episode to center on Howard Sprague. Scenically, it is also an anomaly, as it presents extensive location shots of Howard cavorting on the beach. Again, we realize that the Jack Dodson character is one of the most fascinating on the show, and we share his pride in having gone against his stereotypical image and at least tried to add excitement to his life. The superb script is aided immeasurably by some funny supporting characters, including Harry Dean Stanton as the brain-dead owner of the general store. Yet, Jack Dodson dominates the entire show, in a wonderfully multi-layered performance. **FAVORITE DIALOGUE:** In his nightmare, Howard sees himself as a zombie-like beach bum who greets Andy and Aunt Bee with the only dialogue he is capable of uttering: "Wanna buy a ship in a bottle?"

Episode 235: "Goober, the Executive" (12/25/67) •••1/2

DIRECTOR: Lee Philips; **WRITERS:** Michael Morris and Seaman Jacobs **CAST:** Andy Griffith, Ron Howard, George Lindsey, Paul Hartman, Bo Hopkins, James McCallion, Sam Green **SYNOPSIS:** When Wally decides to sell the gas station, Goober, fearing being put out of work, buys the place himself. Andy and Emmett reluctantly cosign a loan, and soon regret it. While an excellent mechanic, Goober proves to be an incompetent owner and lets the station fail due to constant indecision. However, after Opie reads him an inspirational article about an executive who overcame similar problems, Goober gets is confidence back and the station begins to make money again. **CRITIQUE:** Goober is forced to mature in this episode, as he embarks upon the biggest decision of his life; although it appears he has bitten off more than he can chew. Fortunately, there is no sappy ending, with Wally retaining the filling station. Instead, we watch the character of Goober continue to evolve, and George Lindsey's performances become more endearing and watchable with every episode. **FAVORITE DIALOGUE:** Goober's motto for the filling station: " 'The only thing we don't wipe clean are the smile on our faces!' "

Episode 236: "The Mayberry Chef" (1/1/68) •••

DIRECTOR: Lee Philips; **WRITER:** James L. Brooks **CAST:** Andy Griffith, Ron Howard, Frances Bavier, George Lindsey, Don Keefer, Jack Bannon, Richard Poston

Episode 237: "Emmett's Brother-in-law" (1/8/68) •••1/2
DIRECTOR: Lee Philips; **WRITER:** James L. Brooks **CAST:** Andy Griffith, George Lindsey, Jack Dodson, Aneta Corsaut, Paul Hartman, Dub Taylor, Mary Lansing

Episode 238: "Opie's Drugstore Job" (1/15/68) •••1/2
DIRECTOR: Lee Philips; **WRITER:** Kent Wilson **CAST:** Andy Griffith, Ron Howard, George Lindsey, Jack Dodson, Robert F. Simon, Jim Begg, Sheldon Collins, Diane Deininger

Episode 239: "The Church Benefactors" (1/22/68) ••1/2
DIRECTOR: Lee Philips; **WRITERS:** Earl Barrett and Robert C. Dennis **CAST:** Andy Griffith, Ron Howard, Frances Bavier, Jack Dodson, Aneta Corsaut, Paul Hartman, William Keene, Hope Summers, Mary Lansing, Vince Barnett

Episode 240: "Barney Hosts a Summit Meeting" (1/29/68) ••••
DIRECTOR: Lee Philips; **WRITER:** Aaron Ruben **CAST:** Andy Griffith, Don Knotts, Ron Howard, Frances Bavier, George Lindsey, Paul Fix, Richard X. Slattery, Michael Higgins, Alan Oppenheimer, Ben Astair, Hollis Morrison, Charles Horvath **SYNOPSIS:** Barney convinces his police chief to recommend Mayberry as the site of a top-secret summit meeting between two high-ranking U.S. and Soviet officials. But when the house he intended to use proves to be off-limits, he convinces a reluctant Andy to allow him to utilize the Taylor home. The politicians are initially outraged over having to stay in such a modest place, but gradually Aunt Bee's hospitality wins them over. In fact, the setting is so relaxing that the summit ends early due to some late-night negotiating which occurs when the U.S. and Soviet dignitaries bump into each other while raiding the refrigerator. Barney ends up getting an official commendation for his inspired choice of the Taylor house. **CRITIQUE:** Don Knotts's final guest appearance on *The Andy Griffith Show* was every bit the equal to his preceding Mayberry visits. Barney's ego is still his biggest problem, and his presumptuousness in assuming he can use a cranky old man's mansion for the summit leads to an amusing scene in which the old coot mistakes him for a juvenile delinquent! However, the script occasionally borders on the absurd when it deals with the political elements. (As lovable as Aunt Bee is, it's doubtful the Secret Service would allow her to serve pie to men who are presumably discussing top secret plans that will affect the balance of world power.) Despite Frances Bavier's scene stealing, Knotts is the focus of the show, and his last sequence with Andy Griffith is an appropriate one—engaging in some small talk on the Taylors' porch. In its own way, this comforting image is every bit as exemplary of American culture as are the paintings of Norman Rockwell. **FAVORITE DIALOGUE:** Barney, reflecting on those unknown individuals who helped arrange great meetings in history: "Those of us who chart the course of world events shall forever remain nameless."

Episode 241: "Goober Goes to an Auto Show" (2/5/68) •••1/2
DIRECTOR: Lee Philips; **WRITER:** Joseph Bonnaduce **CAST:** Andy Griffith, Ron Howard, Frances Bavier, George Lindsey, Noam Pitlik, Jack Good, Patty Regan, Freddy Roberts **SYNOPSIS:** While attending an auto show with the Taylors in Raleigh, Goober is reunited with an old buddy who claims he has become the vice president of an auto company. Ashamed at his relative lack of success, Goober pretends he owns a chain of

"Hail! Hail! The gang's all here"—and looking better than ever, reunited in 1986 for *Return to Mayberry*.

gas stations. When his lie is uncovered, Goober is humiliated by his friend and becomes deeply depressed. While leaving town, the Taylors and Goober gas up at a local service station, and here they stumble upon Goober's "successful" buddy working as a mechanic. Rather than humiliate the man, however, Goober decides to go home quietly, his pride having been restored. **CRITIQUE:** Where once Goober was simply a buffoon, here he is simply naive and eccentric. The evolution of his character over the years is a positive one, because it would have been impossible earlier for George Lindsey to bring the dramatic shadings to Goober that he does here in an excellent, heartrending performance. **FAVORITE DIALOGUE:** Andy to Goober, after the latter chooses not to humiliate his old friend: "Goob, I wouldn't worry anymore about trying to be a big man." Goober: "Why not?" Andy: "You already made it."

Episode 242: "Aunt Bee's Big Moment" (2/12/68) •••1/2
DIRECTOR: Lee Philips; **WRITERS:** Dick Bensfield and Perry Grant **CAST:** Andy Griffith, Ron Howard, Frances Bavier, George Lindsey, Jack Dodson, Paul Hartman, Aneta Corsaut, John McLiam

Episode 243: "Helen's Past" (2/19/68) ••••
DIRECTOR: Lee Philips; **WRITER:** Douglas Tibbles **CAST:** Andy Griffith, Ron Howard, Frances Bavier, George Lindsey, Jack Dodson, Aneta Corsaut, Ruth McDevitt, Monty Magretts, Michael Freeman, Peter Hobbs, Connie Sawyer **SYNOPSIS:** Andy accidentally discovers an old newspaper article from Kansas telling of Helen Crump's arrest in connection with organized crime figures. While he conducts a secret investigation, word of the scandal leaks out and Helen is threatened with termination by the school board. However, Andy arrives to explain that the "scandal" was due to Helen's work as a college journalist, when she went undercover to expose a crime ring and was arrested by mistake and then acquitted. The embarrassed school board apologizes and commends Helen on her bravery. **CRITIQUE:** The way the Mayberry locals react to a potential scandal in Helen's past, one would think she was Bonnie Parker. Granted, the prospect of the town's respected teacher being involved with organized crime surely justifies some eyebrow-raising, however the immediate rush to judgment on the part of the locals is unbecoming of the friendly folks of Mayberry. Particularly painful is Helen having to hear the misinformation that Andy is attempting to oust her from her job. The only major support Helen finds is from good ol' Howard Sprague, who may be square but certainly is loyal. There's more drama here than laughs, but a good spirit and excellent performance by all make it an engrossing episode. **FAVORITE DIALOGUE:** Opie learns of Helen's scandal just before the Taylors sit down to dinner with her: "I got a feeling it's gonna be one of those jittery suppers!"

Episode 244: "Emmett's Anniversary" (2/26/68)   •••1/2
DIRECTOR: Lee Philips; **WRITERS:** Dick Bensfield and Perry Grant **CAST:** Andy Griffith, Ron Howard, Frances Bavier, George Lindsey, Paul Hartman, Mary Lansing, Ruth McDevitt, Alberta Nelson, Ronnie Schell **SYNOPSIS:** Martha wants a mink coat for her twenty-fifth anniversary, but Emmett, unable to afford one, is taken by Flora from the diner to see a wholesaler. When Martha spots them together she fears an affair is taking place. To calm her, Andy tells her the truth about the mink Emmett is buying. Martha is thrilled and promises to keep the surprise. However, Emmett has decided to buy a bathrobe instead. Tipped off to Martha's expectations, Emmett asks Andy for a ride back to the whole-

TV GUIDE

15¢

Tell television what you like

VOTE!

AWARDS BALLOT
SEE PAGE 13

Don Knotts of
'The Andy Griffith Show'

The success of *The Andy Griffith Show* put the cast on magazine cover stories from coast to coast. (courtesy Dennis Hasty collection)

saler to buy the mink! **CRITIQUE:** A true comedy of errors, and Emmett initiates Ralph Kramden when his big mouth prevents him from getting out of buying the costly mink. Paul Hartman is a wonderful actor who never got his due, but there is no denying his comic timing which is amply demonstrated in this fine episode. *Gomer Pyle* star Ronnie Schell appears as the fur wholesaler. **FAVORITE DIALOGUE:** Goober suggests an anniversary gift to Emmett: "I can get you a good deal on a set of nylon tires for her car!"

Episode 245: "The Wedding" (3/4/68) ●●●●
DIRECTOR: Lee Philips; **WRITER:** Joseph Bonnaduce **CAST:** Andy Griffith, Jack Dodson, George Lindsey, Aneta Corsaut, Paul Hartman, Mabel Albertson, Teri Garr **SYNOPSIS:** When his mother suddenly ups and marries and moves to Mt. Pilot, Howard Sprague decides to turn the house into a "bachelor pad." He redecorates with a flair for the garish, and installs beaded curtains, a bearskin rug, large throw pillows, and ugly paintings. He decides to have a swinging singles party, much to the chagrin of Emmett, whose marriage precludes him from attending. The party sours, however, when neither Howard nor Goober can get dates, leaving Helen Crump the only female in attendance. The evening is a disaster, and at nine o'clock, the party breaks up from boredom. Emmett, though, makes a surprise appearance and reinvigorates everyone with some lively dance routines. **CRITIQUE:** Thanks to Jack Dodson's consummate skill as an actor, there are scenes that rank as classic comedy moments from the show. Howard's noble but pathetic attempt to change his image is a true "Mission: Impossible" despite his taking to wearing ascots and kimonos. His idea of partying is to offer soft drinks (and some cider that has hardened) as well as a seemingly endless supply of cheese sandwiches. This segment is proof that the quality of the later episodes ranked right up there with those from the Barney years. **FAVORITE DIALOGUE:** Howard to Goober, as he answers the door to admit Andy and Helen, the only other guests at his swinging singles party: "And still they come!"

Episode 246: "Sam for Town Council" (3/11/68) ●●●
DIRECTOR: Lee Philips; **WRITERS:** Dick Bensfield and Perry Grant **CAST:** Andy Griffith, Ron Howard, Frances Bavier, Ken Berry, George Lindsey, Paul Hartman, Jack Dodson, Aneta Corsaut, Gil Lamb, Don Sturdy, Denny Kunard, Roy Engel, Dick Johnstone, Mary Lou Taylor **SYNOPSIS:** When Emmett declares his candidacy as head of the town council, his friends predict disaster if he is elected. They persuade genial Sam Jones to run, but he must compete against Emmett's strategy of promising personal favors in return for votes. Severing his friendship with nonsupporters, Emmett wages a spirited campaign, but Sam wins by a narrow margin. Emmett concedes and resumes his friendship with his former rival. Sam becomes disheartened, however, by his own supporters' immediate request for favors. Andy convinces Sam that it is up to him to end such expectations and help bring Mayberry politics into a new era. **CRITIQUE:** A lightweight episode, which eased Ken Berry into the show in anticipation of Andy's departure, that could have benefited from a stronger script, with too much time being spent on inconsequential talk, while the campaign itself is barely glimpsed. Also, the friction in the story between Sam and Emmett is resolved in seconds in a rather unconvincing scene. Nonetheless, there are a few bright spots and Paul Hartman and Jack Dodson provide most of the laughs. **FAVORITE DIALOGUE:** Emmett on his motivation to run for office: "I think it's a man's duty to serve when he's called." Goober: "Well, who called you?"

The author with Don Knotts in Atlantic City, July 1993.

Episode 247: "Opie and Mike" (3/18/68) ●●●
DIRECTOR: Lee Philips; **WRITER:** Douglas Tibbles **CAST:** Andy Griffith, Ken Berry, Ron Howard, Frances Bavier, George Lindsey, Buddy Foster, Diane Winn, Kellie Flanagan, Russell Schulman

Episode 248: "A Girl for Goober" (3/25/68) ●●●1/2
DIRECTOR: Lee Philips; **WRITER:** Bruce Howard; **STORY:** Bob Ross **CAST:** Andy Griffith, Ken Berry, Ron Howard, George Lindsey, Aneta Corsaut, Nancy Malone, Maggie Peterson, Tod Andrews **SYNOPSIS:** Goober sends in an application for a computer dating service. His date is the owner of the service, Edith, a doctor of psychology who is eager to see if the applications sent in result in appropriate matches. Unfortunately, Goober has misinterpreted certain key questions, leading Edith to expect him to be a man of sophistication and culture. Her shock at finding this is not the case causes the first part of their date to be a disaster, although she warms to Goober's naturalness and charm. **CRITIQUE:** When Goober interprets the question on the dating application about his interest in painting to mean his ability to coat a barn, there's inevitable trouble in the cards. He brags of reading thirty books a month, but neglects to mention they are comic books. However, as played by Nancy Malone who has gone on to become a prolific TV director, Goober's date is never mean or belittling toward him and, in fact, "The Goob" wins the girl in the end. (He even takes her to Morelli's Italian Restaurant—home of Barney's infamous "pounded steak"!) This amusing tale is the last true episode of *The Andy Griffith Show*. As such, it is rather a bittersweet experience—and we are left with the knowledge that the end of a TV era was at hand. **FAVORITE DIALOGUE:** Goober recommends a favorite dish at Morelli's Italian Restaurant to Edith: "The pounded steak dinners are nice. They pound them right here on the premises!"

Episode 249: "Mayberry R.F.D." (4/1/68) ●●1/2
DIRECTOR: Peter Baldwin; **WRITER:** Bob Ross **CAST:** Andy Griffith, Ken Berry, Frances Bavier, George Lindsey, Aneta Corsaut, Jack Dodson, Buddy Foster, Hope Summers, Gabriella Tinti, Bruno Della Santina, Letitia Roman, Almira Sessions **SYNOPSIS:** Sam Jones invites Mario Vincenti, an Italian immigrant he befriended while in the service, to live on his farm outside of Mayberry, only to find that Mario has also brought his sexy sister and elderly father with him. The clash of cultures wreaks havoc on the farm, and Sam prepares to ask them to move in with another family. However, he is so taken by the enthusiastic reception Mayberry accords the Vincentis that he becomes committed to make their assimilation a success by having them all work and live on the Jones Farm. **CRITIQUE:** Compared to today's highly publicized "farewell" episodes, *The Andy Griffith Show* simply departed quietly. Given Andy Griffith's low-key style, that's probably just the way he wanted it. (Technically, the last episode of the series to be filmed was "A Girl for Goober," but, as frequently happened, the shows were not telecast in order.) However, this final show of the series is not really representative of the preceding seasons. For one, Andy and the series regulars (with the exception of Aunt Bee) are strictly window dressing here, with the focus on establishing Ken Berry as the star of the forthcoming *Mayberry R.F.D.*, of which Andy will be executive producer. The episode isn't bad, just unremarkable. Like most of the episodes featuring Ken Berry, the absurdities that often plagued the town were replaced by a more subdued form of humor. With the airing of this episode, a major

chapter in the history of television comedy was closed. Few shows have come close to equaling—and none have surpassed—the unique blend of laughter, sentiment, and love that so consistently characterized this series. **FAVORITE DIALOGUE:** Goober admires Mario's taste in clothes: "I got a coat just like that. Over here, we call it Ivory League!"

"Mayberry R.F.D—The Premiere Episode" (9/22/68) ●●●1/2

EXECUTIVE PRODUCERS: Andy Griffith and Richard O. Linke; **PRODUCER:** Bob Ross; **DIRECTOR:** Christian I. Nyby II; **WRITER:** John McGreevey **CAST:** Ken Berry, Andy Griffith, Don Knotts, Ron Howard, Frances Bavier, Aneta Corsaut, George Lindsey, Jack Dodson, Paul Hartman, William Keene, Buddy Foster **SYNOPSIS:** Andy and Helen finally tie the knot and move away, and Aunt Bee announces that she plans to leave Mayberry to move in with her sister. Simultaneously, Sam Jones and young son Mike desperately need a new housekeeper and ask Bee to move to their farm to see if she likes the atmosphere. Bee cannot adjust to working with the animals, though, and is so intimidated she resumes her plans to move to her sister's. When Mike shows Bee a family album, she is encouraged by the bravery of the pioneer women who preceded her and becomes determined to make a success of herself on the farm. By story's end, she is firmly in control of the situation and relishes taking charge of "her" new kitchen. **CRITIQUE:** While not technically an episode of *The Andy Griffith Show*, this premiere episode of the spin-off wraps up many loose ends concerning important characters. We finally see the long-awaited marriage of Andy and Helen, and in the best Mayberry tradition, it is an understated, dignified affair that most appropriately allows Barney Fife to return as Andy's best man. The Andy-Barney presence is low key, however, and the story's main focus establishes Aunt Bee's link to Sam and Mike Jones—a relationship that would help ensure the success of *Mayberry R.F.D.* The wedding scene has its share of laughs, primarily due to Don Knotts's nervous fidgeting. Knotts later turns up in an amusing epilogue in which we find he has invited himself on Andy and Helen's honeymoon! This episode established Ken Berry as a successful leading man, and replaced his slapstick image from *F Troop*. He would receive substantial help, of course, from such veterans of *The Andy Griffith Show* as Frances Bavier, Jack Dodson, George Lindsey, Paul Hartman, and Arlene Golonka, and *Mayberry R.F.D* would continue achieving the ratings enjoyed by its predecessor for three years. It was still the number-six show in the nation when it became the victim of CBS's notorious purge of the rural sitcoms in 1971. The cancellation of such shows as *Mayberry R.F.D.*, *The Beverly Hillbillies*, *Petticoat Junction*, and *Green Acres* was explained as a method of putting a new "sophisticated" image to the network. It is not without irony that over the years, actors from these shows were asked to re-create their roles in reunion movies that enjoyed tremendous ratings success. Their continued popularity in reruns is indicative of their lasting impact on American culture. **FAVORITE DIALOGUE:** Howard advising Andy on his honeymoon trip to Florida: "If you're lucky as Mother and I, you may get to see the mating dance of the scarlet egret!"

The 1993 CBS reunion special, with the guys sporting
the latest designer wear from "The Mayberry Collection."

Return to Mayberry (1986)
EXECUTIVE PRODUCERS: Andy Griffith, Richard O. Linke, and Dean Hargrove; **PRODUCER:** Robin S. Clark; **DIRECTOR:** Bob Sweeney; **WRITERS:** Harvey Bullock and Everett Greenbaum **CAST:** Andy Griffith, Don Knotts, Ron Howard, Jim Nabors, Aneta Corsaut, Jack Dodson, George Lindsey, Betty Lynn, Howard Morris, Maggie Peterson-Mancuso, Denver Pyle, Hal Smith, Karlene Crocket, Rodney Dillard, Doug Dillard, Mitch Jayne, Dean Webb **SYNOPSIS:** Andy Taylor, now a big-city postal inspector, returns with wife Helen for a visit to Mayberry to help Opie and his wife Eunice, prepare for the birth of their first child. For the most part, time has stood still in Mayberry, and that's just the way Andy wants it. Tired of the city, he thinks he might just run again for sheriff—picking up where he left off almost twenty years ago, following his marriage of Helen Crump. It's Andy and Helen's dream to spend their golden years in the peace and quiet of the town they love so dearly. Once in Mayberry, Andy is plagued by car problems and seeks help at Wally's Service Station. The business is now known as the "G & G Garage," reflecting the names of its owners—Gomer and Goober Pyle, both of whom are as friendly and dense as ever. Andy then visits Opie, now editor of the town paper, who surprises his father that Barney Fife is running for sheriff. He encourages Andy to remain in the race as Barney is certain to lose to his opponent, an obnoxious loudmouth named Ben Woods. However, Andy changes his mind about seeking the sheriff's office again out of respect for his friendship with Barney. Visiting the courthouse, Andy greets Barney in an emotional reunion. Barney confirms that he is running for sheriff against Woods, who is waging a dirty campaign aimed at Barney's reputation for being a burglar. More reunions follow. While visiting Aunt Bee's grave, Andy runs into now divorced Thelma Lou, who has also returned to town for a visit. Andy arranges a get-together with her and Barney, and it becomes immediately apparent the old sparks are still there. There is more excitement when Eunice gives birth—with Andy delivering the child in the backseat of his car! With a new addition to the family, Opie makes the gut-wrenching decision to relocate to New York with a larger newspaper. A disruptive reminder of the past appears in the person of Ernest T. Bass, who throws rocks as indiscriminately as ever, and warns Andy about the presence of a monster. Andy disregards this as more gibberish from Ernest T., and is introduced to a young businessman named Wally, who is attempting to revive a failed restaurant on the outskirts of town by Myer's Lake. Shortly thereafter, Mayberrians begin reporting sightings of a monstrous serpent rising from the lake. Barney immediately jumps to conclusions and classifies the beast as a legitimate threat, and despite public ridicule, launches an expedition to capture it. Unbeknown to Barney, Andy suspects Wally and Ernest T. are behind the incidents. He proves his suspicions correct and manages to get Barney credit for uncovering Wally's scheme to use the monster to increase business at his restaurant. With Barney now a hero, he seems headed for certain victory in the election. But he makes an emotional plea for his supporters to vote for Andy Taylor. Visibly moved, Andy accepts the nomination. The outcome is a victory for the Sheriff Taylor/Deputy Fife ticket. Barney and longtime girlfriend Thelma Lou then wed in a barn with all the locals in attendance, including the Darlings, who provide their own unique, foot-stompin' music. After the ceremony, Andy and Barney pick up where they left off—teaming up to keep the peace in their beloved Mayberry. **BEHIND THE SCENES:** In the 1980s, television reunion movies peaked with seemingly every hit

Return to Mayberry proved to be one of the highest rated TV programs of all time.

series from the 1960s returning in one format or another. Some were well done, and captured the quality of the original series. Among the best were TV movies revivals of *The Man From U.N.C.L.E., Get Smart, Gunsmoke*, and *Perry Mason*. Others were ridiculous even by the most liberal standards. (This writer somehow found the willpower to resist seeing how the Harlem Globetrotters ended up on *Gilligan's Island*.) Andy Griffith, critical of the "quickie" nature of many reunion flicks, did not want the carefully cultivated image of Mayberry destroyed in a one-shot film. He insisted that any reunion would have to involve most of the talent from the original show—a tall order in 1986, even though only three prominent *Griffith* alumni had passed away: writer Jim Fritzell and actors Paul Hartman and Howard McNear. (Frances Bavier, who had shunned most acting jobs since she left *Mayberry R.F.D.*, was too ill to appear in this film.) Andy also wanted a plausible script that capitalized on, rather than disguised, the aging of the cast members, and had stated that he dreaded the prospect of not having had the characters evolve. As one of the three producers, Andy could exercise creative control. This lead to his rejecting the initial script, and calling in the cream of the original show's writers—namely Everett Greenbaum and Harvey Bullock. To ensure the movie captured the true feel of the Mayberry atmosphere, Bob Sweeney was signed for director. Virtually every important cast member expressed their willingness to be associated with the project. There were sixteen "originals" returning before and behind the camera. In May 1986 the reunited Mayberry crew "invaded" the small town of Los Olivos, California—a suburb of Santa Barbara, now doubling for Mayberry. For Andy, the opportunity to work with treasured friends from the old series made the passage of time seem minimal. Said "The Big Guy": "It's like we finished the old show on Friday and started this one on Monday." Ron Howard, the instigator of the reunion, confessed that the prospect of successfully re-creating the old atmosphere made him concerned: "I can sleep through anything, but I was tossing and turning because I was nervous about this. I'm so relieved the feelings are good." When the nineteen-day shoot was completed, Andy seemed to speak for the entire company when he reflected on the glory days of *The Andy Griffith Show*: "Those were the best years of my life." **CRITIQUE:** As possibly the most anticipated reunion movie ever, *Return to Mayberry* had to satisfy not only the high standards of the cast and crew, but also the millions of fans who eagerly awaited seeing their favorite actors re-create roles they had not portrayed for almost twenty years. Could characters who were so amusing in 1960 withstand the test of time so many years later? Could the writers and directors capture the innocence of a bygone era without having to "modernize" the dialogue and situations to such a degree that all of the charm was lost? Most of all, there were sociological aspects to ponder. Since *The Andy Griffith Show* left the air in 1968, the American public had become hardened and cynical. Would Mayberry look completely ridiculous in the 1980s? Fortunately the TV movie proved to be a tremendous hit with critics and audiences as well. (The show scored a 53 share in the Neilsens, making it one of the highest television events of all time.) The writers followed the old adage, "If it ain't broke, don't fix it," and restrained from making the characters deal with modern problems and social issues. (The absurdity of trying to update Mayberry was brilliantly spoofed years ago on *Saturday Night Live* wherein guest host Ron Howard returns to town to find a cesspool of crime and corruption: Floyd the Barber is the local pusher! That *Return to Mayberry* is a largely sentimental journey is evident from the first minutes when Andy pauses by the ol' fishin' hole outside Mayberry. As Earle Hagen's classic theme song plays, the title sequence of Andy and Opie walking along the same spot so many

(Left) Barney takes the professional plunge and runs for sheriff, and (above right) later Don ties the Knott (no pun intended) with Betty Lynn's Thelma Lou.

Seems like old times on the *Return to Mayberry* set.

George Lindsey, Don Knotts, and Betty Lynn reminisce with hilarious anecdotes on the TBS thirtieth anniversary special. (photo courtesy of TBS)

Andy and Don, friends for decades, take a sentimental journey on the 1993 reunion special.

Don, Jim, George, Ron, Andy, and Jack on *The Andy Griffith Show Reunion* for CBS in 1993.

If you look up "talent" in the dictionary, you just might see this photo of Don Knotts and Ron Howard, posing at the 1993 reunion show.

years ago is superimposed. It's a touching moment, as is Andy's various reunions with the old gang. The chemistry between all cast members is infectious and instantaneous. No sooner is Andy in town than he finds himself protecting Barney from his own bumbling ways. The scene in which he tries to explain to Opie why he will not run for sheriff against his old friend speaks volumes about the relationship with Barney and Andy. Says Andy of his longtime deputy: "I don't imagine Barney's had too many high spots in these last years. Everybody deserves one. This may be his big one. I won't stand in his way." *Return to Mayberry* is one of those rare projects in which everything jells with a wonderful precision. From the exasperating behavior of Goober and Gomer and the antics of Ernest T. (the only juvenile delinquent with white hair!) to the heartwarming sentiment of Andy and Barney being reunited with their romantic interests and the stoic, reassuring presence of Howard Sprague, this is a rare movie which exceeds expectations. When the final credits roll in *Return to Mayberry* and we see Andy and Barney—both proudly wearing their uniforms as they lower the flag which flies over the center of town—you realize that the old adage that you can't go home again does not always ring true. Mayberry is a town whose geographical size may be small, but whose heart is limitless. **The TBS Anniversary Tributes** It's no secret that one of Ted Turner's great passions in life is *The Andy Griffith Show*. Turner's Superstation TBS has been responsible for bringing repeats of the show into the homes of millions of viewers on a nightly basis. TBS and the many other TV stations which air the series periodically run festivals of *The Andy Griffith Show*, often with inventive themes. For example: a station might show episodes based on the stars' personal favorites, or shows which feature a certain character. TBS runs *Griffith Show* festivals several times a year, frequently featuring voice-over introductions from cast members. Week-long festivals thus far have included "It's Me, It's Me, It's Ernest T!," "Goober's Greatest Episodes," "The Five Best Episodes as Selected by *The Andy Griffith Show* Rerun Watchers Club," "A Salute to Floyd the Barber," and "Aunt Bee's Summer Loves," to name just a few. So potent are the ratings for these festivals, that they are routinely run as eight-hour marathons against the Super Bowl. In 1985, the network telecast its first tribute to the series to be produced in-house. Celebrating the twenty-fifth anniversary of *The Andy Griffith Show*, the telecast featured a tuxedo-clad Don Knotts, looking very dignified, as he introduced various classic episodes and told behind-the-scenes anecdotes. The show was so successful, it has been telecast frequently through the years. In 1990, TBS undertook its most ambitious *Griffith* project to date, by creating a thirtieth-anniversary special titled *Thirty Years of Andy: A Mayberry Reunion*, which brought together Don Knotts, George Lindsey, Betty Lynn, Hal Smith, Jack Dodson, and Howard Morris in front of an enthusiastic audience in Atlanta. Here, the stars enchanted their fans with hilarious and insightful tales of their adventures and misadventures while filming the series. As a bonus, filmed tributes were telecast from other cast and crew members. The special proves even more significant today, as it provided Danny Thomas and director Bob Sweeney with their last opportunity to discuss the show prior to their untimely deaths. A neat little surprise followed the credits, when Andy Griffith appeared in a taped segment with the star simply saying, "Happy anniversary to *The Andy Griffith Show*, from a fan." The network has no intention of slowing down, either, as there are always plans for more Griffith film festivals on the boards. (Especially gratifying is that, on these occasions, the episodes are often shown uncut with their original epilogues).

Andy reminisces with Jim Nabors and George Lindsey in front of a replica of Wally's Filling Station on the 1993 reunion special.

The 1993 CBS Reunion Show
EXECUTIVE PRODUCERS: Andy Griffith and Andre Solt; **DIRECTOR:** Andrew Solt, **PRODUCER:** Stuart Schreiberg; **WRITERS:** Andrew Solt and Peter Elbing **CAST:** Andy Griffith, Don Knotts, Ron Howard, George Lindsey, Jim Nabors, Jack Dodson

As if to prove you can't get too much of a good thing, CBS telecast an "official" reunion special in early 1993. What set this show apart from previous tributes was the active involvement of Andy himself, who served not only as host, but also as executive producer. The show was filmed in Wilmington, North Carolina, where Andy now lenses *Matlock*. Here, Andy was joined by Don Knotts, Jack Dodson, George Lindsey, Jim Nabors, and Ron Howard in recalling favorite memories of the show. As an added treat, Ron showed home movies which were taken on the set of *The Andy Griffith Show* by his mom and dad, Jean and Rance Howard. The movies offer a rare glimpse into the making of a television classic. The brief footage shown on the special only whetted the audience's appetite for more, as scenes included such wonderful moments as Ron skateboarding between takes, playing ball with Don Knotts, and rehearsing a fishing sequence with Andy. In between brief conversations with Andy's former costars, there were generous clips of highlights from the show. Taped segments featured talks with Sheldon Leonard and Aaron Ruben, who introduces the final sequence from his favorite episode, "Opie the Birdman." Andy also paid tribute to Frances Bavier and Howard McNear. Celebrities like Burt Reynolds, Nolan Ryan, Reba McIntire, Randy Travis, Charles Kuralt, and Kenny G. contributed their thoughts on the series. If the special had a fault, it was its brevity. The hour zooms by faster than Bill Bixby's sports car (see the "Bailey's Bad Boy" episode!) No sooner do we start to relish what we are seeing, when the show is nipped in the bud, so to speak. One hour may be ample time to honor most sitcoms, but it would take a weekly special to properly pay tribute to the talents behind *The Andy Griffith Show*. Perhaps, with luck, the areas left to be covered will serve to inspire future reunion specials.

"There's something about Mayberry and Mayberry folk that never leaves you. No matter where life takes you, you always carry in your heart the memories of old times and old friends."

—Andy's farewell speech to Opie in *Return to Mayberry* (1986)

United American Video's series of
tapes restore many of the epilogues
which are traditionally edited from
most reruns.